Buddy System

Buddy System

Understanding Male Friendships

Geoffrey L. Greif

OXFORD
UNIVERSITY PRESS
2009

OXFORD
UNIVERSITY PRESS

Oxford University Press, Inc., publishes works that further Oxford University's objective of excellence in research, scholarship, and education.

Oxford New York
Auckland Cape Town Dar es Salaam Hong Kong Karachi Kuala Lumpur Madrid Melbourne
Mexico City Nairobi New Delhi Shanghai Taipei Toronto

With offices in
Argentina Austria Brazil Chile Czech Republic France Greece Guatemala Hungary Italy Japan
Poland Portugal Singapore South Korea Switzerland Thailand Turkey Ukraine Vietnam

Library of Congress Cataloging-in-Publication Data

Greif, Geoffrey L.
Buddy system : understanding male friendships / Geoffrey L. Greif.
p. cm.
Includes bibliographical references and index.
ISBN 978-0-19-532642-0
1. Male friendship. I. Title.
BF575.F66G735 2008
158.2'5—dc22
                                                      2008004182

9 8 7 6 5 4 3 2 1

Printed in the United States of America
on acid-free paper

Acknowledgments

I received enormous encouragement from so many people I talked to about the book. Everyone has a story to tell about his own friendships. Recently, a 48-year-old reporter told me about his closest friends, all of whom he met in first grade. They have a set of rules under which they operate to maintain their friendship. One of them is that any time three of them are together, they must call the fourth friend so everyone stays included. Sandra Bullock (everything I read about movie stars is true, right?) apparently has a rule with her friends that they incur a fine if they go for more than 48 hours without touching base with each other. These are all strategies to stay connected with friends at a time when friendships are being put to the test by competing demands on our time. I wish to thank all those who have spoken to me both informally and formally about their friendships.

Many students at the University of Maryland School of Social Work assisted with conducting and analyzing interviews. Beginning with the first group of students in a research class in 2002, when I started the semester with a lecture on Aristotle, each subsequent group of students built on the work of the previous group. Their input was highly encouraging and invaluable to my thinking about the meanings of the interviews. The book could not and would not have been done without them. They are: Jean Spence, Maggie Hume, Dawn Swoyer, Rosie Behr, Amanda Bordwine, Derricka Brasfield, Carol Bryant, Tsiona Cohen, Vanessa Dean, Michael Durdock, John DeCosta, Leonard Ellentuck, Stacey Fabian, Jesse Fask, Kristy French, Faith Gofney, Janna Henesch, Carolyn Hoffman, Anne Ingham, Kara Kalbaugh, Jennifer Leib, Monica Lester, Renee Liebnow, Stanley

Linthicum, Tamika Lopez-Ryan, Mende Martinez, Deborah Matos, Zina Miller, Bonnie Milner, Corene Myers, Deborah Paradise, Loraine Pasquantonio, Regina Patente, Bridgette Phoebus, Jeffrey Plankeel, Tiffany Rexrode, Tineka Robinson, Matthew Rosenfield, Laurie Sapperstein, Greg Scharer, Karima Selehdar, Tamara Simmons, Cheri Stanley, Helen Stovicek, Gretchen Strunk, Leslie Styron, Amanda Tabb, Krista Vishio, Sondra Williams Jones, Christine Wiratunga, Cynthia Woodham, Evonne Gershon, and Melisa Poole. And, Roy Furchgott helped with the writing early on.

Most recently, my 2007–2008 Research Assistant was Brett Lebowitz, who helped with the editing and citation research for the book. Chris Davis did an excellent job with ministering to the book and helping it along. My wife, Maureen, was unfailingly patient in listening to me talk about this book for the past five years. A formative dinner at the Shapiros with two other couples a few years back was great encouragement. The anonymous readers from Oxford's stable of reviewers helped put me back on track when I had driven the book into the wilderness. Finally, Maura Roessner, my editor at Oxford, displayed uncommon support from the beginning of the project. She was a fabulous resource throughout the writing. Every author should have such a great editor.

I dedicate the book to those male friends with whom I have played poker, sports, and music.

Contents

Buddy System

Introduction

*I was being interviewed about parenting by a local news anchor in his
30s and, during a commercial break, he asked about the topic of my
next book. When I told him men's friendships, the first thing out of his
mouth was "Men don't have friends."*

*I met a woman at a cocktail party. We were chatting, and I told
her about the topic for this book. "That'll be a short book. Men don't
have friends," she said.*

Wait a minute. I have friends—Don't I?

The knee-jerk refrain "Men don't have friends" often left me wondering. Why do so many people say that men don't have friends? Does it come
down to how one defines "friends," or is it something more?

Must, Trust, Rust, and Just Friends

Mulling an authoritative definition of *friends*, I thought about my bi-weekly
card game. I have been playing poker with roughly the same group of guys
for more than 40 years. It's not the hope of winning the World Series of
Poker or the pitiably low table stakes that pulls us back to the game every
other week—it's mostly the camaraderie. Does that mean we are friends,
or is it just a shared excuse to get out of the house?

I thought about my relationships with these poker buddies. Certainly,
we have a fair amount in common. Everyone in the game is or has been
married. Almost all of us have children. We are all men, within 10 years of
each other in age and educated, successful, professionals. However, despite
our many similarities, my relationship with each player differs.

For instance, one player is my brother Steve, who is three years older than
I am, a computer programmer, and the game's bookkeeper. Certainly, we

3

have the most in common and, after my wife, he's the first person whose counsel I seek when I face a tough problem. Does that make us friends or family or something in between?

Then there's Pub, a former publisher, 58 years old, whom I have known since we were assigned to the same first-grade Sunday school class. Now retired, Pub spends his time volunteering on community boards. Although he might not be the first guy I'd call to hash out a personal problem, I know that I can tell him something in confidence, and he would keep it between us. That ought to qualify as a friend in anyone's book.

And Crow? I've known Crow, an antitrust lawyer, since we were eight. We grew up in the same neighborhood, played sports together. We share many touchstones of a childhood lived out side-by-side. Our poker game is the better for his witty asides that keep the play from becoming too contentious. If I ever want to reminisce about old times or know what is happening in politics, he's the one I can call. Wouldn't he be a friend?

What about Mike? I've known him a comparatively short time. Brought into the game by another player just two years ago, he may be the most dedicated of the players. He's the only one of us who goes to Atlantic City to compete in Texas Hold'em tournaments. Accordingly, he keeps his cards close to the chest, literally and figuratively. Although I don't know him very well, I enjoy spending time with him at the games. Shouldn't I count him as a friend?

The simple answer is, of course, Mike is a friend. My brother, Pub, and Crow are friends, too, as are the other players, Charles, Robert, Alan, and Richard. But they are different kinds of friends. Just looking around the poker table tells me that friendships vary in type and intensity. Reasonably, that means there must be different definitions for friendship. Using the card game as a template, I can see four categories of friendship, each with its own definition: *must* friendships, *trust* friendships, *rust* friendships, and *just* friendships.[1]

A *must* friend is a best buddy, a member of the inner circle, the closest of relationships. If something happens (birth, death, a hole in one, winning the lottery), these are the men I am most close to and whom I *must* call. These are the men I can count on when the chips—poker and otherwise—are down. If I have a personal crisis, I talk to my wife first, then I call my brother. I can count on Steve to listen well and offer a perspective I haven't considered, which often brings me to a solution I might have missed. No matter how personal the issue, Steve won't gossip about our discussion. Without *must* friends like my brother, life is less fulfilling and, in many ways, less fun.

Trust friends are people who, in their interactions with me, demonstrate a level of integrity that allows me to feel comfortable talking with them, but I would not seek them out as a *must* friend. They will keep a confidence, and they will give me feedback that makes me feel understood when I talk with them. I might not consider them in my closest circle of friends, although I like and enjoy them. I might want to develop a closer friendship with them but have never had the opportunity or time. Although I usually see Pub only at our games, if I do run into him, and the context is right, I trust him enough to feel comfortable talking with him about a personal problem.

Then there are *rust* friends—people (like Crow) I have known for a long, long time. My elementary school friends could be *rust* friends. We know each other because of our history together and, when I see them, I may fall back into old patterns formed when I was 10 years old. A *rust* friend may or may not be especially close (note that many *must* friends are also *rust* friends) but exists because of the length of time I have known him. These friendships are locked like rust to iron over time. A *rust* friend is closer than a *just* friend whom I recently met, but nothing incandescent exists about the relationship except its length (Crow's case is an exception, but I'll get to that). My *rust* friends are unlikely to change into a higher level of friendship—I have known them for years and have already assessed their potential—unless we find some new way of interacting. It is even possible to have a *rust* friend who is not well-liked; the kind of friendship that leads others to ask, "Why hang around with that guy?" The answer, with a shrug, might be, "I've known him a long time."

The men in our poker game are naturally closer to some players than others—we are not all *must* or *trust* friends. A few of us have no urge to socialize outside of the poker game, although we all like each other. Our getting along serves the purpose of filling the card table. These friendships I call *just* friends because these people are, in fact, just friends. They are a little closer than acquaintances and are pleasant to be with, but we don't expect to socialize outside of our poker game. Just like guys who get together out of an interest in basketball, golf, or stamp collecting but gather only for sports- or hobby-related contact. I'd count Mike as a *just* friend. Enjoyable company, but I haven't known him long enough for him to be a *rust*, or well enough for him to be a *must* or *trust* friend—although, as the newest acquaintance, he is the most likely to change friendship status over time.

These categories—or Buddy System—aren't strict pigeon holes; plenty of overlap exists. For instance, I cited Crow as a *rust* friend, and he is, by dint of our long association. But he is also a *must* friend. Not only did we learn to play tennis together as children, we still share that interest and have attended the U.S. Open tennis tournament together annually for more than 35 years. Even more complex is my relationship with my brother. He's a *must* friend, a *trust* friend, and one who can't get more *rust*.

It's even a little more complicated, because a level of friendship with a particular person can differ depending on the social settings. For instance, one player in our game is my accountant. I trust him with my financial matters, so that is a trust relationship when it comes to business, but the social relationship could still be *must* or *rust*.

Another complicating factor in understanding friendships is that people make friends in different ways and within varying timeframes. Some men say that a buddy has to become a *rust* friend (be a friend for a few years) before he can become a *must* friend. Others say they can make a *must* friend in a much shorter period of time. Sometimes friendships are a matter of circumstance. People who move into a new neighborhood at the same time often become *must* friends quickly because they are eager to develop a social circle. Freshmen roommates in college are another example. Soldiers often immediately become *must* or *trust* buddies due to the intensity of the shared experience and because their lives may depend on it. Whether these kinds of friendships survive after someone moves out of the neighborhood, graduates from college, or completes military service remains to be seen. A less dramatic example is my mother, who at my daughter's wedding gravitated to the other 80-plus-year-olds because of their common age. That relationship might only last a short time; still, it could be a *just* friendship for the duration of the reception, but offer the possibility of meeting again at future family events.

But, back at the poker table, after 40-plus years of card games together, one might imagine that there is no topic we can't discuss openly as we deal the hands. Well, not really. We're guys. We don't talk a great deal about feelings, personal relationships, and our vulnerabilities unless it is in a self-deprecating, joking way.

This a principal difference between the way men see friendships and women see friendships. It may be why so many women insist that men don't have friends, because men don't have friendships in the way women define friendships. Guys get together and have shoulder-to-shoulder relationships—we do things together, as compared with women, who are more apt to have face-to-face relationships. At the poker table, personal news is shared, but not with the expectation of a long support session.

Someone might say he didn't get a job he was hoping for, and the response might be something like, "Wow, that's a tough break. Deal you in this hand?" Deeply personal topics are reserved for discussions with *must* friends, not for table talk.

Although assessing my card game helps me clarify my friendships, much more information is needed to help other men clarify theirs. Hearing from other men is one way to do this.

Friendship Study

This book is about friendships between men. It is designed to help men better understand how to function in their friendships and how to think about them in new ways, so that they can be improved if necessary. Many men have close male friends and derive a great deal from those relationships. But another large segment of men do not feel they have enough close friends, cannot easily identify who their close friends are, and believe that friendships between men in particular are rare. I believe that, because of how we are socialized, raised, nurtured (call it what you will), men miss opportunities to understand, appreciate, and build new or existing relationships. Our friendships are sometimes left undeveloped.

What is a great friendship? For me the answer is "Let me sit and watch TV and not talk with my friend about anything other than the game. But, let me also know that if I need to talk to him about something bothering me, I can." Many men believe they do not have these or similar options in their friendships. By providing a road map about friendships in this book, I hope that men will be able to have the friendships they want.

Study Group

The intention of this book is to improve male friendships. The book is based on almost 400 interviews with a diverse group of men who were asked about their friendships. To learn about men's friendships with other men, we constructed a questionnaire that had both open- and closed-ended items—meaning it had questions that could be answered at some length with a description or a story, or could be answered briefly with a yes or no. Over the course of two years, 39 graduate social work students interviewed 10 men each, using the questionnaire. They analyzed the responses individually in a lengthy paper and also spent time as a class presenting their findings and debating the meaning of their interviews. More recently, 12 students interviewed 10 to 11 women each using the same questions, with the terms amended to be applicable to women (the results of these interviews provide an interesting counterpoint in Chapter 6). This approach resulted in 386 useable interviews with men and 122 interviews with women.[2]

The men who were interviewed are diverse in terms of age, race, religion, occupation, and relationship status. Two-thirds of the men are white, 29% are African-American, and the rest were evenly divided among Latino/Hispanic, Asian, and Arab.[3] The men ranged in age from 21 to 85 and had an average age of 38. Most were Christian/Protestant, with the remainder being Jewish, Muslim, or without religious affiliation. Sixty-seven percent were married, and 2% identified themselves as gay, although the actual number might be higher if a respondent concealed his sexual orientation.

Fifteen percent had no more than a high school education, with a few finishing only eighth grade.[4] Seventeen percent had at least some college education, 34% had completed college, and 34% had at least some or had completed graduate education. As far as employment is concerned, 21% were professionals and 44% worked in sales, business, or other non-professional white-collar jobs. Twenty-two percent were blue-collar workers, and the remaining men were either unemployed, students, or retired. Slightly more than half the sample grew up outside of Maryland and slightly over half said they were raised in an urban environment. The women, described in depth in Part II, are similar to the men in terms of age and race.

The interviewers were also highly diverse. Slightly more than half are white, over one-third are African-American, and the remainder are Latina. Five out of six are female, and the interviewers ranged in age from their 20s to their 50s.

The input from these more than 50 students, both verbally and in writing, has been extraordinarily helpful to me in formulating my thinking on this topic. We debated ideas about the meaning of friendships for hours, and we looked for similarities and differences between and among the men (and women) concerning how race and sexual orientation shape friendships. This process led to the formulation of the *must, trust, rust,* and *just* categories of friendships—what I came to call the Buddy System.

I have also interviewed other men and women over the years, which brings the total to about 400 formal and informal interviews of men and more than 130 interviews of women. Some of these interviews have been infused into the chapters. I also specifically sought out men in each of the decades of life for more extensive interviews. These conversations, recounted in separate chapters in Part III of the book, are meant to provide an in-depth look at the nature of male friendships across the lifespan.

Finally, I interviewed a group of men who attend a Saturday morning men's group at a local church. Their pastor had heard me lecture on my research and invited me to talk with this group about the findings. Their stories provide an additional dimension to the project. I also provide in Chapter 16 specific suggestions for men as to how they can improve their friendships. These suggestions are based on the responses from the study as well as my own ideas. Please see Appendix A for more information about the study methodology and Appendix B for questions that can be used informally with groups of men as well as in the classroom setting to guide discussion.

Study Questions

The questions we asked the men, answered in the following pages in their own words, include:

1. What is a friendship—what does a friend mean to you? With this question, we set the scene for the interview. We found a good deal of consistency in what constituted a friendship. Readers can build better friendships by understanding how other men think about them.
2. Are friendships important to you? We did not want to assume that all men necessarily thought friendships were needed. Although the vast majority did think them important, there were some interesting comments from those who did not value them as much.
3. Do you believe you have enough male friends? Most do believe they have enough friends but that belief often depends on their expectations about the number of friends they have time for, given the competing pulls of family and work.
4. How have friends helped you (are they a source of social support)? How have you helped friends? Friendships are thought of differently, from the concrete help men receive from one another to the personal availability a friend may provide. Most often, the way a man was helped was the way he helped others. Here readers can learn more about the steps to making friends and about the expectations friends may have.

5. What are examples of what you do with your male friends? Is it all sports and hanging out in the bar? To some extent yes, but to a large extent, it is more complicated than that. As with the previous question, the men gave concrete examples of activities that build friendships.

6. How do you establish friendships with men, and how do you maintain them? The men's responses here provide sound advice for those who have trouble making and keeping friends.

7. Do you ever lose male friends and, if so, how do you get them back (if you do)? The intent was to learn how friends resolve their differences when they have a falling out. Many men do not like to look back at a relationship after they have been hurt—they move ahead and form new friendships rather than try to repair the old (a finding that did not please many of the female students who were looking for long-term relationships with men).

8. Did your father (or other significant adult male) have many friends and, if so, what messages did you receive about friendships from him? Almost half said their fathers had few or no friends. Thus, role models were not always available for them to rely on when they tried to make friends themselves. These responses can encourage men to form stronger connections with male mentors if their fathers were unavailable.

9. Do you have friendships with women that are nonsexual in nature? Most men said they do although marriage can put a crimp in these friendships, as their wives might become jealous.

10. Do you learn about friendships from observing female friendships? This question drew the greatest range of responses. Some men thought that women's friendships, because of their closeness and levels of intimacy, were ideal. Others, however, looked at women's friendships negatively and saw them as backstabbing and "catty."

11. Have you made friends through your wife? Some people have written that men need women to form friendships for them. For those men who were in marriages or committed relationships with women, we asked to what extent they had made friends with their wives' or significant others' friends' male partners. The responses will help men to better understand the role that women can play in their relationships with other men.

12. Is there a link between masculinity and male friendships? This was the most misinterpreted question (some men thought it had to do

with homosexual relationships). The intention was to learn if a man's conception of masculinity included friendships, and whether a man linked his sense of self as a man to his friendships. This issue was raised at the end of the interview and is reported on here in Chapter 3. It turns out that some men seek in other men the same level of masculinity they see in themselves.

These twelve questions form the backbone of the book and guide the chapters that follow. You will hear how other men, many like you, view friendship. Perhaps you will recognize patterns in your own friendships and see what makes them so strong (or weak). Maybe you will decide that you can do more to connect with your old friends or to build new, long-lasting friendships. The decisions you make can have a significant impact on your life—friendships can make you happier and healthier. This book will take you into the world of men's friendships with other men.

Study Limits

Although this book is based on a study, the interpretations are often mine and derived from those of my students. Limitations exist in the study—we heard only from those men who wanted to be interviewed, and we have a sample that is largely currently living on the East Coast, although many grew up elsewhere. So, when percentages appear in the next few chapters as to how many men answered certain questions, it is not representative of all men—just those in this study.

Also, sometimes it was difficult to categorize answers—for example, defining friendship as "having someone to rely on" can be a reference to trust, loyalty, or dependability, depending on the speaker and the context. Thus, without relying heavily on the exact number of responses to any one question, the data should instead be used as a foundation for building knowledge around this most important feature of modern life.

About This Book

In writing this book, my goals are to:

- Highlight the strengths of male friendships despite the messages men have received about such relationships

- Help men understand friendships using the categories of *must, trust, rust,* and *just* friends
- Get friendships started or going again for men who need more friends
- Build stronger communities by helping men become more connected to each other

Despite all of the good that friendships can bring, obviously friends can be bad influences by supporting or encouraging negative behaviors. Especially in the teen years and into young adulthood, friends can encourage friends to drink too much, smoke too much, have unwise sexual encounters, cheat on exams and papers, drive too fast, and treat others badly. These adolescent friendships must be altered and replaced with adult ones that will benefit rather than hurt the person. This tends to happen with age, as young adults let go of the antiauthoritarian behaviors that drive so much of adolescent behavior. But adults get caught up in bad friendships, too. Substance abuse programs often advise their clients to drop their old friendships and make new ones among nonusers. In this book, I will talk about the positives that derive from contact with people who are beneficial to growth.

Also, from the interviews, I am convinced that friends are not needed by everyone. Some men seem quite content to have few social contacts. They may be absorbed with a significant other, children, work, or religion. They may also just be solitary souls who prefer being alone.

The 16 chapters are divided into four parts. Part I explains the results of the interviews with the 386 men and focuses on 10 men (a few additional men are quoted in these chapters when I think their comments illustrate a new point). Chapter 1 discusses how we, as an American society, understand male friendships. Chapter 2 features the first of the study findings, asking how the men defined friendships, and Chapter 3 deals with the mechanics of friendships: how friends help each other, what they do together, how they maintain the friendship, and what they do when the friendship is in trouble. Chapter 4 illustrates how men view their fathers' (or other authority figures') friendships.

In Part II, I look at the role of women in friendships, as men often compare their friendships to those of the women in their lives. Chapter 5 deals with women's influence on men's friendships: Do men emulate women's friendship? Do men have platonic friendships with women? And, finally, do women (wives) help men with friendships? In addition, Chapter 6 features the results of the interviews with 122 women, asking the same questions of the women as the men to get a female perspective on same-sex friendships.

Part III includes the interviews with men separated by decade of their lives. Friendships do vary by age. Chapter 7 features a single man in his 20s, who has not yet established a family. Chapter 8 introduces a man in his 30s, who is balancing family and work commitment and struggling to keep up with his friends. In Chapter 9 is a man in his early 40s, who is married and raising two children. He feels work pulling him from his family yet maintains very strong contact with his three closest friends. In Chapter 10, a man in his 50s is able to pursue friendships again now that his last child is in high school. Chapter 11's interview with a 64-year-old offers a more reflective view of relationships in later life. Chapters 12, 13, and 14 are one-on-one conversations with men in their 70s, 80s, and 90s, men who may need to find new friends in later life because their former friends have died.

Finally, in Part IV, I provide some additional perspectives and guidance on male friendships. Chapter 15 focuses on what the Saturday men's group thought of my findings from this study. Chapter 16 frames the importance of friendships and gives men pointers on establishing new friendships or improving the ones they have.

Back to the Poker Table

Do I feel closer to my poker buddies from having looked at them through this lens? Yes. This Buddy System helps me understand the ebb and flow of the game, and helps me appreciate it for what it is—camaraderie and entertainment. Does it help me play poker better and win more? Am I a better bluffer and less able to be bluffed out? Do I now, as Kenny Rogers advises, "Know when to hold them and when to fold them?" Unfortunately, no. That would require more of me than I now possess and more than this book offers. But at least I am having more fun.

I
UNDERSTANDING MEN'S FRIENDSHIPS

1

How Do We Understand Men's Friendships?

At a wedding, I ran into an acquaintance, Harry, who is 70. He is a runner. Three times a week, for years, he ran with men from his neighborhood until joint pain and arthritis reduced the frequency of the runs. Insinuating myself perhaps more than an acquaintance should, I asked if his running mates are friends. Harry answered immediately—he considers them friends. When they run, they talk about their concerns about their children, their work, and whatever else is happening in their lives. The discussions help these men normalize their own experiences—hearing that another person is going through something similar makes them feel better. They are not alone with their experiences and have bridged both the loneliness that people fear but also the isolation that one's problems can force on oneself.

Despite running together frequently, these men do not talk much in between their runs. Even though they are neighbors and "friends," they do not get together as a group with their wives. They tried that once, and it was awkward—no one knew how to act. There is a code of silence that says they should not share with their wives what they hear from someone in the running group.

Would they get together and talk without running? Harry says no. Like many men, these guys are engaged in "shoulder-to-shoulder" friendships, friends who interact while doing some activity. Women more often have "face-to-face" friendships, in which talking is the primary activity.

Jeff, who is in his 60s, wonders if something is wrong with him and his friendships. He knows a group of guys who talk by phone, e-mail, and get together every day in Florida, when they migrate from the north for the winter. He can't imagine communicating that much. He has friends, but they are almost all contacts he has through sports. "What could these guys have to talk about?" he wonders.

I had been thinking about men's friendships for a while; it wasn't until I talked to other men that I realized how little understanding men have of their own friendships and how awkward they often feel about them. Men can talk about their relationships with their wives or girlfriends at great length (partly because women often push men to talk about relationships). But, when it comes to understanding their friendships with men, many never examine them in any depth.

Guys are interesting—they can watch the Super Bowl together every year yet not know how many children the other guy has, that he just broke up with his girlfriend, or where he works. They will get a great sense of the other guy's football knowledge, though. Does he grasp the nuances of the salary cap, no-huddle offense, and the challenges that a coach faces? So, is the lack of interest in his personal life emotional constriction? Fear of closeness? Or just how men are constructed?

It is important to men's survival that they figure out friendships and improve them if they are unfulfilling. Studies have shown for years that both men and women benefit from friendships. Friendships help us live longer and healthier lives.[1] Having friends means having people who look after you, keep you up to date on the latest health news, and pick you up when you are feeling blue. Isolation is not good for people.[2]

Look at the actuarial charts: men do not live as long as women. This may be due in part to men being raised to not ask for help when they need it and to try to handle their problems on their own.[3] Friendships, where help is given and received, can be one way of helping men communicate their needs better to others. If men can improve the number and quality of their friendships, they may live longer and healthier lives.

They will also, I believe, live more fulfilled lives. At a time when people are seeking greater personal and spiritual meaning, friendship can be especially important in providing that meaning.

It is believed by some people that men do not have friendships. They're wrong! After delving into this topic and leading groups of research teams, it is clear to me that, although men have friendships of many flavors, histories, and intensities, they are friendships nonetheless. And although these men can talk about their friendships when asked, almost universally they said they had never considered some of the questions posed to them. Men don't think about their friendships—they don't examine them and may not appreciate them. But, through thoughtful examination, men can get more from their friendships.

"You've Got to Have Friends"

Despite Bette Midler's sound advice in the song, we are a society that glorifies friendships on a superficial level without ever defining them. Every book, television show, commercial, movie, or play deals with relationships that, if not sexual in nature, involve friendships. From the time a young child first interacts with a potential playmate, the doting parent hopes the child will make a friend. When the child comes home from the first day of school, the parent asks, "Did you make any friends?" For a conference with a teacher in kindergarten or elementary school, a teacher will describe on report cards not only the child's schoolwork but how well the child gets along with the other children. Whose telephone numbers does a teen first plug in to be speed-dialed when he gets a new phone? Not mom's and dad's—his friends! Teens choose classes or extracurricular activities in high school and college based on their friends' similar schedules and interests.

But, somewhere along the line, men have gotten the reputation of being unable to have close friendships with other men. Many men have come to believe at first blush that the friendships they have are not good enough, are superficial, and not meaningful. Not so. Most men, when you talk with them in depth, realize this reputation is not consistent with reality. Most (although not all!) of the men in this study have at least one or two close friends. They can talk about those friendships and of their enormous value.

Don't take my word for it—read their stories in the chapters that follow, as men talk about what friendship is, how important it is, and how they make and maintain their friendships. Also, listen to the men talk about their fathers' influences on their friendships and how knowing women has (or has not) shaped relationships with other men and women.

This does not mean that the state of male friendships is fully evolved and does not need help—far from it. Friendship is an untapped resource for men. A friendship can be like a ship twinkling in the darkness far out at sea—a man knows it is there, but he can't enjoy its warmth. Many men, after being interviewed for this book, came to re-evaluate the importance of their friendships.

Men's friendships are definitely different from women's friendships. For example, men do not show as much physical affection or offer as many compliments to each other as do women. They do not require as much or as intense verbal communication from their male friends. Men compete more openly than women, and do so by following pre-set rules in that competition, like those established in sports. For example, men can always find a professional sporting event on which to bet. They can play a pickup game of basketball in any city and know that they keep the court if they win. Every golfer knows what match play is, and every football fan understands the point spread. For many men, these are universal and acceptable forms of competition. They are a form of communication, and they define the way that male friendships are played out.[4]

Women, on the other hand, openly show affection and compliment each other frequently. When it comes to their interactions, they sometimes size each other up by less clear standards than men. Who is the best mother, the best worker, or the most emotionally giving is difficult to quantify, but these are areas of comparison in which women might engage. Communication differences also exist. Brant Burleson, a professor of communication, notes that women learn that talking is the manner through which intimacy is created and maintained, whereas males use talking to accomplish things.[5] This is not to say that men and women do not want the same thing—intimacy, empathy, and trust in their close relationships. It is just that men have different ways of getting there.

Unfortunately, it appears that people are connecting less with friends than before. Public policy expert Robert Putnam writes, in *Bowling Alone*, of the increasing separation between Americans as those networks that used to bring us together, like bridge clubs and religious institutions, dwindle in membership. In our neighborhoods, Putnam explains, we spend less time chatting over the back fence, and we know our neighbors less well. We are more centered in our homes, away from others outside our family.[6] A survey that captured attention in the news found that Americans today had fewer confidants, an average of 2.08, than 20 years earlier, when the average was 2.94. On the other hand, it was reported that spouses/significant others are playing an increasingly important role as confidants,[7] a finding similar to what is happening in Great Britain.[8]

How can we account for this shift from the importance of friends to the importance of spouses? As more women entered the workplace, greater financial and professional equality emerged between men and women than in previous generations. This equality led to roles being less starkly defined;

many men appreciate their spouses more and are more apt to consider them true friends. The survey also found that, not surprisingly, men said they had fewer confidants than did women.

One unsettling conclusion of this research is that Americans are more socially isolated than before: If the spouse dies or a divorce occurs, the support network will not be as large as before. (Many divorced people often lose a set of friends after the breakup if their friends have to pick sides.) Putnam's research provides a similar perspective on this. With women entering the workplace in greater numbers, women's ability to organize neighborhood activities and to have time for community connectivity has diminished. We all are more isolated.

Men can improve their friendships and communicate better among themselves (and not necessarily through a female version of that communication). Most men will tell you they have a buddy they can depend on, someone who is there when they need him. Some can talk with this friend about their deepest fears and greatest joys, whereas others will reserve their most personal feelings for their wives, although still considering the buddy a "best friend." Other men have friends with whom they can do their favorite activities but with whom they would never discuss anything personal. Fish together? Sure. Talk? Never. And yet that friendship works for them. These are all parts of their way of classifying friends, their Buddy System.

Despite the many friendships that work, I think men miss opportunities to "do friendship" better. Fear holds them back. For example, they worry too much about appearances when they want to show camaraderie with other men. They get embarrassed by hugging men, unless it is a group hug after a sports victory. Showing affection raises fears that a man might be perceived as gay, as does calling up a guy and asking him to go out and do something. Men don't like appearing needy, especially in front of other men. Calling up another guy puts the caller in a vulnerable position, a place men do not like to be.

We find it difficult to tell men we like them—unless it's in front of somebody else and in the context of saying he is a "good guy." Lionel Tiger, an anthropologist, wrote over 30 years ago that men have trouble showing tenderness unless it is within the context of sports, politics, or memorializing war heroes. What do sports, politics, and memorializing heroes have in common? They are all virile activities. We can be tender if we are being masculine at the same time. No one questions a war hero's virility.

Tiger also believes we have not evolved that much from cavemen. Participation in sports is popular because it has replaced the earlier hunting behavior that was required for survival. We can not hunt together for dinner like we used to but we can still get together and hit a baseball.

Men also maintain a sense of closeness through friendly teasing. Teasing allows a man to specifically comment on another man's behavior, one he has obviously been observing, but to do so in a slightly pejorative way. The message is that "I notice you. But I am keeping you at a safe distance by teasing you."

Friendship, like love, works best, I believe, when a person can be himself. If a man is *himself* with another man, the friendship should work. Getting comfortable with oneself and seeking out men who are a good counterpart is the best way to have meaningful friendships. Holding back on relationships because of trepidations does not make sense. I am not advocating for men to "dump" their emotions onto a friend. Rather, I am arguing for the judicious exploration of what may occur if a man slowly opens himself up to an investigation of his current friendships and the consideration of future ones.

Friendships Throughout History

The concept of friends and friendships is everywhere we turn. The term *friend* comes from *freogan* (an Old Goth root) meaning "to love." Friendships have existed throughout history and have challenged the philosophers who have tried to define them.

Friends first were partners in survival. Early men (various herdsmen, clansmen, tribesmen) chased food together. They sat around the campfire and figured out game plans when fighting other tribes. Whether these were "friendships" as we think of them is debatable, but they served the key survival functions of eating and fighting. And when a man "got his friend's back," he had to hope the friend had his, too, to protect each other from spears and saber-toothed tigers.

The nature of friendships began changing during the shift from the Paleolithic Age to the Neolithic Age. In the Paleolithic Age, small tribes traveled from plain to plain searching for food and shelter. At some point, about 10,000 years ago or so, some smart person determined that everyone might be better off staying put for awhile. During this Neolithic Age, farming began, and more stable communities were first established.

This stabilization resulted in a need for a different type of friendship.[9] It also meant more complex communication between people was needed.

When you are on the move all the time, the loudest, strongest, and fastest hunters lead the pack. In a small community, wiser heads start to prevail—those who can plant, plan communities, and build them gain ascendancy. Negotiation skills, rather than brute strength and speed, become more important. To negotiate and be a good citizen, you need to get along with people interpersonally.

As tribes became communities, more stable and less threatened by the elements and seasons, survival became a little less tenuous. The nature of relationships and friendships, how people got along within the community, changed, as villages developed into towns and then into cities. With survival more assumed, wise heads began to consider more existential ideas about life and friendships, and the study of philosophy grew. Fast forward to ancient Greece, where Aristotle, Plato's most famous student, began writing about the nature of friendships and pushing the understanding of friendships further. Although both teacher and pupil saw friendships as useful for survival and important for a higher quality of life,[10] Aristotle was more explicit. He wrote that you could only be friends with a peer (not someone from whom you have something to gain financially) and that you must have shared "salt" or a common problem with someone (like a battle experience) to be a true friend.[11] He also believed that friendships took time to develop and that, because true friendship was of such a high order and so difficult to achieve, a person should not have too many friends. Each friend required much time and effort.[12]

Banding together out of professional need became formalized in the Middle Ages with the formation of *guilds*, or places where people in similar professions could help each other in times of crisis. Cobblers and other craftsmen realized they would be better served by forming a united front and regulating their business. These were essentially work relationships (not friendships), and they continue today in the workplace as unions and professional associations. The Friendly Societies of the 18th and 19th centuries were just that—institutions formed to protect members against undue hardships as a result of natural causes. In that way, they operated like insurance. The term "friendly" was used, but in a way far different from the more modern consideration of friendship and even further away from Aristotle's notions of friendship. It may not, however, be a far cry from the relationships formed by men in the armed forces, in which they come to rely on each other, although they may not like each other or be friends. Many of these were group-based or small-community relationships.

The one-to-one relationships that are the focus of this book were also common by the 18th century, according to Sociologist Peter Nardi. Men, he notes, would freely express their innermost feelings to each other in writing.[13] Some of these letters survive today. One example, from 1779, was American statesman Alexander Hamilton's note to a friend: "I wish, my dear Laurens, it might be in my power, by action rather than words, to convince you that I love you."[14] Although close relationships were maintained over the course of a lifetime, they were, like today, apt to be most intimate and intense during the teenage years and into young adulthood, a time when men break away from their families but have not yet established a career or gotten married.

U.S. President Abraham Lincoln had a close friend, Joshua Speed, with whom he roomed for four years while living in Springfield, Illinois, before Lincoln was elected president. The two men shared a bed, which has led to speculation by some 20th century historians that Lincoln was gay—one sign of how close friendships between men can be misinterpreted. However, in earlier days, it was common for people to share beds when there was little space, and bed sharing was a protection against the cold. Both men later married and stayed close friends for years.[15] The 19th century was perhaps the last period in U.S. history when men could easily hang out together without fearing that people would believe they were gay.[16]

Over the last 100 to 125 years, Nardi writes, concerns about homosexuality have crept into American consciousness, and these concerns have a profound effect on the way that men structure their friendships by making these friendships much more circumspect. What happened? Piecing together the thinking of several historians and sociologists,[17] it appears a number of occurrences near the end of the 19th century began to fuel the rise of homophobia. Prior to that time, no widespread fear of same-sex relationships existed; in fact, the term *homosexuality* did not exist before the 19th century. Sex between men did occur, but it was not always labeled deviant, and it was not an issue on many people's radar.

Most importantly, by the end of the 19th century, women's roles began to change. Along with black and immigrant men, women were entering the workforce and competing for jobs with the dominant white male culture. Men wanted to stop that encroachment and hold on to their position of power. Effeminate behavior became something "real" men wanted to avoid. Gay men, increasingly evident in urban centers, often displayed effeminate behavior to signal their sexuality to each other.[18] Acting in a masculine way, according to Michael Kimmel, a sociologist who has written extensively about men's roles, was one way of differentiating oneself from women and homosexuals, who then came to be characterized negatively.[19] As middle-class culture pushed this ideal of masculine behavior forward, it was reinforced by the burgeoning field of Freudian psychology, with its emphasis on "normal" development. Beliefs about "healthy" sexuality (which had to include heterosexual sex) began to take hold, with the result that sexual acts between men were seen as wrong and something to be avoided.

The growing concern in the early decades of the 20th century was to be masculine and maintain a physical distance from men to prove you were not homosexual. In some circles, there also existed, according to Kimmel, a rising concern about the feminization of American boys by female teachers and caretakers. Making men out of boys became paramount[20] and masculinity continued to be defined as heterosexual behavior. This fit very nicely with the rugged individualism that came to capture so much of the American spirit of entrepreneurship: rely on yourself and not others, and don't get too close to men who might be competitors, men are told.[21] By the 21st century, sharing a bed with another man and maybe even having a quiet dinner together with a good bottle of wine at a French restaurant are perceived in some circles as questionable behaviors for heterosexual men. Masculinity, although defined in different ways within different U.S. cultures, remains an important ingredient in how men define themselves and how they form friendships.[22]

Learning About Friendships

How do men learn about friendships? Parents and grandparents set the tone for the early years. Parents have a powerful influence on friendships by providing access to peers by picking the neighborhood in which the child lives and the school he attends and by overseeing how the child spends his time (not easy to do in adolescence). Parents also influence children by being good citizens themselves, by not engaging in illegal activities, and by having a loving relationship with their child.[23]

Children watch their parents interact with friends, figure out which friends are good people, observe whether friends are invited into the home, and come to understand whether friends are an important part of the family tapestry. Children get a sense of the value of friendships by hearing their parents discuss juggling time spent with friends versus time spent with family and at work. Children notice if their parents hug their friends when they see them, and are excited about running into them at the mall, the movies, or the park. All these hopefully positive responses by parents give children a sense about the importance of friends.

But children also learn more complex and troublesome lessons. Children may hear how their parents were betrayed by their friends either in business or romantic relationships. Children then learn that friends can not always be trusted. Children learn the differences between friends and acquaintances, between new friends and life-long friends, and the differences between work friends and non-work friends. Work friends may be those with whom they go to lunch. Non-work friends may be grouped into sports buddies, home repair guys, or church friends. If such delineations are made by parents, children pick up on it; they learn whether it is okay to stop off at the bar on the way home from work to have a drink with the guys.

Finally, children learn how important friends can be in a crisis, particularly if family members are unavailable or are unreliable. Learning about friendships continues throughout life as new information about friends comes in even as parents reach old age and are nurtured or ignored by friends.

School is another source of information about friends. Without friends at a young age, children usually suffer (unless they are uniquely self-sufficient). On the playground, boys in particular learn about the hierarchy of sports and friendship. The skilled 10-year-old athlete gets picked first—children want to be with him because, as a teammate, he can make them a winner. His abilities give him cachet and friends. It is rare that a great athlete will have no friends. Group activities, whether sports, class elections, in-school and after-school academic and nonacademic activities, or being attractive to the opposite sex are venues for acceptance, status, and friendship for a child. Those children who are good at something socially acceptable will naturally have more people around them. Bad parental examples can be trumped by good peer experiences, when it comes to children learning how to make friends.

Psychology textbooks[24] seek to explain friendships. In children, friendships (also called *peer relations* or *social support*) offer a huge protective barrier against loneliness and provide access to other friends, activities, and self-esteem. Those studying children's friendships tend to define them as voluntary, close relationships between two children founded on cooperation and trust. Very young children's friendships often take the form of *parallel play* (two children playing side by side but not playing with each other). The notions of community and relating to larger groups have not entered their world yet, as young children are only interested and able to cope with one person at a time.

Older children have more direct interaction with each other and thus form stronger bonds than young children. They develop a social need for each other; this need increases during childhood and will come to include numerous others. Adolescents develop strong peer relationships. Teens spend an enormous amount of time with each other as they simultaneously gain independence from the family. Hormones are bubbling up, too, making feelings about others more intense. But, as intense as these adolescent friendships seem, many of those friendships spontaneously combust at some point and never make it into adulthood.[25] The best friend at 13, for whom a child would sacrifice a kidney or studying time for a final exam, can drop off the face of the planet a year later if a change occurs in school, neighborhood, or peer group. So, although adults often talk about their childhood friends, they are highly selective with their memories: many friends fall by the wayside at one or the other's initiation.

Some of these youthful friendships *do* endure into adulthood and, when we get together with that childhood friend, we are young again. Seeing my high school buds returns me to my adolescence. I once again am playing in the rock band. I don't get that type of buzz from people I first met since I became an adult. For people who have had good childhood or teenage years, being with friends from those days recreates those youthful, exuberant relationships.

Forming Friendships

Across all ages, people become attracted to each other based on physical attraction (liking the way the other person looks), similar interests and traits, feeling accepted by the other person (which makes you feel better about yourself), proximity, and that undefinable something—chemistry. These elements also are influenced by age, religion, culture, race and ethnicity, class, and sexual orientation.

Physical Attraction

Young people tend to be attracted to those who look like themselves. Although it is politically incorrect to acknowledge that not all people are made beautiful, it is also foolish to ignore the fact that the Prom Queen and the Quarterback go out together more often than either of them would go out with someone seen as a "geek" (except in teen movies where inner beauty prevails). How often do we look at couples who are of unequal attractiveness and wonder how they matched up? In fact, some men in this book talked about seeking friends whose level of masculinity (or appearance) was similar to theirs—they are searching for that same level of attractiveness.

Similarity and Feeling Accepted

People are usually (although not always) drawn to each other based on race, ethnicity, age, religion, education, family structure,[26] and even genes (identical twins, those sharing 100% of their genes, are more apt to pick friends similar to each other than are fraternal twins, those sharing 50% of their genes).[27] Similarities also occur when tastes and interests match up, and similarities make friendships easier to maintain. And, unless you are interested in hanging out with people who make you feel bad about yourself (not a good interest to have), finding someone who conveys that you are likeable to them will be very reinforcing to your self-esteem.

Proximity

Friendships are more apt to be formed and maintained when there is ready access to the other person.[28] However, in today's society, with its cell phones, e-mail, and text messages, long-distance friendships have a greater chance of survival than ever before. E-mail, in fact, can be a major source of friendship maintenance,[29] allowing for brief updates with individuals as well as group communications that prior modes of communication, aside from the bulk letter stuck in the holiday card, did not permit. Online friendships (defined as connections between people who have never met but have a shared interest established through the Internet) are also maintained through e-mail and, like many friendships, usually are strengthened with time.[30] Mick, who is highlighted in Chapter 10, describes his experience with an online friendship built around a love of guitars and music. He and Jorge have never met face-to-face, yet they have shared a great deal of intimate details online, including problems with their children.

Chemistry

Chemistry is different from physical attraction, because sometimes we are pulled to people whom we do not find physically attractive. *Chemistry* refers more to a form of magnetism between people that attracts them to each other (yes, even opposites can have the chemistry). Psychologist Daniel Goleman writes that, when the connection or chemistry is there, it may be reinforced by a biological reaction.[31] For example, if you see a close friend upset, it may make you upset on a biologically measurable level (such as blood pressure). This chemistry is hard to quantify, but men who were interviewed for this book often said essentially that they "just liked the guy" without being able to say more about why.

Sometimes something happens between people that draws us together. There may be no understandable reason for why we like hanging out with them. But, if no chemistry exists, even though the other four components are there, it is unlikely that the friendship will get off the ground.

Age

A man's age and stage of life can also play a significant part in friendship formation. Younger men with more leisure time have the greatest need for friends, while married family men with child care and work responsibilities have the least apparent need (because they have the least time). When their children leave the nest and their work lives slow down, the need for friends increases again. As I show in later chapters, older men also express their need for friends differently from younger men, as they are less able to ask for help.

Religion

Religion can also affect friendships, particularly among adherents of more conservative religious sects. Orthodox Jews and Muslims, for example, are not permitted much casual contact with women outside of their family, thus emphasizing male friends and making their relationships with those men more intense. Faith communities often provide such friendships to their members (the church group interviewed in Chapter 15 is an example of men getting together to bond based on a common religion). The structured interactions supported through common religious practices can make it much easier to form life-long friendships by providing safe environments for getting together with others.

People who do not attend religious services will, in general, have fewer opportunities to make friends, especially friends who share similar family values with them. Although differences may exist between highly religious and less religious men in their level and type of interactions with other men, comparing the nature of friendships between religions is difficult.

Culture

Culture affects how men interact and how their friendship patterns develop. Southern European men—for example, Greeks—with their high degree of interpersonal expressiveness, may do better at connecting with others than Northern European men, who are believed to be less demonstrative. According to one study, suicide rates for men in Russia, Finland, and Denmark, are substantially higher than for men in Southern Europe.[32] And, in another study, suicide and depression among men have been noted to be increasing in Eastern Europe. Why? One hypothesis presented by the researchers is that Eastern European men have too strong an orientation toward traditional masculinity. Traditional masculinity is defined (perhaps unfairly) as using dysfunctional coping strategies like not expressing emotions and not seeking help when needed.[33] The Mediterranean culture, in which men hold hands and kiss each other on the cheek, provides access to higher levels of interpersonal happiness.[34] Is this a coincidence, or is there a connection?

Other studies also have found cultural differences in interpersonal relationships. Polish people are thought to have less intense and intimate friendships than Americans.[35] Chinese express themselves with more subtlety than Westerners, who use more explicit means of communication. Meeting the needs of the individual at the expense of the group is less likely in China, where it is important not to upset the community.[36] Thus, individual friendships may be more difficult to build in China.

Race and Ethnicity

Any member of a minority group in a majority culture is likely to form an immediate bond with other members of that minority group for reasons of identification and, in some cases, protection. A sense of solidarity exists between members of some groups, particularly if they identify highly with their group.[37] Walk into a large gathering where you see only one or two other people who resemble you in race, gender, or age, and you are likely to want to connect with them in the belief that some commonality exists.

African-American friendships, according to sociologist Clyde Franklin,[38] are formed partly around the shared experience of being a member of a minority group as well as being a member of a group that has not always been welcomed by certain segments of society. African-American men have a natural affiliation for each other based on this experience and based on a greater sense of collectivism.[39] Both verbal and emotional expressiveness are highly valued in forming friendships, perhaps to a higher degree than among white men, according to psychologist George Roberts.[40] Although working-class friendships among African-American men are seen as warm and self-disclosing, with the men interacting with each other as if they are family members, upwardly mobile African-American men have friendships that, according to Franklin, tend to mimic broader society—they are neither close nor intimate. This group of men spends their time trying to get ahead, and they do not put as much time into their friendships.

Less research is available on Latino men and their friendships. In the United States, the Hispanic population is now second in number to the white population. (*Latino* or *Hispanic* is a catchall term used to describe peoples from a number of countries whose cultures may vary markedly from each other, but whose language is based on Spanish or Portuguese.) Latino men's behavior is often thought to derive from a traditionally *macho* culture, a culture in which, according to sociologist Scott Coltrane, men parade their masculinity through combative posturing and sexual conquests. Others have written that the *macho* stereotype includes men being denied permission to cry, being always competitive, trying to be the best, never retreating, and not getting emotionally involved.[41]

Such stereotypes are, of course, just that—stereotypes—and do not apply to all Latino men in or outside the United States. Clearly, men born and raised in the United States and of non-Latino backgrounds demonstrate such behavior also, although it may be more socially supported among Latinos. These stereotypical behaviors would not seem to engender easy friendships between men due to their competitive slant and lack of interpersonal giving. Yet, as we hear from a few Latino men in this book (including Casey, introduced in Chapter 2), their friendships are quite giving and are often physically affectionate. Stereotypes should not always be considered as reality, and cultural behavior may shift over time. For example, in a study of Latino families living in the United States, a great deal of role-sharing between husband and wife occurs, despite the macho tradition of these families.[42] Such change could affect how men relate to each other, too.

Class

Another important consideration is the impact that economic class can have on friendships. A high school peer group may begin to break apart after graduation when the more academically gifted and financially secure members of the class have the option to pursue college out of state. Lower-class students have fewer choices,[43] often stay in-state, and maintain their peer group through continued association with their high school buddies. Once careers start, the more highly educated and upwardly mobile men have increased options for pursuing relationships that are more work-related. They are less apt to return home, and they may leave a whole cadre of friends behind who are not on the same career path.

This was also true in the 19th century, when middle-class men who had formed deep attachments to childhood friends left those friendships behind when it was time to begin the responsibilities of marriage and career. The individualism that came to characterize much of the growth of the United States during the 19th century fostered competitiveness rather than cooperation for those aspiring to get ahead.[44]

Once settled into a socioeconomic class, other differences appear. Working-class men, sociologist Ted Cohen believes, may place a higher value on peer relationships at work and may stay at a job longer because they like the guys there.[45] Working class men are more apt to develop friendships in the workplace, according to Peter Nardi, and are less apt than middle-class men to entertain at home.[46] The more upwardly mobile men, in a way to similar to what Clyde Franklin described for African Americans, will pursue the next rung of the career ladder, even when it means leaving behind men they like. When work is the focus, the peer group will be secondary. Friendships between working-class men, according to Cohen, will often be more fulfilling emotionally.

The workplace is a good place to foster cross-class friendships, as neighborhoods are often home to people of the same class. Cross-class friendships usually begin when people are starting out at a new job and are at the same level of employment. But, if one guy gets promoted and begins earning significantly more money, class differentials can begin to intrude and break apart the friendship.[47] If the friendship was solid before the promotion, it may survive. Of course, people do form friendships at work with people from a different class, but these are more likely to be true friendships if one does not have control or influence over the other's job.

Sexual Orientation

What about sexual orientation and friendships? As we will hear from gay men later, being gay does matter. Sexual orientation affects the way that gay men interact with each other as well as how they interact with straight men. Sociologist Peter Nardi describes the intensity of gay men's first meetings.[48] Not only are two men members of a minority group getting together and sometimes sharing fears and feelings about being a member of a minority group, but the meeting holds the potential for a sexual or love relationship to be established (as does a first meeting between a man and a woman). Straight men do not engage each other with this type of intensity. Thus, even if the friendship between two gay men remains platonic, the bond formed is apt to be deeper, based on their initial exchanges and their membership in a minority group.

Sociologist Jammie Price studied friendships between gay and straight men, which are discussed later in this book. Gay and straight men often struggle with acceptance of the other and operate at some level of distrust. They can be "casual" friends but are rarely emotionally close with each other. Only about one-third of the men she interviewed truly accept and respect sexual differences in men of another sexual orientation and consider them close friends.

Ways to Think About Friendships

So, how do friendships work today? They usually begin with a *meeting*— when strangers first interact and become acquaintances—then proceed to a period of *mating* or bonding—when an acquaintance becomes a friend.[49] Believe it or not, a Web site is dedicated to helping build friendships, www. celebratefriendship.org. This group defines a *friend* as a beloved companion, someone you break bread with, and a *comrade* as someone you live with, like a roommate. Although meetings can happen by serendipity, they are more likely to occur among people who have similar interests or are close in proximity (like neighbors). Meetings can occur on the Web, in the multitude of chat rooms devoted to people looking for connections around hobbies, interests, activities, medical information, and, yes, even in chat rooms that help with friendship problems.

Social psychologists point out that what helps us to like people is how we feel when we associate with them—a "reward theory of attraction." When a relationship gives us more, or at least as much as it costs us, we like it.[50] Another way of thinking about relationships is in terms of equity.[51] Ideally, what two male friends get from a friendship or a relationship should be similar to what they put into it. If imbalance exists, the friendship will not work or will not work as well. Striking a balance may be especially important at the beginning of a relationship. When people first meet—let's set the scene in a bar—they are likely to buy each other a drink. "Let me get you that beer," says one to the other. "Okay, but I'll get the next one," which he is likely to do if the acquaintanceship is going to continue. Not enough history exists to know that payback will come. With an established friendship, the reciprocity does not have to be immediate. A man may buy a drink or a round of golf for a friend and not expect payback the next day, but will wait until the next weekend or the next golf season. Because of the existing friendship, the other man knows the payoff will come with time.

Friends reveal increasing amounts of information as they deepen their commitment to each other. They may share things with their best friends they do not share with others. They come to know each other better over time[52] and can predict responses. This helps to define the friendship and is based on a level of trust that assures that the receiver of the self-disclosure will accept the information in a way that makes the sender feel okay about himself and will handle the information in a trustworthy manner.

Fraternities, most common in colleges, also provide a basis for friendships. Lionel Tiger writes of them as being a safe way for men to find friends. Secret handshakes and rituals are ways of binding men together in the company of other men. When I pledged a college fraternity 40 years ago, the vast majority of freshmen joined for social and economic reasons. If I did not join, I would either be seen as "unattractive" or counter-culture (I was not cool enough to be counter-culture). My options for living arrangements during the rest of my college years were greatly enhanced by having the frat house as an option (wild beer parties and all). At some colleges, in the old days, fraternities accepted or rejected guys based on race or social class (mine did not, I am proud to say) and were a great venue for future professional networking (mine was not, I am sorry to say). Frats were a safe and masculine way to join together with men in living arrangements. I consider how much time was spent together planning mixers with the sororities, heading out to bars together, going to the college football games as a fraternity, and, although less common, forming study groups. The fraternity was also a place to form cross-class friendships. Now, although fraternities are less popular, they are still a safe way to make friends that may carry over into young adulthood.

A century ago, the fraternity brother might enter the work force as a young adult and keep such relationships going by joining a fraternal order. The Odd Fellows, Freemasons, and Knights of Pythias were all venues for men to continue their fellowship and escape the influence of women.[53] Sociologist Michael Kimmel believes that the fraternal order promoted male bonding through secret rituals and initiation ceremonies. Yet, like the fraternity, these too have diminished in importance due, in part, to work and family demands and increasing participation in sports or watching sports together.

As we leave college and young adulthood behind, a "best" friendship can turn out to be a more stable relationship than a friendship with a spouse, especially given the high rate of divorce. Such a "best" friendship usually involves people of the same sex[54] and has been of some considerable duration. As we age, friendships persist in playing an important role as they buffer us against loneliness, particularly in later life, and may, if they are with a life-long friend, help us to feel young. Women may need these friendships more than men do, as they tend to live longer and, if married, to outlive their husbands. But men still need them.

Family Ties

How should we consider family in light of friendship? As family therapist Anna Muraco writes, enormous overlap exists between friends and family, because both provide trust, respect, intimacy, and caring.[55] Family relationships are much better understood and have been written about more than male friendships. And although multiple theories of family therapy exist for dealing with family problems, no tested theories exist for solving adult friend problems. Family members are often one's best or closest friends, as we hear from the people interviewed for this book. People from large families in particular often feel less need for friends outside of the family— someone is always around.[56] People with small families are forced to make friends with others to gain companionship.

One important and obvious distinction exists between family and friends—biological and legal bonds hold families together whereas, with friends, the more elusive concept of choice maintains a friendship. But this is also where friendships may provide more support than family. Friendships can substitute for a lack of connection with siblings.[57] Friendships can be less stressful than relationships with family—less historical baggage is present, and friends can be added if you like them and dropped if you don't (although, as you'll read later, dropping a friend isn't always easy).

Although siblings are the obvious first consideration for family friends, some people also consider their children or parents as friends. Men will describe their father or their son as their best friend. It is wonderful when such relationships exist and are satisfactory for both parties, although I believe these are rare. Warm relationships between fathers and sons are not rare, but I think generally people also benefit from having close friends outside of the immediate family. One study of older adults found that friends often matter more than adult children do because of their discretionary nature (you can pick your friends but not your family). This may be especially true for older adults, who become more selective in friendships as they age.[58] So, if you have chosen to spend time with a close friend, he is probably quite important to you.

Are Male Friendships Difficult to Establish?

Given that friends are made and the models we have for them in movies, books, and television are diverse, why do men have a difficult time making friends? Robert Lewis, a social scientist, gives four reasons. First, friendships are maintained at a physical and emotional distance because men fear emotional and physical closeness, which they link to homosexuality.[59] Second, adult role models are lacking—because their fathers did not have many friends, today's men did not learn how to make friends from them. Whether because of their father's own socialization patterns or the dire need to work during the Great Depression (see, for example, Michael, who is in his 60s and featured in Chapter 11), the role models, particularly for older men, are not there. The third and fourth reasons are a fear of being vulnerable and competition between men. If we add to these four a fifth reason—that men are taught to control their emotions,[60]—then the opportunities to connect with other men are greatly restricted, even though, since the 1960s, men have become more open with their feelings.

As a result, men develop shoulder-to-shoulder or side-by-side friend-ships based on doing activities together, like sports,[61] as compared with women, who develop friendships in which they interact more personally or intimately. Several caveats are important here, however. With deep and longstanding friendships, some evidence suggests that interactions between male friends can be more personal.[62] We also need to be careful when assuming that sports, mentioned so often in what males do together, is the best venue for building later strong friendships. Sociologist Michael Messner writes that the structure of sports, with its emphasis on competi-tion, does little to help young boys transcend their fear of intimacy.[63] At the same time, sports do allow boys a socially acceptable way of touching each other on the field of competition through knocking into opponents to hugging or high-fiving a teammate, something they cannot do in most other venues.

The early upbringing of boys in the United States plays a part, too, in how men do or do not form friendships. Psychologist William Pollack describes how boys are raised to be tough and unemotional as part of the growing up process. Even as early as three years, boys learn to be careful about being too emotional and vulnerable. They adopt a macho veneer that can affect building friendships. Thus, the difficulties can begin at a young age. But all is not lost. When Pollack gave the boys he interviewed the opportunity to speak in a safe environment, it was clear that they sought connection with others through friendships and relationships.[64]

The separation of boys from their feelings is considered a major imped-iment in men's ability to form connections with others. If boys are trained at an early age to get by without experiencing their own and others' feelings, as adults, it is hard for them to become connected with friends, spouses, or significant others.

At issue too are unclear definitions of masculinity and what men need to develop emotionally. Some who have written about men's relationships view men as not aware enough of their "maleness." They see men as being unable to deeply relate to each other as men. Robert Bly, the author of *Iron John*, believes men need to be with other men to experience collective masculinity and that some men have become too feminized and "soft" by surrounding themselves with women. For Bly, doing things with men and finding male mentors are the answers and would, by extension, lead to more fulfilling friendships.

Raewyn Connell, an Australian professor of education and expert on masculinities, wrote about understanding masculinity and men's roles in a context that includes women. Men make choices about how to act from "a cultural repertoire of masculine behavior."[65] Men are not passive recipients of this set of choices but are involved in setting up the choices. These choices differ greatly from one country to the next. For example, the way that masculinity plays out in Mexico among the working class is different from how it plays out in South Africa among those with a history of colonizing others and being colonized. Friendships in Russia, where a totalitarian government has been in place, are different from those in the United States.[66] Ultimately, Connell defines masculinity as related to and embedded in culture and personality, a very different view from Bly's.

Why else might men have trouble making friends? In a study comparing men ages 25 to 34 with men ages 35 to 50, the older men were found to have fewer friends. The authors believe this is due to the increasing time invested in a relationship with one woman, usually a wife.[67] As families are formed, the wife and children increasingly pull men away from friends. Even with women, men's emotional intimacy can be problematic. One research team argues that the socialization of men makes intimate relationships with women and the discussion of emotions difficult—men withdraw when expected to articulate emotions.[68]

Much of what is understood about men's friendships and the potential difficulties they have in being formed come from comparing them with women's. Sociologist Lillian Rubin, in researching deficits in men's lives, wrote, "At every life stage during those years, women have more friendships . . . than men, and the differences in the content and quality of the friendships of women and men are marked and unmistakable."[69] A "best" friendship in particular may not be easy for a man to get. In her research, women were much more able to name a best friend than were men.[70] Some men reported that best friends were for kids, and others said that it was difficult getting close to other men. More recent research on friendships have described women's friendships as more self-disclosing,[71] emotionally closer,[72] and more oriented toward one-on-one relationships rather than toward group relationships.[73] Friendships continue to be important as we age, but friendships are seen as more important to women than to men over time.[74]

These are the many reasons, including the inappropriate comparison with women's friendships, why men may have difficulties with friendships. I say "inappropriate comparison" because, if you tell men enough times that their friendships are not as good as women's, some men—and women—will believe it, and that will affect friendship building.

But, not so fast. Other research offers a less dire picture of men's friendships when compared with women's. In some quarters, friendships are thought to be equally important to both men and women, and only the definitions of friendship vary for men and women.[75] One researcher described men as having more friendships than women, although they were less close friendships.[76] In a different study of adolescents and adults, women and men were found to equally value friendships.[77]

One last thought—the ability of men or women to receive support from others may be, in the final analysis, linked more to one's genes than to one's gender.[78] We are not all wired the same when it comes to dealing with each other on a personal level. Because women's and men's brains are different, our ability to interact within relationships will be different.[79] Biological male–female differences can not be downplayed. Even in the first few days of life, boy babies are attracted to activities different from those of girl babies. In one study, girls were more drawn to faces and boys to mechanical objects.[80] Does this mean men's friendships are deficient? No—but they may play out differently than women's.

Ultimately, barriers may exist to men's friendships. The way friends are defined by men and women needs to be taken into account because the social context, even when genes are involved,[81] can influence personality and how we interact. Although comparisons are certainly made in this book between men and women's friendships, it is not useful to dwell too much on differences (our similarities may be more interesting), as the purpose is to help men build new friendships and appreciate those they have.[82]

Real-Life and Fictional Friendships in the Media

We build friendships, in part, based on our family, our school, our community interactions, and on the portrayals in the media to which we are exposed. Stories about friendships between men are plentiful and have helped shape how men interact. These span the Bible (note the friendship between Jonathan, son of Saul, and David, the future king, in which Jonathan warns David his father is out to get him and thus sides with his friend over his father) to the Stephen Ambrose books about war buddies (*Band of Brothers*, for example) to the more personal accounts in which one-to-one friendships are captured. Some are stories specifically about friendships, such as *Brian's Song* about football legend Gale Sayers and his cancer-stricken teammate Brian Piccolo.

In 1978, author Willie Morris wrote extensively and admiringly about his friendship with James Jones, who authored *From Here to Eternity* and *The Thin Red Line*. Morris recounts their long relationship and also describes Jones's friendships with authors William Styron and Irwin Shaw. Morris refers to Jones as one of the two great presences in his life, along with his mother. Morris had known Jones personally for 10 years at the time. "Why did we become like brothers?" Morris asks in the opening pages. In considering how friendships develop, he wonders, "Among the countless people you meet in a lifetime—in a classroom as a child, on a plane, in a bar, through friends—is it possible when you first begin talking with them to foresee that someday they might be among the very few of all human beings or perhaps the only one of all of them, to share something immeasurably close and enduring?"[83] Is there a special chemistry to friendships? he is asking. In fact, Morris and Jones met at seminal turning points in both of their lives, and that, I have learned, and as Ambrose describes with his accounts of war, is one reason why people become life-long or close friends. They meet at the right time—whether on the playground, in the neighborhood when new families are moving in, or at work when co-workers share a challenging assignment.

David Michaelis dedicates an entire book to famous friendships between the well-known (e.g., comedians Dan Aykroyd and John Belushi) and the less well-known (Vietnam veterans Leonard Picotte and Michael Edwards).[84] In describing Aykroyd's response to the death of Belushi, whom Aykroyd had been trying to salvage from a drug-induced downward spiral, Michaelis writes, "Dan Aykroyd was suddenly on his own. His best friend was dead of an overdose of heroin mixed with cocaine. Aykroyd felt as if he had lost a brother. Gone was the business partnership, and the strong friendship, which had provided for both men an emotional support system as well as a permanent base from which they had launched their careers in tandem. . . . Together they had shared their twenties, and had talked of growing old together. It had been, in Aykroyd's words, 'a full friendship. There was no dimension of it unexplored, except the sexual one. This was friendship between two young men, two young Turks, young rogues.'"[85]

In this passage, Michaelis touches on several themes about friendship: (a) it is, for some, like a relationship with a brother, a notion also subscribed to by Willie Morris; (b) it is an emotional support; (c) it has the hope of lasting a lifetime; and (d) it is nonsexual (as defined in this context).

We return to these ideas later in the book, when we hear from some of the nearly 400 men who were interviewed.

David Halberstam's book, *The Teammates: A Portrait of a Friendship*, on the friendships of the baseball players Ted Williams, John Pesky, Dominic DiMaggio, and Bobby Doerr, which endured for 60 years, is an example of a series of shoulder-to-shoulder friendships. Only they had pursued World Series rings together, so only they could understand the complex team relationships that had been forged over the years. When they stopped playing ball, they maintained the friendship by working at it—they relived their past successes on the ball field while fishing or talking on the phone.

Is every close relationship a friendship? Probably not, especially when it is between teacher and student, mentor and mentored, coach and player. Mitch Albom, in *Tuesdays with Morrie*, learns about friendships from Morrie, his former college professor who has a terminal disease. What is a perfect day for the dying Morrie? "I'd get up in the morning, do my exercises, have a lovely breakfast of sweet rolls and tea, go for a swim, then have my friends come over for a nice lunch. I'd have them come one or two at a time, so we could talk about their families, their issues, talk about how much we mean to each other."[86] His friends give his life meaning. Two weeks later, they have their last visit, as Morrie's death is imminent and he can barely talk. Albom recounts the exchange, "'My . . . dear friend . . .,' he finally said. 'I am your friend,' I said."[87] Yet Morrie then asks to be referred to as Coach. After his death, and in the final paragraphs of the book, Albom refers to Morrie as his teacher, his professor. They return to their preassigned roles, even after spending such intimate time together. These close relationships may become friendships if they achieve parity, but more often they remain in the form they started.

Fictional male friendships are easy to find in classic American literature. Mark Twain's Tom Sawyer and Huck Finn may be the prototype for childhood friends. Yet they were quite different in both their family connections, their interest in girls, and in their willingness to form relationships with others, with Tom being the more socially connected of the two. Somehow, they were drawn together, not just because they lived in the same town, but by a penchant for adventure sprinkled with a healthy dose of antiauthoritarianism. They had commonality, proximity, and chemistry going for them. Mark Twain himself looked at friendship through various lenses. At one point he noted, "The proper office of a friend is to side with you when you are in the wrong. Nearly anybody will side with you when you are in the right."[88]

Lenny and George in John Steinbeck's *Of Mice and Men* are also friends who need each other. Although they are quite different in many ways, George is drawn to Lenny's mental limitations and finds in Lenny someone he can take care of. Lenny relies on and trusts George totally. Without Lenny, George's dream of buying a farm cannot be realized. George arguably proves the ultimate friend by swiftly and mercifully killing Lenny at the end of the book rather than turning him over to the authorities to die a slower execution.

Butch Cassidy and the Sundance Kid, two real-life outlaws immortalized in a 1969 movie, are shoulder-to-shoulder friends who bond while robbing banks. It doesn't take the viewer too long into the movie to see that they are noncompetitive friends who rely on each other yet have a teasing component to their relationship. They are both heroes and antiheroes depending on how you look at it.[89]

The list of buddy movies is long and includes the motorcyclists played by Peter Fonda and Dennis Hopper in *Easy Rider* and the oenophiles Miles and Jack in *Sideways*. Movies have also shown friendships that are extraterrestrial as well as human. Think about the youthful focus on friendships in *ET: The Extra-Terrestrial* and the Harry Potter movies (sometimes between a boy and a girl), as well as the *Star Wars* movies with their cast of galactic characters banding together to save the universe.

And let's not forget TV friendships: *Friends*, *Seinfeld*, and most cop shows all portray male friendships from the funny to the serious. Too recent for you? How about Buffalo Bob and Clarabelle, Captain Kangaroo and Mr. Greenjeans, and Andy Griffith and Barney Fife? We learned growing up how to be friends from watching these old shows, and we learned from the more recent ones how friendships play out in adulthood.

Classifying Friends

I like to think of men in a Buddy System as having four types of friends—the *must* friend, the *trust* friend, the *rust* friend, and the *just* friend (and it is remarkable how many of the men we interviewed came up with their own classifications). Many men have friends whom they need to see to maintain their well-being. These are their closest (*must*) friends, and they would miss them sorely if they were not in their lives. If something good or bad happens—a child gets engaged, a job is lost, or a marriage breaks up—the *must* friends are called.

Many men have a few people whom they trust, but with whom they do not feel extremely close. These are friends from work or the neighborhood, but are not the closest buddies. They may be told the same personal information about the engagement, firing, or breakup, but that sharing will happen more by chance. Sometimes, such friends provide space from a too-intense relationship with a *must* friend. A few men I have talked to do not share some of their closest secrets with their *must* friends because they believe those friends are too close to others in their community. They talk instead with people outside of the community, those who they do not worry will share the secret with others in the hometown. If there is, for example, a difficulty with a *must* friend, the *trust* friend can also provide a sounding board that does not carry the emotional weight that a *must* friend does.

Men also have *rust* or old friends. These are friends that have accumulated over the years and may also be a *must*, *trust*, or *just* friend. They are close to the man by dint of time and, with time, comes at least a modicum of trust and knowledge. Families that grow up together, in which the children know each other and then their children know each other have *rust* friends. If you grew up with someone in the same town and see him all the time, he could be a *rust* friend. *Rust* friends differ from *just* friends in that longevity underpins the relationship. They could be the golf buddies from the past 25 years or a running buddy. A work colleague told me about going to his 35th high school reunion and finding classmates whom he couldn't stomach many years ago, but were now enjoyable to be with. He has started to get together with them. "Now we can just be ourselves. Before it was all about competition and everything," he told me. Time has made these *rust* friendships work, and they are usually not highly intense.

Men also have acquaintances that they consider *just* friends (and nothing more), those with whom they would not share upsetting news because they would be unsure of the reaction and whether the recipient would keep it private. People who are *just* friends are people with whom you might get together casually to share an activity. Joseph Epstein writes that people in casual relationships have no responsibility to each other.

Throughout this book, we discuss the Buddy System of *must*, *trust*, *rust*, and *just* friends. Regardless of how you consider your friends, there is one more idea to discuss—that the nature of friendship changes with age. As we read these men's stories, it is clear that older men are different from younger men—the guy in his 20s needs his friends more than does the man in his 40s, who is balancing family and career and has formed a meaningful relationship with his wife. The guy in his 70s has time again for his friends and comes back to them as his children consume less time. So, the need for friends ebbs and flows throughout life and is greatest at the beginning and the end of life.

Conclusion: Understanding Friendship

What we have learned from this chapter is that friendships come in many shapes and sizes. They are a vitally important part of life and they vary by context, culture, and class. If you want to live a longer, healthier life, you should gain an understanding and appreciation of the friendships you have, figure out how to make them as meaningful as possible, and accept that great diversity exists when it comes to how they operate. Your friendships only have to be meaningful to you.

2

What Do *Friendship* and *Friend* Mean?

I am riding in the back of a taxi in Sydney, Australia, where I have traveled to learn more about men's friendships. My cab driver is a recent Pakistani immigrant to Australia, a man probably in his mid 20s. We begin talking about why I have traveled so far. I ask if he has made friends in his new country. He has not, and he longs for them. He tells me, "A friend is the most important thing to have in the world. If you have a friend, you have everything."

Friendship, like love, has always had important and universal meanings to people. But, like love, the definition varies from person to person, with no universally accepted notion. Ask 100 people what friendship is, and you will get almost as many unique responses. Over time, though, and like love, some similar themes emerge despite individual differences. Take the next three quotes. These were given by typical men who were interviewed for the study and were asked what friendship meant to them. Their quotes set the stage for the discussion that follows, as they show both the range and similarity of definitions.

- "It's a relationship between people that is amicable and helpful, and where there is good will. You count on your friends to be tough on you. Real friends tell you things that are difficult to hear."
- "You can't really define it. . . . Some of these sound like clichés, but a friend is someone who is there for you when you have a need, somebody that isn't judging you, someone who is going to be understanding, somebody who is going to support you even though they don't agree with you all the time."
- "A true best friend is someone you can count on in all circumstances, under all conditions, and who you understand very well and share many common goals and interests."

Defining Friendship and Friends

To get a sense of how men thought about friendships, in our study, we asked a broad, two-part question: "What is friendship, and what does a friend mean to you?" Although no universal definition of "friend" exists,[90] for the men in the study, and I believe for most men, friendships include the ability to communicate with and be understood by another person. Trustworthiness, loyalty, and dependability are also essential. Throughout the interviews, the men said similar things and used remarkably similar words: *Sharing, honesty,* and a level of mutual *acceptance* had to be present for a friendship to exist. Honesty can include being understood when honest and also trusting a friend with your honesty.

The men in the study gave the following responses to what friendship means:

- Being understood (communicating, sharing, caring, not being judged, and includes having the friend give feedback), 57%
- Trust and loyalty, 50%
- Dependability (have someone to rely on, someone to count on), 42%
- Doing things with/hanging out with, 24%
- Commonality (are similar in important ways), 18%
- Demonstrates friendship with concrete acts (helps move, loans money), 2%

The men highlighted in these pages, with a particular focus on 10 men who are followed throughout the next four chapters, give answers that often include more than one of these responses. I include at least one example under each of these responses to give the flavor of what we heard in the interviews. They also give examples of *must, trust, just,* and *rust* friends. Early in the interviews, it is clear that some men compartmentalize friends by topic or activity, and others separate them into levels that range from close to distant. They also talk about whether they have to be in constant contact with their friends.

Being Understood

Everybody wants to be understood and accepted by others. This is the cornerstone for men. Whether the men interviewed talked about this issue in terms of communication, giving feedback to someone, or having a friend to share with, being understood was essential for the majority of men. A few men said a friend would listen and accept them whether they were right or wrong. A few mentioned that a friend is like a brother, or like family.

But the notions of unconditional acceptance and friendship varied. Some men described in macho terms that a friend would tell them when they were wrong and would "keep them in line." These men felt that they were a little tougher if they had friends who would "tell them off" and who felt free to speak their minds. They were proud of appearing that they could go "toe to toe" in a friendship by openly speaking their minds. That was how they felt understood. In the case of Al, being understood included keeping confidences.

Al, a 45-year-old white nurse, has been married most of his adult life and is the father of a son. Interviewed over a cup of coffee at a diner, Al introduces very quickly the importance of being one's own person in a friendship, a sentiment that is key to a friendship's long-term health. In his description, he nails the concept of a *must* friend. "A friend is someone you can confide in, talk with if you need to talk with. Someone to joke around with, let your hair down with, you don't have to worry about offending. But even there, you base it on personalities. I have some pretty religious friends who I do not tell off-color jokes to. Trust is a big thing—trust and confidentiality. I wouldn't want them running right back to their significant other on some topics."

Note how Ben, the next man, looks for good communication with his friends. Age 27 and white, Ben has been working with children and adolescents as a social worker for two years. He is also a married father and doesn't think friends have to be in frequent contact to sustain their friendship. "I think a real (*must*) friendship is something where the relationship will endure anything—good times, bad times—pretty much unconditionally. And that's what friendship is. I'm not sure if the criteria should be that you have to see each other that often. I have friends I haven't seen for months, or as much as a year, and when we get together, it's like we were never apart. So, enduring, unconditional—people who can be there for you at the same time they can give you both kinds of feedback—they can give you the positive, and they can tell you when you are ridiculous."

In my dialogue with Hal, the final example here, the importance of being understood comes through loud and clear. Hal, 59, has a Ph.D. in chemistry and works at a large university where he conducts research and teaches. White and married for 23 years, he has two sons, ages 20 and 18. He has lived in the same university town for 17 years, after moving around from the West, the Midwest, and the East. His mother lives 100 miles away and is blind, having suffered from macular degeneration for the past 40 years. His father, who was her primary caretaker, died of prostate cancer 10 years ago. Hal is an only child and believes he needs friends to a greater degree than he would if he had siblings. His parents only had one child, he told me, because that was all they could afford, given his father's income from an electronics repair business. He is a thoughtful guy and paused for long periods of time during our conversation to consider the question that is posed. Our interview took place in his office.

"My perspective on friendship is based on my being an only child. I never had many people around, so people are a big deal for me. It doesn't seem to be that way for others, but people are a big deal for me. When I look at my wife, who has a large family, following up on friendships does not seem as important for her, and she is a much more loving and giving person than I am. So, looking at the world as we do, one would say that she should be much more into people than me because I am into science and don't cut a lot of people slack. But I am more into people. A (*must*) friend to me is someone you look up to as you would your family. Family is someone who is blood and responsibility, and someone can be a friend and enter into that sphere. That's where I would put a friend, in the inner circle.

"They have to be truthful to a point—sometimes you have to handle truth and grace together as a juxtaposition. Sometimes you have to handle things with grace and sometimes you have to be the truth teller. So, someone who will hold me accountable but realize the times when I need to be handled with grace would be a good friend."

His response pushed me to comment, "Your answer really speaks to the duality or the gray area that exists in friendships—I have heard from some men that they want someone to tell them the truth all the time, and from other men that they want someone to watch their back. Your statement about grace and truth spans that by saying that such actions are contextual. You are giving a more bifurcated view of how this works." These themes return later in our conversation.

One interesting study finding comes from the older men interviewed. Whereas 57% of the entire group of 386 men talked about the importance of "being understood" when they described what a friend was, among the 73 men in the sample who answered this question who are age 50 or older, 68% included this in their description. Men increasingly recognize and want a friend as they age who they can communicate with and who is accepting. Also interesting is that, of the 10 openly gay men in the sample, nine also mention "being understood" as a key component of a friendship, a higher percentage than in the sample overall. If gay men are more emotionally expressive (more apt to exchange fears and feelings, according to Peter Nardi), defining communicating as key to friendship is consistent with that belief.

Trust and Loyalty—"Having Your Back"

Trust was a key component of friendship, and it does not always mean the same thing to everyone. Robert Putnam, in his book *Bowling Alone*, describes trust as the cornerstone of social connections. If I do something for you, I must trust that, at some point, you will do something for me.[91] Without trust, friendships do not work.

Echoed by other men, the notion of loyalty and protection is very important and harkens back to earliest humans. Tribes or clans survived in part through members relying on each other. If you cannot trust your friend to protect you, then who can you trust?

Loyalty has been identified by philosophers as a key element of friendship. For example, a philosopher, Sarah Stroud, on the ethics of friendships, wrote, "One particular aspect of that loyalty, it seems, is sticking up for your friend. If someone pokes fun at one of your friends . . . or says something false or misleading (and derogatory) about him, it seems to be your responsibility as a good friend not to join in the fun; not even simply to remain silent and withhold comment; but, on the contrary, to stick up for your friend."[92] This is "having your friend's back" and vice versa. Stroud is saying that, even when the friend is not present, you will defend him.

Occasionally, the men in the survey said that trust meant lending money or providing a specific service. The men mentioned that a friend was someone who would give you a loan or come to your assistance at a moment's notice (Although this was represented by the separate response of demonstrating friendship with concrete acts, it could be subsumed under trust and loyalty.)

Casey, 35, describes himself as single, and part Hispanic, part Korean. He is involved in construction and has an engineering background. For him, loyalty is the key to friendship. "A friend is somebody who is loyal and really warm. He shows his friendship to you, not only with words but *con hechos* [with acts]. If you are sad, sometimes a good friend can catch your energy and say, 'Hey, you look sad. Can you tell me what's going on?' That is friendship to me. They show interest without making you feel bad. Some people are your friends because of the things you have, material things, but, to me, a real friend is the one who gives you friendship without asking anything in exchange" (a good description of a *must* friend).

David is 24 years old, African-American, single, and, like Ben, also counsels children. His response reveals the enormous changes he has gone through in relation to trusting males. Early on, his gang involvement pushed loyalty without friendship, in part for safety reasons. He had to grow up to learn the true meaning of friends. "I think friendship extends to commitment, support, encouragement, and someone who will raise you up when you are down. It didn't exist for me in the early part of my life. I had no idea. Honor and loyalty equal friendship now. When I was 13, I was running with the Crips, so it's loyalty but not about friendship. It was 'I die for you,' and nothing in between and no emotions are discussed and no support except 'let's get this hustle.' As I progressed through life, because of that initiation, the trust factor of other males was never there. It was like, 'you're trying to get my hustle' or 'you're trying to get my girls or my money.' So, I actually came to despise males and stayed away. I would smile at you or whatever, but if you messed with me, it's on. And I look back at how sad that is now, but realize the functioning of that. So, the definition of friendship changed as I grew older."

David talked also about the importance of age and maturity in understanding friendships and the continuing transformative role that fraternities can play for men. Fraternities for men who have been a part of a gang or even a sports team can help them continue to be together with other men in a socially acceptable way.

Finally, we meet Jack, who describes a friend and business partner who is loyal and also has his back. He could be a *rust* and a *must* friend given the longevity and closeness of their relationship. Jack, a white, 43-year-old married father of an eight-month-old named Roger, is in the most unusual situation of the featured men. He is a stay-at-home dad, and his wife is a surgeon at a major hospital in Chicago. They moved to Chicago from Baltimore one year ago because of the academic position she was offered. Female surgeons are as rare as stay-at-home dads.[93] Jack works out of the home as a parts supplier for cars, a job he was able to travel with when they moved to Chicago. It is mostly phone sales, but he also does a few trade shows a year that take him around the world, without his wife or Roger. Jack offers an interesting perspective on his role and what it is like to maintain friendships from afar, struggle to make new friends in Chicago, and raise a young son. Our interview took place in a neighborhood bar.

Jack brought Roger along in a stroller and sat him on his lap during most of the interview. Roger is incredibly mellow and, aside from a little fussiness, and one diaper change (the men's room did not have changing facilities, which Jack pointed out to the bartender), was a welcome addition to the conversation.

I met Jack at a party the week before, at which he and I were talking about this book. So, when I asked Jack how he defined friendship, he had a ready answer. "Loyalty, someone you can count on, someone with the same interests as you. Someone who would have your back. I was in another city at a trade show last week with a co-worker and we were always watching each other's back because the show was not in a safe part of town. So, friendship can mean literally and figuratively watching each other's back. This was someone I grew up with, and we ended up working together. This is someone who is personal and business. We enjoy each other's company in both realms. We were at each other's weddings and at other important junctures in each other's lives. Friendship is calling each other when the other is down. I'd call him, and he'd call me. Respect is also important. I need their respect and they need mine."

Dependability

Trying to parse out dependability—having someone to count on—from loyalty can be a wordsmith's chase but the sense gained from the men was that *dependability* was different from *loyalty*. They wanted someone specifically who they could rely on to be there when needed. They did not talk about being understood as much as the belief that they could call someone up in the middle of the night, and that person would be there for them.

A brief response given by a 41-year-old white electrician, Arnold, epitomizes the responses related to dependability that we got from the less loquacious men. "You can count on them, on a moral basis, more than anything else. They are going to be there for you if you need them, and you do not have to jump through hoops."

A more in-depth example is from one of the 10 men we are following, a response that could be grouped with these other responses. A few minutes into Felix's answer, I hear the sense of dependability that he provides for his friends.

Felix, age 50, white, and gay, lives in a condominium in a New York low-rise that he helped designed when he was with an architectural firm and before starting his own firm. He is not in a committed relationship, having broken up two years ago with his long-time significant other, Bernard. When we began the interview in his home, Felix asked me how many gay men had been interviewed for the book. Two percent had self-identified as gay, I said, but the number could be higher in case someone wished to conceal his sexual identity. That led me to cast the first question in light of his being gay, "What does a friendship mean to you, and do you think that being gay has a different meaning for you and your male friends?"

In his response, Felix turns away the question of being gay with a clarification about his self-definition before he speaks directly to friendship. "Maybe not for me—I consider myself more straight than gay. Gay is the fact that, as a sexual orientation, I prefer men. But I don't think I fit the stereotype of gay men, and the stereotype of gay men is so unfair and there are so many who do not fit the stereotype, whatever it is. Friendship for me is loyalty, and that is the basis for my philosophy, whatever the situation is. The best sign of a (*trust*) friendship is when you are having a problem and people come through for you. But if people are not loyal to me, basically they do not exist. I am not a good poker player, and I show my emotions and am very forward. When I broke up with Bernard, with whom I am still very close, I went into a local café by myself for dinner, which I do fairly frequently. I value being alone, but I also value being with people. I am very reclusive and very social at the same time. I approached a table of three friends, and they knew I was alone and they didn't ask me to sit with them. From that day on, I have never had anything to do with them."

I asked if it was because they were aligning with Bernard after the breakup?

"No. In relation to friends, gay men are very cliquish. I am not cliquish, but I find the gay community more cliquish than any other community I knew growing up, and I have no use for that in any shape or form."

I pointed out to Felix that he valued loyalty and asked if that includes having a friend support him, regardless of the situation. "When I think of loyalty, I think of a friend being there for me when the chips are down and when they are not down. I have friends from high school and college, and I put a lot of effort into friendships. I don't chase people, but the mother of one of my friends from high school said to him a few years ago, 'You'll be getting a card from Felix until you are 100.' That's the kind of person I am, and that is how I operate. I recognize there are people who adore me and those who can't stand me, and I am okay with that. I can be very warm and friendly with those I like, and I can be very aloof and removed from those I don't like and I am not ashamed of that. So, there has to be loyalty for this to work."

The third example is of someone who also values being understood and demonstrating loyalty. His response includes the notion that he can go to his friends in a pinch, and their responses will be consistent.

Ed, age 55 and white, drives a taxi. Twice-divorced with two children, he has come to rely on his male friends a great deal but withholds his friendship until the situation is right. "I'm pretty selective. I have a hundred thousand acquaintances (*just* friends), but very few move to a (*must*) friend. You have to be understanding, have a good sense of humor, and you must be trustworthy. If I say something a good pal doesn't like, I don't expect him to fly off the handle and vice versa. If I need a favor, if they need a favor, we will be there for each other. . . . [A friend is] someone you can beat up and they can beat up on you, too, and still be friends."

Do Things With: Hanging Out

Being able to spend time with a friend was very important, especially to younger men, for whom "hanging out" was frequently mentioned. One lengthy example is provided by Kenny (not one of the 10 featured men), who describes many aspects of friendship and also reflects on his youth, when he made friends through distinct activities.

A white 57-year-old married mental health practitioner with a master's degree, Kenny categorizes friendships with great complexity: "Friendship is a relationship between two people who like each other, who trust each other, have a reasonable number of commonalities that bring or bind them together, and communicate often enough to support, build, and maintain that friendship. I expect a friend to be like a Boy Scout. A scout is trustworthy, loyal, helpful, friendly, courteous, kind, obedient, cheerful, thrifty, brave, clean, and reverent.

"From a friend I expect more than from other people. I expect him to be there through thick and thin. As a teenager, I had three close friends: Jeff was my 'athletics friend'; we played tennis and basketball together; Rick was my 'intellectual friend'; he taught me about astronomy, chess, and word games. Joel was my 'social friend'; we went to the YMCA dances, double dated, cruised around, and talked about life, family, and feelings. But with each of us, there were other overlapping commonalities. We lived within reasonable proximity of each other, we were raised Jewish, we went to Hebrew School together, we were in the same Boy Scout troop, none of us smoked or did drugs, we were each from two-parent families with siblings, and we went to high school together and were college-bound. It is important in friendships to have the same behavioral and communication styles."

Jeff, Rick, and Joel were his *must* friends, and each was there for him in different spheres of his life. Men can have very close friends with whom they do different activities or who fulfill different needs. It is part of a maturation process, I believe, when a man realizes that no one person can be expected to meet all of his needs.

Commonality: One Basis for Building a Friendship

We can see the importance of commonalities in making friends in the concluding chapter, where suggestions for forming friendships are given. Without some sense of shared interests or history, it is difficult to establish or maintain a friendship over time. In Chapter 1, commonalities of race, religion, age, class, and sexual orientation are also discussed as a basis for friendship. One-fourth of the men mentioned being similar as a basis for friendship. Isuko provides an example of what the men were saying about the link between commonalities and friendship.

Isuko is a 37-year-old, Asian-American businessman who describes himself as gay. Perhaps more so than the others, he feels comfortable with opening up to other men. But a common link has to exist first. "What is a friendship? Someone you've somehow bonded with. You have something in common with them—it could be locality or interests. It can be spending time in each other's homes. I could think about my childhood friend: that's easy, because we have our childhood as our commonality. In friendships now, sharing humor is really important. Once we can make each other laugh, that would be it.[94] Definitely, when you are going through hard times, they are there for you (the *must* friend). They are interested listeners. It is definitely sharing your dreams with someone, what you want to do in the future. What comes later is that you tell the person how important they are to you. It's subtle. You could say it outright, or it's watching over each other when you have too much to drink and you puke. It could be very emotional. You remember that bond, and you open up your soul."

Although Isuko does not specifically refer to whether he means friendships with gay men, straight men, or both, it is interesting to look at the description he uses: "you tell the person how important they are to you."

Isuko may be more comfortable opening up to men in general and uses terms that imply greater intimacy than the other men use.

From reading the responses, I picked up on three other trends relating to how men define friends and friendships. First, a few believed that friendships must evolve over many years and that they have only truly good friends from their childhood or high school years. These men appeared unwilling to explore the opportunity to make new friends.

Second, men with limited exposure to others are most apt to maintain friendships they had from their youth. Men who grew up and stayed in the same small town are likely to hold on to those experiences and value long-term high school friends as compared with men who have moved often and have been forced to make new friends.

Third, men whose high school years were filled with unhappy circumstances and friendships will most likely not hold on to those relationships. They will be interested in maintaining friends they made from a time when they were happier with themselves.

Finally, let me mention Larry, who is different from almost all the men interviewed in that he admits to being a loner. He is not one of the 10 featured men, but provides a valuable counterpoint. A 31-year-old African-American engineer who is single, his relationships epitomize the nature of the *just* friend, as he has no close friends. To some extent, he is pessimistic about friendships. Although he has only acquaintances, he is well aware of what friendships could be. "I don't really consider any men my friends. I look at them as associates. There are individuals who I communicate with on several different things. I have associates who I communicate with on strictly business matters. There are others who I can just hang out with and have fun. With these individuals, I go out to a sports bar, athletic games, and fishing trips. I have a lot of fun with them but I do not really look at them as friends, just associates. . . . I wouldn't say I have a lot of friends." When asked what a friendship means to him he says, "It means someone who is really honest, loyal, and trustworthy. I just don't know anyone who fits into that category that I would consider a friend. It seems to me that no one is really honest when you get right down to it."

Although Larry says he has no friends, these "associates" clearly provide at least two of the benefits that friendships offer. He spends time with them, and he has fun with them. He has not, however, allowed himself to let down his guard with these men. He keeps them a bit at arm's length, consistent with what men do with their *just* friends.

Are Friendships Important to You?

The perception out there is that men are uninterested in friends, do not seek them, and are uncommunicative with the friends they have. But almost every man (90%) we talked to said that friendships *are* important. As some men answered this question, they elaborated more on their definition of friendships. What follows are comments from some of the men we've just introduced, as well as comments from the tenth man, Greg.

Greg is a 43-year-old white film production supervisor. To him, loyalty and a connection through sports or some other activity are important components of friendship. He describes friends on a continuum, and says friends connect us to the broader world. "Friendships are very important. I don't think I have a great number of people that I consider to be good friends because, based on my definition of it, there's a great deal of time and commitment required. I suppose you can have different grades of friendships—primary, secondary, tertiary, that kind of thing. It's one of the major ways you establish a link to the community, to the world that you live in, so you're not completely focused on yourself. It's a way to grow: through their problems, or through listening, you can gain insight or avoid certain pitfalls."

Greg's primary, secondary, and tertiary could also be the *must, trust,* and *just* categories. His notion of connecting to the broader community is consistent with the view in this book that friendships can help build better neighborhoods and broader support systems.

Al, the nurse, has grown away from his high school friends and finds his new friends re-enforce his marital relationship. "Friends are absolutely important. Guys have a bonding thing. I'm in a profession where I do not have a lot of work-related male friends. My male associates primarily come from the racquet club. I play a lot of racquetball. I wouldn't call most of those close friendships. I would call them associations (*just* friends). I have always broken friends down. There are good friends and [there are] associations. My high school buddies were friends in high school but now they are associations (*rust* friends). I basically don't know them anymore because I've been away so long.

"My close friends now come basically from the parental side of things. They are parents of my children's friends. We have developed strong friendships both as a couple and individually. For instance, my friend Mike and I ride motorcycles. He is the father of my daughter's friend. You make associations along those lines. An association is someone you do like but do not see outside of the arena in which you met them. Even these friendships are important (*trust* friend). There is a certain bonding that goes on."

Casey, who works in construction, believes friendships are vital to him because, "It's important to have somebody I can talk with, somebody who can support me, and I can give my support to. It's for both of us. I give my friendship with all my heart, and that means a lot. Good friends always keep secrets, and friendship entails never giving away what I know about my friends, and vice versa. That's important to me. I support my (*must*) friends in any way I can, and I get the same from them."

David, the mental health worker replied, "If I'm a friend, I would give you the shirt off my back because it takes a lot for me to consider someone a friend. That means I know as much history as you're conscious about, and you know the same about me. We share personal things. That's stuff that most males, particularly African-American males, don't share, and it just doesn't happen because it supposedly shows weakness. To have a (*must*) friend means to have a belief in another individual, which is a great prize for humanity with all the mistrust in this world."

Felix talks about the importance of friendships that are made up of *must* friends and also *just* friends. This latter group is, in his description, one that he uses and who he believes use him. "Friendships are very important. I like quality friendships. I don't like a lot of friendships. I like to know the people I am friendly with I can count on, that they are there for me. My whole social life has changed in the last five years since my business has taken off, and I have a high-profile account, and I've been told I need to be careful to separate out those people who want to be friends with me because of the account and those who want to be friends with me because of me. And I have made some very good friendships from the account, and I know that if you have a few good friends at the end of your life, you are doing well."

So, what about the men who said friendship was not important? Who are they? This small group raised issues about the roles that spirituality and family play in their lives. Some men linked friendships to God, and others saw God as a substitute for friendships. A 40-year-old African-American special education teacher said friendships were not important because, "You don't need friends to live. A person can live if he is spiritually in touch." Another teacher, a 33-year-old Orthodox Jew, said a great deal of his time was spent in observance rituals or with his wife and family, leaving little time for friends.

So, for a few men, spirituality or family replaces friendship with other men. These obligations may prevent the maintenance of friendships, but they also reduce the need for friendships (we come back to the role of family in reducing the need for friendships later).

Do You Have Enough Friends?

Malcolm Gladwell, the journalist who authored *The Tipping Point* and *Blink*, writes that, if you make a list of people whose death you will be truly devastated by, you will come up with around 12 names. Some of those will be family members and others close friends. "To be someone's best friend requires a minimum investment of time. More than that, though, it takes emotional energy. Caring about someone deeply is exhausting."[95] For many people, a circle as large as 12, including family members, is more than enough.

Questioning whether one has enough friends begins in childhood. Children and teenagers often complain to their parents that they do not have friends or that they do not have *enough* friends. Do adults say this to themselves also? For some, one friend is enough; for others 12 is not enough. As adults, if we do not have many friends, we often adjust by filling in the gap with hobbies, forming a significant relationship with one person, or becoming absorbed with work or family. In fact, some men we interviewed "blamed" work and family for hindering friendships, saying, "I'd like to hang out with the guys but I have to (fill in the answer): (a) go to the office or (b) be home with the wife and kids." Obvious problems arise when work and family prevent a man from having enough friends.

When asked if they had enough friends, the men in this study answered:

- I have enough friends, 60%
- I do not have enough friends, 25%
- I am unsure, 15%

Some men said they have enough friends, given the constraints on their time.

Yes, I Do

About six out of every 10 men in the study felt they had enough friends. The African-American men were more apt to say they have enough friends than were the white men, with almost three-quarters giving this response. This may be a result of the collectivism that is more apt to mark African-American friendships than white friendships.[96]

Older men, the 50 and over crowd, were also slightly more likely to say they had enough friends—67% of them versus 60% for the whole sample. It is difficult to say whether these differences are significant, given the possible ways men could interpret the question, but it may be that older men have learned better either how to construct friendship networks or how to accept the networks that they have. But, for the oldest men, danger lurks. Having friends who are still alive into their 80s and 90s is not common.

Greg describes how changing circumstances affect his need for friends. "I do have enough friends and don't crave more, but I am also not shunning more. I'm not saying my dance card is full with male friends, and you can't get on it. I think it's more that I pick and choose. It takes me a while to figure out, 'Hey, they are a good friend.' Am I open to meeting more? Absolutely, and as you move through life, circumstances around you change, and you can meet more people, but I don't think I'm waiting for more male friends."

Isuko makes a distinction between friends he sees frequently (his *must* friends) and those from the past (his *rust* friends) whom he sees occasionally. He said he had enough but, "that doesn't stop me from making more. There's enough occurrence of seeing so many people and knowing what I've talked about with them that I know they'll be friends for a long time with me. That's enough, because I remember the feeling from being with them, and it's a good feeling. I have friends also that I have not seen for a long time. What I've discovered is, even though I haven't seen them in a while, it picks up from where it left off. So that is enough, because I feel I can easily open up."

Felix is working on the number of his friends. "Well, I have male friends in New York, but because I don't hang out with a group of guys, I don't have people here like I could call back in Atlanta where I grew up. I have that in New York with women friends but not with male friends here. One woman kind of adopted me when I moved here—I feel like I have a family here and have worked hard to not feel like an outsider here. So I would say I would have enough friends, ultimately. In the last six to eight months, I am making a greater effort to make friends. I've been traveling a lot so people don't think I am here that much. But I am reaching out more and have become more gregarious."

Some men felt that they had enough friends given the time they had, but that they never had much time because of work and family demands. Ben said he could be happy with the number of friends he has, but it is hard for him to make new friends now that he is out of school. He worries he doesn't have time for the friends he already has.

Jack said, "You can't have too many friends. This one here (referring to baby Roger, whom he was bouncing on his knee) is enough of a friend for me now." I pushed him as to whether he had enough friends now that he was a stay-at-home dad and a relatively new transplant to a big city. "I don't have any friends here, but it is hard to make them when you have a kid going and you are working 10 hours a day. You need to have someone who has a baby, also. Being a dad, it is difficult to make friends because I am into doing the same thing like carousing, going to the gym, going to the sports bar. It is a pretty significant change. I *did* go out to a restaurant with a friend back home and took Roger with me. But I have no other friends in my same situation."

Hal believes he has enough friends to "go about the business of life."

No, I Do Not

The men who said that they did not have enough friends (one in four in the study) felt they were missing out on something. They can perhaps benefit most from reading this book.

Al says, "Actually, I could use more. The friends at the club, the racquetball guys (*just* friends), I see them at the club but not outside. I have a small social circle. It is partially my family, partially myself and my wife, our relationship. I probably had more male friends before I was married because I spent a lot of time at the club and played ball with them. It was that type of friendship, light, not deep."

Some men did not lament not having enough friends. For example, the oldest man in the survey, Frank, an 85-year-old white retired poultry dealer, was resigned to his number of friends, given his age and family and work obligations, "I don't have any (friends). I had them in the past. Part of the reason is that most of my friends aren't alive. Even when I was young and raising a family, I never had time for friends. I always had to work very hard, and we were a close-knit family. So, friends weren't really a part of the family. As a surrogate father to some nephews and nieces, that took up time, too."

Another interesting example of a man who feels he does not have enough friends comes from Chang, a 24-year-old Chinese American. His family's history in the United States has had a deep impact on his friend-making skills, and he may epitomize what other immigrants experience. "As a kid, we weren't allowed to have any friends. My father came over to America as an illegal immigrant, and my parents were always afraid that they would be found out. We lived in an apartment behind the hand laundry business that we ran. My parents were very embarrassed about where we lived and the business that we had, so we never had people over nor was I allowed to make friends."

I Am Unsure

About one in six of the men in the study were unsure if they had enough friends. Ed questioned the notion of what constitutes *enough* friends and also cited the difficulty in making true friends, "I don't know if you can quantify. A half a dozen might be too many. I'm talking about true friends (*must* friends). There are not too many who meet the requirement of a true friend. I could call four to six people and ask them for money or Ravens' tickets but they are not necessarily true friends. My best (*must*) friend—we can sit beside each other for hours and not say anything. We are really solid. He's a retired police officer. One of my previous best friends (a *must* friend), another taxi driver, was shot in the head and killed. We had the same kind of relationship. We'd hang out together until 1:00 A.M. at a local diner. What a shock when I heard he had been killed. That was five years ago. Like me, he was a Vietnam vet."

One unexpected finding from the men in the study was that those who grew up in Maryland and have lived there their whole lives were more apt to say they did not have enough friends. Another way of looking at this is that people who have moved around may be more apt to believe they have enough friends than those who have remained in their home area their whole lives. It could be that once a man begins to move, his expectations about friendships begin to change. The bar may be lowered when he leaves his hometown, and he may expect that one of the losses from moving may be the loss of friends. Also, a man may remain in his hometown into adulthood to maintain friendships. If he watches those friends then leave town or not remain a friend, he could conclude he has lost friends and does not have enough.

Using Work as a Substitute for Friends. Some men work all the time precisely to avoid others—they may be afraid to establish close relationships and so turn to work as an excuse. Others come to believe they don't need friends at all. Many of us know people who are obsessed with work. Academia is rife with men who work long hours in the service of research. One fellow I know, although there are others like him, is not especially social and puts in long hours at the office. If he had more friends, would he work less hours?

There are many excellent reasons why men work hard. For many men, it is a way of giving their all for their family and defining themselves as a successful breadwinner and man. If we *temporarily* seal ourselves off from others to finish building a new room in a house, to complete a dissertation, or to cover a series of swing shifts at the factory, we are not acting in a dysfunctional way. We all get busy, but it is important to maintain balance and leave room in our lives to attend to our relationships.

Relying Instead on Family. It is interesting to consider that society has the term "workaholic" but not the comparable "familyaholic." A man can be accused of being too consumed with work to the exclusion of other activities, but not too consumed with his family. But what if his absorption resulted in a lack of friends? A man's first obligation *is* to his family, although many who have longstanding friendships would argue that a friend, say an old Army buddy, could be a very close second. When you toss the children into the mix, the scale tilts even more toward the family obligation.

During long periods of a man's life, a wife (or significant other) and children often take precedent—and by lengthy periods I mean from the children's birth into their teenage years. Even as the teenagers are struggling with independence, the man's obligation to his children and partner do not disappear. Where does time with friends fit in? Is it okay if the father has no time for friends?

Like absorption in work, it is a problem if the balance the father has struck is tilted too far to the family, with no attempt made to maintain outside friendships, because those friendships are needed for his continual growth. In fact, if the father has tilted too far toward the family, he may be sending a dangerous message to them that family obligations should be all-consuming and that people should not explore outside relationships. Children learn from their fathers about friendships, and so fathers must model healthy friendships with other adults.

A 48-year-old Latino counselor, Oscar, talking about the family and friend balance he tries to strike said, "I don't have enough time for them. I don't have enough time for my kids, my wife, or even me. When I do try to get together with my friends, it can't be spontaneous. I have to plan. It's sad, and I really long for more."[97]

Blaming Ourselves. Some men are raised to accept responsibility for their own actions at an early age; others come to that point later in life and may tend to externalize a lot of behaviors that get them into trouble. For example, work problems may be blamed on the boss, bad grades on the teachers, and losing competitively in sports on the (pick one): referee/umpire, bad line call, weather, or bad luck. Recognizing that one's own behavior can contribute to the ability (or lack thereof) to make friends is one way of understanding why some men may not have enough friends. We heard from a few men who have the insight to look at their own behavior and feelings as the root cause for not having enough friends.

A 44-year-old white married social worker, Dylan, blamed himself. In part, he does not feel masculine enough and equates masculine behavior with friendships, a theme explored in greater depth in the next chapter. "I think that I have a lack of confidence in male friendships. I have trouble finding men who are truly similar to me. I am not entirely comfortable with men. I am not into 'locker room talk,' and the football game atmosphere really gets to me. I dislike the macho stuff, drinking, etc., that many men do."

A 78-year-old white retired minister, Geoff, also had doubts about his abilities to make friends. "I blame myself because I tend to be introvertish. It is a matter of trust. You want to have a friend you can spill your heart to, and I am not sure I trust people to really hear objectively what I may have to say."

Conclusion: Defining Friends and Friendship

No matter how they are defined friends and friendships are vitally important to men's lives and are based on being understood, trust and loyalty, dependability, and doing things together. Some men feel they do not have enough friends and want more of them. Others are torn between wanting more friends and believing their first obligation is to their families or their jobs.

3

So, How Do Friendships Actually Work?

Recall that one of the purposes of this book is to help men make friends by working on their friendship-building skills. In my study, I was interested in the mechanics of friendship—how they worked or didn't, and whether the men were able or had a desire to restart a friendship once it had been lost. As we will see—and this also can have implications for women's relationships with men—once something has gone wrong in a friendship, men often abandon it, regardless of its previous intensity or benefits. Finally, I wanted to explore whether a connection exists between masculinity and male friendships.[98]

The study questions "How have friends helped you?" and "How have you helped friends?" are meant to get at exactly what men do for each other in a friendship. In most cases, the answers turned out to be similar—the ways men are helped are the ways they, in turn, help their friends. Without a sense that one will get back what is given, a sense of equity, the friendship fades.

A sense of equity through mutually beneficial assistance is what sustains a community. Neighbors and the larger community function best when people expect certain rules and societal expectations to be followed. In many surveys of how Americans spend their time, it is clear that we are less engaged with others than in previous generations.[99] A lack of engagement, or social responsibility to each other, can lead to further disconnection. Studying how friends help each other can lead to a reconnection with others (neighbors and communities) by providing a roadmap for how relationships with others can be built and sustained on a one-to-one basis.

How Men Help and Are Helped

In my study, when asked how friends have helped them, the men answered:

- Supporting me/encouraging me/being there/taking care of me, 65%
- Listening/talking with me/sharing with me, 45%
- Giving me advice/providing perspective, 32%
- Providing companionship/hanging out, 15%
- Loaning me money, 15%
- Helping me with home and car maintenance, 15%
- Buoying my spirits, 10%
- Helping me move to new residence, 7%

The men could give more than one response. The sense of being there for each other in its broadest sense is what comes through most clearly from the interviews with these men. Listening and talking were also described as key to helping and being helped by a friend. Sometimes this latter activity would take place in the context of shoulder-to-shoulder activities that men engage in to feel comfortable while relating to each other. For men, helping each other is a sign of stability and steadfastness, deepening relationships and allowing them to be built and sustained through concrete activities. At the same time, helping is a nurturing activity because it involves taking care of someone else. These activities draw on the softer, nurturing side of a man while also allowing him to be quietly or nonverbally strong. If I help someone out by driving him to a doctor's appointment, I am nurturing him.

The examples given of how men were helped by friends range from the mundane to the extraordinary and further flesh out the various meanings of friendship. I wanted to include the answers given by these next two men, who are not among the 10 featured men, because they help to frame the discussion. Friends help each other in both concrete and emotional ways: It is not always just about loaning money or coming over to the house in an emergency at 4 A.M. It is also about "being there" in ways that can vary greatly from one man to the next. The *must* or *trust* friend is someone who is "there" for you when the *just* or *rust* friends might not be.

A 60-year-old white administrator, Tab, gave a straightforward answer that encompasses what I believe many men want—a supportive, noncritical ear, someone who "has their back." "Close (*must*) friends are there for you in adversity, in family situations, and at work. They listen and offer information that is based on their own experiences. Or, they just listen and say nothing, which is also good at times." (Significant others should also pay attention here.)

A 56-year-old white economics professor, Scott, who is helped more by the emotional connection of friends than anything concrete, gave an example that typifies men who don't need much verbal communication to feel close with another man. "I don't know how to define how they help me. There's a certain extension, a sharing of some part of life, mutual caring. Something is there, and it is really easy to converse. You can sit on a boat, whatever—you don't have to talk; stare at the sky—but there's a feeling that this person loves the same things I love, and so I don't feel I have to talk about it."[100]

Men often need shared, shoulder-to-shoulder activities to feel comfortable being together, as compared to women, who have face-to-face friendships that imply greater intimacy. Many men are not comfortable just sitting around and talking with each other face-to-face. When men do listen or give support, it is often in the context of some other activity. The appearance of too much intimacy gives rise to the fear of appearing gay.

Al talks about how his friends help him. It is interesting that, even though he is in a traditionally female profession, nursing, his friendships look typically masculine. "You can always seek advice. The closer friends are helpful in various situations. I have a good friend right now who has been helping me with a motorcycle I just bought. I met him through my wife, who is also a nurse. I would consider him a good friend. He has been over and has gone with me for rides while I still had my learner's permit. If I needed something, I could ask him for a loan. We've got a bond."

Asked how he has helped friends, Al said, "When the friend I just described went through a divorce, I was there for him. I gave him moral support. I listened to him complain, talk, whine, whatever."

Ben describes being helped through his willingness to connect with another man, rather than through anything specific or concrete. He feels quite comfortable with closeness, perhaps because of his training as a mental health therapist. "Here, at this job, I made a male friend who became a close colleague and friend. I really think my whole interactional style was affected by his influence. He feels the same way. I think real friends grow with each other. Friendship is interactive. It is two people who become something different because of their friendship. I really believe I became a better person and a better therapist having been this person's friend."

Ben also offers insight into why some men feel both close to and distant from high school buddies and how they can help but may also drag one down. "The high school (*rust*) friends who were there through every good time and bad time—they're encouraging and belittling. They knock you down if you get too high and build you up when you are feeling at your worst. As far as helping others, I have been there for friends. I am a good friend, available, validating and attuned, and always wanting to do stuff and organize stuff."

It is difficult to tell here if Ben is saying he is belittled in a good way or if he resents his *rust* friends knocking him down. For some men, it is with a sense of pride that they describe such interactions in which they are knocked back a notch by a friend. Others, though, feel these interactions are demeaning and prevent their more adult side—a side they have been trying to cultivate since school—from emerging. This can be the downside of staying around *rust* friends—they remember you at your most immature and often treat you as if you were still that younger age.

While Ben is philosophical in describing friendship, Casey is more concrete. Money is a key component, as is physical assistance, like helping a friend move. Casey describes friends who are always there for him, and he feels more comfortable with a high level of intimacy than other men. "When I am in trouble financially, Nick, who is my best friend, and also my dad, they ask, 'Do you need help? How much do you need? Do you need help with the apartment?' Things like that when you are moving. There's not that many people who offer help. But good (*must*) friends do. And I do the same thing. Right now it is only with Nick—he's always asking me if I am okay and if I need anything. If he's out of town, I'll call his wife and ask her and the kids if they need anything. My mom says we are *amantes*, lovers. I like that. I'll take my mom to church and then go visit him. She knows him, and they get along well. I do the same thing. I know his mother and get along well with her."

David's answer covers many topics. He speaks to the equity of the friendship and the unstinting support. "They (friends) have helped me financially, spiritually, emotionally, guidance-wise, and even a friend younger than me has helped me correct my ways. It is a checks-and-balances system of friendship, and a lot of acceptance takes place. The greatest gift I can give a (*must*) friend, in turn, is time, because we can never get that back. So time [it] could be if they want to sit and stare at their feet; but they want someone there, or a shoulder to lean on, or someone to wrestle with to get the frustration out, or if you want to scream at me as a sounding board, or if you need financial support, or if you need to drive somewhere—I got your back, and you're never going to be alone."

For Ed, friends are a significant source of support and are connected to him through an equitable relationship. He refers to them as being important particularly in case of an emergency, "It was good to have a few buddies just in case something happens. If I needed emotional help, like my aunt just passed away, my three closest (*must*) friends have offered to help. The reciprocal is also true. One of my friend's dads is in bad shape, and he knows I'll be there for him."

When Felix was asked how friends helped him, he immediately described the support he received from a close friend when he needed help in dealing with his family. "When I came out of the closet to my parents, my father was *really* upset. We got through that, and a friend from high school was very supportive. We knew each other's families, and he was there for me." "Being there" without detailing *how* someone is there is the process of what men friends do for each other. Men don't talk about it, and they often cannot articulate it (although I tried to get Felix to be specific)—friends just show up like a guard at the door. This is revisited when Felix was asked how he helped friends. "Same way. Let me give you an example: A friend's mother died, and I flew back to Atlanta for the funeral. I showed up and gave of myself tremendously." When you give of yourself, what do you mean? I pressed again for specifics but again got nothing more concrete than an answer that reinforced what Felix had said already. "I think when you show up for somebody, just being there is a support."

Hal illustrates how (*must*) friends can assist each other by helping them to follow through on things, including activities that can be health promoting. "My involvement in the church group holds me be accountable for things I may not have the wherewithal to do myself. Like running as an analogy. My friend and I would meet and run, and I know he'd be there and he'd know I'd be there so we both would get there and run. Then we'd talk, and he would ask me the next day, 'Did I talk to my son about sex? How did it go?' holding me accountable. So not only being held accountable for running, but also for other things in our lives."

After reflecting for a while, Hal brought up an example of how *trust* friends help each other. "A really interesting thing happened last week. I don't have many friends on campus, not someone I can confide in, but I saw a friend the other day, and he had a cane and I asked him what was up. He came back two days later and said he wanted to tell me he had just gotten a diagnosis of prostate cancer that was all in his body, and he was in

the throes of trying to decide what to do about it. It was very raw emotionally, and he was talking to me about it, and I was surprised by the level of
intensity of the discussion. He was really vulnerable. I would never have
opened up to him the way he did to me—I would wait until it was settled,
but he needed to talk about the process and needed help deciding what to
do. So, I was surprised by the timing, not that he told me about it. I was
grace giving. I did not tell him what to do."

This *trust* friend did not deliberately seek Hal out, and Hal was taken
aback by the intensity of the encounter. A *must* friend might have purposefully called Hal to discuss the cancer diagnosis.

Isuko reacts to the question on a practical and on an emotional level.
He was one of the few in this study to raise the issue of touching as a form
of help, while clarifying how touching is done. "There are times when I'm
really stuck with a problem. Given that friends are outside the problem,
they have a perspective I hadn't considered before. They help me think
clearly. I guess there are times when I realize I need them. They come by.
It's really a great feeling. They're supportive. Is that a way of helping? Even
when they disagree with me, that is a good thing.

"I help them with money sometimes; it could be anything from treating
them to dinner to helping them get what they want to buy. Definitely
listening. Sometimes you don't know what to say, but they just need a
presence, instead of trying to interject, 'This is what I think you should do.'
I've tried that, and it helps sometimes, but listening is even better and
touching them, you know, on their shoulders. It helps feel like you are
there for them.

"With my closest friend (*must* friend), I've recently offered to have him
live with me because he's going through a rough time. He hasn't done that,
but he does spend a lot of time at my place, which is great. Also, when
there are special occasions, like birthdays, I'll get him a gift of something
I would like and he can think, 'Wow, someone did something for me!'"

And Jack, who is still bouncing baby Roger on his knee as he and I finish
a beer at the local bar replied, "Giving emotional and moral support is
how I help them and how they help me. Be a positive influence. Tell him
when he shouldn't do something, and he tells me the same. Like, I lost a
job, and my friend said it was no big deal. I got a better job and, because
I lost the first job, I've seen more of the world; he showed me that it was
no big deal to lose a job." I wondered if this was his best friend, the one
described in the previous chapter with whom he now works. "Yeah. I've
known him 28 years. I hang out with about four guys from the old days."

This *must* friend of Jack's is also a *rust* friend. He is someone who has been supportive of him when he is down, which is one way that Jack and his friends help each other.

The men also talk about the reciprocity of relationships. They often say they were helped the same way they helped others. Their responses reflect this similarity: 70% said they helped by supporting, encouraging, being there, and taking care of friends; 44% said they helped by listening, talking, and sharing with friends; 20% said they helped by providing companionship; 18% said they helped by giving advice or perspective; 14% said they helped with moving; 14% with home and car repair; 14% with loaning money; and 6% by buoying spirits.

What Men Do with Friends

What do men actually do when they get together? Many men gave more than one response; in my study, they said:

- Sports-related activities, 80%
- Communicate, 55%
- Drink/party/hit the bars, 45%
- Go to lunch/dinner, 25%
- Watch movies at home, 7%
- Chase women, 7%
- Travel together, 5%
- Hang out with our children, 5%

Sports

The most common answer to this question—playing or watching sports—is no surprise. Many sports activities were mentioned: bowling, fishing, shooting pool, hunting, golfing, playing tennis, running, playing cards, biking, working out at the gym, roller blading, ice skating, playing chess, and watching sports together at home or in a bar (one man also mentioned playing video games). Men frequently mentioned more than one activity that they did with their friends.

Sports loom very large in many men's lives. To understand men and their friendships, one has to understand the role of sports across the lifespan. Those who can compete physically, do; those who do not compete physically compete vicariously through watching. Competition often finds form in betting, teasing, and subtle or overt acts of one-upsmanship. Dealing with defeat and victory are all connected to sports and the way that men interact. They are also all connected closely to friendship.[101]

For many men, much hinges on the "game." Watching sports, even while alone, helps men form a common bond; it is a way of being with friends because knowledge of last night's sports event connects men to friends the next day at work and outside of work.

Sports involvement does not seem to vary by age, although some differences do exist. Older men may participate in less vigorous sports like golf and fishing, whereas younger men are more apt to participate in active sports like football and basketball.

For example, I was once at a party thrown by my wife's boss. I met a man 15 years my junior who was from a different racial and work background than me. After attempting a little conversation and failing, he wisely asked me if I was into sports. The conversation took off from there. For many men, it is the universal ice-breaker and the universal connection.

Typical of what the men said are these responses from Ed and Jack. Ed said, "You hang out for three to four hours. Get together, and we talk sports, we banter, until we have a fight about it and then laugh it off."

I asked Jack what he does with his guy friends. "We talk about sports, trips, going away places. Trying to make the house better." What about feelings? I ask. You are in this nontraditional role as a stay-at-home dad. This has forced you to think more about men's roles than most people. Does that make you more open about stuff? "We talk about feelings, but probably not more than most guys." Jack leaves me with the impression that he is a pretty traditional guy who just happens to be living a nontraditional, role-reversed lifestyle. It does not seem to have reshaped his relationships with his (*must*) friends except in the way it affects his availability to do things with them because of child-rearing responsibilities.

Communication

The second most common thing that men do with friends is communicate, one-on-one, by phone, or by e-mail. What do men talk about? Everything—from politics to sports to children to work. We could make the case that sports qualify as a form of communication but most of the men separated out sports from talking in their answers.

How might conversations between friends evolve? Usually, they become more highly personal as trust is established. For example, there is a local group of men in Baltimore, primarily in their 60s and early 70s (one guy is in his 90s), Jewish and African-American, who call themselves the "Hebros," a combination of Hebrews and Brothers. Their attraction for each other initially was their racial and religious difference, not their similarities. They talk about race, religion, their children, politics, and sports. They travel together every year for a few days, specifically to play golf. They get together with their wives from time to time. Essentially, according to one member of the group, everything can be talked about, and they kid each other mercilessly about their race and religion. This is a "no-holds-barred" style of communication, and the members of the group revel in their ability to be open with each other despite their diversity. There is a certain amount of risk taking with each other that also serves as an attraction and has a very masculine feel to it, similar to what other men have described about their ability to have friends to whom they can say anything and still be accepted.

Another Washington, D.C.-based group of men, all born in India, get together with their wives on occasion. Their similar backgrounds bring them together. The women drift off and talk about shopping, and the men talk about politics in India and the economic situation worldwide. Sports are rarely mentioned. In this case, the immigrants talk about topics that few others outside of their group can discuss. In addition, people from similar backgrounds may feel comfortable with each other just because they will not be expected to talk about certain topics.

One recent study asked men and women what they talked about when they discussed important matters with others. The question posed to them was "From time to time, most people discuss important matters with other people. Looking back over the last six months . . . have you discussed important matters with anyone?"[102] The next two questions asked (if something was discussed) what the general topic was and who the person conversed with about it. Interestingly, men reported that they were more apt to talk about important matters in general than were women (men may believe that they generally have more important topics to discuss than women), and men said they talked more to their friends about relationships whereas women said they were more apt to talk to their spouses about relationships. House and money (a combined topic) and health were the two topics most often discussed by men and women. Ideology and religion, community issues, politics and election, work, relationships, and kids and education were the next most frequently topics.[103] Note that sports, the most frequent activity for men in this current study, did not show up at all as a topic of discussion. This is most likely because men are aware that, despite sports' importance in their lives, they realize sports is not an important topic.

Hal gives an answer that includes sports, and then he goes on to talk about the importance of communication. "Drink a beer, baseball, shoot pool, horseshoes, unorganized stuff. The men's group and their families all went off to the beach for the weekend last year. When we talk as a group, we talk about bible some but more about family and that kind of thing. The kids are all the same age, they are all going off to college; we talk about wife problems and about taking care of aging parents. For example, my mother's blind, and she needs help and some love some time."

Drink, Party, Hit the Bars, Go Out to Eat

One-quarter of the men interviewed reported going to lunch or dinner with their friends, and an even larger number, almost half, referenced drinking and partying. Some variation by age occurs, with the younger men more apt to go out to bars, and the older men to a restaurant. In *Bowling Alone*, dining at a restaurant and visiting someone's home for dinner were the most frequently mentioned social and leisure activities.

Al mentions sports, and includes dining activities. Conversation, however, is not an integral part of the communing. "We play racquetball, ride motorcycles, and work with a few friends. We used to play cards with a lot of friends. I grew up in the Midwest, where you have to play cards. We also bowl and have backyard barbecues. We used to have fondue parties and play cards. We get the families together. We just go out and horse around a lot."

Ben also likes to party. He describes himself as a simple guy with simple needs, but he touches on the duality of growing up and ceasing wilder activities coupled with the advantage of maintaining childhood friendships as a way of staying young. "I'm into wings and beer. Is there a better social experience? We're getting older now, so there are family parties and kiddies' parties. Hit the town and try to relive high school—which is impossible."

Ed, who we already know likes to talk about sports, introduces another way men relate—through joking and teasing, often while going out for a drink. "We play practical jokes. Most of us are single. You'd like to think we'd talk about women but then you say, 'Nah, let's go to the bar and drink.' We'll tease each other about attractive women we are taxiing around. I'll set up a practical joke at the bar and have a woman call another cabbie on a cell phone and send out a false call."

Felix provides an example of going out for dinner and traveling with a friend. He is not into sports or teasing. A lot of his time is spent with men over food or in work-related activities, specifically around architectural trips with friends. "Dinner mostly. But I also have friends that I travel with to look at examples of good architecture. One of these, who is a straight friend, just happens to love design, much more so than his wife. So, she is thrilled that he wants to travel with me to see these homes as it takes the pressure off of her to be with him doing something she has absolutely no interest in. I don't like movies or theater, and I am not a bar person."

And the Rest, Including the Men's Weekend

Mentioned occasionally as activities with friends were watching television or movies, traveling together, fixing things around the house, playing music, attending Alcoholics Anonymous meetings, praying together, picking up women, and hanging out together with children (one man even mentioned shopping!).

A few men in the study were members of men's groups. These groups have structured meetings specifically designed to allow men to be with other men. Men join men's groups for a number of reasons from wanting to make more friends to wanting to understand better the male friendships they have and the role of men in current society. For example, a 45-year-old married white psychologist, Carl, had been unhappy with his male relationships. He decided to rectify it by starting a group for men. He describes here how his men's group started and how it is run. "I had a sense that other men were in that same situation, where they would kind of like to have a way of meeting and getting to know other men but there wasn't an outlet for doing that. I guess about 10 years ago, I tried to have some intentionality about developing a different kind of friendship with men. After feeling out a few people, we started what we call a men's group that meets on a monthly basis. We get together, talk on the phone, things that you would not typically do. At our monthly gatherings, it is fairly open. It starts out light, and we talk about sports. A lot of times, people will begin to get comfortable talking about what is going on with them, and things that are going on between guys in the group will come up occasionally.

Most of us are fairly similar, though we wish we had more racial diversity. I would say the group of guys has been the core of the inner circle of my friends." In the Buddy System, Carl is saying these are *must* friends.

A number of men I know have longstanding traditions of going away with male friends for a weekend (or week) of golf, Las Vegas gambling, fishing, hunting, tennis, NCAA basketball, and the like. A few I know get together weekly with men they know. I have talked with a number of men who take part in these get-togethers, and they vary tremendously in nature. Younger, single men are apt to combine sports-related activities with a certain amount of women-chasing or extreme sports participation. Older, married men are more apt to use the time together to focus on sports, as a respite from family and work, and to relate to each other. Regardless of the composition of the group, these times together help to forge friendships. For some groups, personal disclosures may occur, but this is rare; it is not the intention of these get–togethers to help men get closer. Friendly competition, teasing, joking, politics, and business-related talk are the subjects and modes of communication.

I asked Tony, 58 years old, about his annual golf outing. Do you guys have serious discussions about feelings when you are away together? "No," he chuckled. "We aren't those kind of guys and that is not the kind of thing I do." I felt like I was speaking to someone from another culture, even though he lives less than a mile from me.

I go away with Crow and my brother Steve for a weekend at the U.S. Tennis Open in New York. We have been traveling together to that event since the early 1970s. For us, it is like going to group therapy. We talk on very personal levels about our work, wives, children, sports, and the state of the world. We value the time away, and it has become a vitally important experience and the capstone to the summer. Comparing myself with Tony, we both look forward to these annual trips for their camaraderie and their fun—but the atmosphere and interactions are very different. Yet, these trips are highly satisfying to each of us.

For Tony, these guys are mostly *trust* friends; for me, they are *must* friends. For me, they would be *must* friends even if we did not go away together. It was the desire to be with these friends as well as watch tennis that made the trio initially so much fun. So, men's weekends can be initiated both ways—a man can decide to get together with his closest friends and find something fun to do with them, or a man can decide he likes to do an activity, like golf, and look for a bunch of friends to do it with. Men who initiate these types of weekends or join an existing group that has been going away for a while might find great joy in the company of men, assuming the intensity of conversation and expectations fit their level of comfort.

Although not a weekend group, I know of another bunch of men who get together over breakfast once a week on Sundays in a nonreligious setting (different from the guys in Chapter 15). These guys are in their 50s and 60s. One man in the group, Yul, made the observation to me that, when men get together in a group, they tend to talk about two things: sports and politics. The topic of health, on the mind of everyone in the group including Yul, who was operated on for prostate cancer five years ago, has been forbidden by the group leader. Yul doesn't read about or watch sports, and he finds endless arguments about politics boring. He has had a hard time his whole life connecting with men because he is so sports-adverse. He believes men have to be in dyads or triads to get into more meaningful and personal material. He may quit the group, even though he told me he is lonely for male companionship. Talking to him, I wonder how many other men there are like Yul, who try to connect with groups but can't because they are marching to a slightly different, non–sports-related drummer.

How Do Men Make Friends?

We asked, "How do you establish and maintain friendships with men?" to get specifics on how men build and keep a friendship. Below, in order of frequency mentioned, are mostly action-centered suggestions. (The men could give more than one response.) I will return to these points in the concluding chapter when the discussion turns to how to make better friendships in the future.

- Find commonalities, 60%
- Make friends through work, 33%
- Reach out and be friendly to others, 27%
- Make friends through going to school, religious institutions, armed forces, 23%
- Meet friends through wife and through other friends, 17%[104]
- Make friends through sports, 16%
- Spend a long time with people (i.e., friendships take time), 11%
- Be yourself, 10%

Find Commonalities

So, how does this play out? In sports, men make friends by engaging them in a socially acceptable, masculine activity. They contact other men to go fishing, play golf or tennis, or shoot some hoops, as in the example given by 52-year-old African-American pharmacist, Adair: "I may call someone that I know likes to play tennis and set up something. After we play, we may notice that we have other things in common, and a friendship begins." Here, the sporting activity leads to one important criteria mentioned by the men for starting a friendship—having something in common. Over half mentioned looking for commonalities in making friends.

Al makes a similar suggestion about looking for commonalities in sports, in family situations, and through the church. "You make friendships through some sort of exposure, like racquetball or motorcycle. You have to have some place to start, a son or a daughter. Associations through family members, through your kids. I have a few through church. They have bible study groups, and I meet people there. You get to know them, and you get to chat and find other common areas, and at some point in time you ask them if they want to go for a motorcycle ride or go have coffee or a beer. It develops from there."

Jack explained how he makes friends with guys; again, it is clear that commonalities set the stage—but something more is also required. "You have to have the same interests. Like a friend in Baltimore and I each had dogs, so that started the friendship. Then we each found that we liked the same music. He lived around the corner, so proximity was important. Also, I trust him. You have to establish that trust in this day and age." I wondered what he meant by trust and whether that was something especially precious to him. "Well, Roger, for example. Can I feel safe leaving Roger with a friend for a bit if it is an emergency. Can I leave money out?" What about feelings, I asked, can you say anything to the friend and he won't freak out and take it the wrong way? For Jack, trust and sharing feelings are all related to making friends. He has to share commonalities, but he also must have a basic sense of trust in the friend.

Through Work and Other Friends

Over half of the men interviewed suggested that they establish friends through work or through other friends. Isuko talks about the part that work can play and then introduces the importance of cultural similarity in friendship building. "Work is a good place because of proximity. (Some men we interviewed maintained clear boundaries between their work friends and their personal lives and consider work friends only as acquaintances.) If you are lucky enough to have personalities that you find interesting, it starts there. Interests outside of work, too, like tae kwon do, have been a good example. Sometimes it can be ethnic commonality. You don't necessarily get along with someone of the same [ethnic] group, but it can be a factor. There might be some similar struggles you're dealing with—as a member of a minority—or positive stuff like food or your placement in society."

Work and other friends provide a "safe" way to meet people and establish relationships. It is often necessary to make acquaintances or *just* friends at work first, before they can become closer friends. This is because some guys feel they must be careful when making friends—keeping a physical and emotional distance—so that they don't appear gay. Having friendships with women (discussed in Chapter 5) protects men from this fear.

When asked how he made friends, Tom (27 years old) raised this concern. "It's hard. People think you're gay. You do it through athletics or work. Maybe you join a business or political group. . . . It's really hard for me because I am not into sports that much, but to make other male friends, you almost have to be."

Another man, a 39-year-old Asian-American businessman, Lou, describes many of the fundamental impediments to making friends for many U.S. men—having the time, the fear of appearing gay, and the lack of community connectedness. "At this time in my life, there is a time constraint and in the urban U.S., you have to seek out ways to make friends. It's not like you're friends with your neighbor. Spontaneous male bonding is much different in the U.S. because of deeper ingrained taboos against homosexuality and getting in people's space. In other countries, if you play soccer, everyone is friends by the end of the game. Here, you wouldn't pat a guy's shoulder or hug him. You have to make more of an effort to connect. I've been in a lot of other countries, so I have a good perspective. In other countries, you can make friends easily at a bar. Here, you have to seek out a specific activity to bond with someone. I found that smoking is a good way to bond."

Young men may be more skilled than their fathers and grandfathers were at their age about sharing closely held feelings with men, but they need a context, like work, in which to first establish themselves so they feel comfortable being themselves.

Be Yourself

Of interest were the handful of men who talked about making friends not through specific activities (like sports) but through being themselves. Their answers to making friends included being friendly and outgoing and starting conversations. In other words, be the "right" kind of person and the right kind of friends will follow. For men who gave this type of answer, activities were less important than their own integrity.

Ben at first said he doesn't *establish* friendships with men, an answer that implies he is being himself and not doing anything in particular. When questioned further, he inferred that chemistry is needed. "For me, it has always been right off the bat. This sounds almost like a romantic relationship. Either you click or you don't. I can tell when I've met somebody who I'll get along with. I met this guy here, and the first thing he did was make a joke about my appearance. I gravitate toward someone who is genuine, expressive, and doesn't hold back and can take a joke themselves. It's right off the bat. In my friendships we have always hit it off—we have not worked through a significant hating thing and then become friends."

Casey does not focus on doing things with people to make friends; he makes friends by responding to vibes and looking at the character of the man. "You can have a nice way of saying things but if you are not honest, I can perceive that. If you are sarcastic or just trying to make me feel good, I can figure that out in a man. Sometimes I tell people, 'Listen, you are just trying to make me feel good but I don't think you mean it.' You can tell when someone is your friend: the way they look at you, the way they talk to you, how close they get to you."

Ed also considers who the person is more than anything else. Ed, like many others, makes a reference to gay men when asked about how he makes friends. When asked about his male friendships, he replied he is more interested in who the person is than in what he does, and, like others, reciprocity is a component. "Well, I don't kiss them, " he chuckled. "You meet someone and start a conversation—if that person demonstrates characteristics that might fit my idea of a true friend, I will consider getting to know him better. With time, if he shows reliability, trustworthiness, etc., he may become a true (*must*) friend. But he has to give 100%. I give 100% and want that back. It's not that I go out looking for a new friend, it just happens. Once you get through the acquaintance (*just*) stage, and that takes time, then you say he is a friend—he will still have to demonstrate some more trustworthiness—being there when you need him or when someone else needs him. He has got to be interested in helping other guys, too. And then he's into my inner circle of true friends."

Ed's answer was unique in that he is drawn to men who also show caring for other people, not just for him. This reveals interest on a level beyond someone's immediate need for gratification from a friendship. It speaks to looking for people as friends whose concerns are more universal.

Reach Out

Reaching out to others is also important, and it requires an active attempt on a man's part to make a friend. Sometimes men won't reach out for fear of being rejected or for fear of appearing needy, as was noted earlier. For Felix, reaching out to others is something that can be difficult at times. Felix reveals anger at having to do it. I think this speaks to the core desire that many people have about wanting to be approached or pursued by others for friendships rather than being the one who is always making the effort. Making the effort, especially in Felix's case, also opens him up to being rejected. "I go to that café a lot, and I often sit by myself. It is not a gay bar, and it is a comfortable place to be, and I run into people that I know. I travel a lot, so I want to be nested here in New York when I am back, so I go to the same haunts. I find that I have to make the effort, and sometimes that gets on my nerves, and I resent it, and I want people to make the effort toward me. But that's the way it is."

A few men noted that friendships can only be established over time, such as in high school or college, or through shared experiences, such as serving in Vietnam or Iraq. David is one who gives time as a prerequisite. For David, a *must* friendship does not have to begin in childhood, but it does have to be longstanding. "I establish friendships with men through time because of the trust factor. I don't trust you, period, because it takes time and it takes situations. It's not like I have a piece of paper and I am checking it, but it is proving yourself. So, with me, it is definitely time put in because interest can be lost so soon in this world."

How Men Maintain Friends

It is not just important to know how to make friends; friends also have to be maintained. When asked how the men kept their friendships, they said:

- Communicate, 65%
- Do things together, 37%

- Reach out, 24%
- Be yourself, 13%
- Be there to give emotional support, 10%
- Stay in frequent contact, 10%

The men's answers focused, for the most part, on being actively involved in the process. They sometimes gave answers that included multiple approaches. In addition, some of their responses overlapped: communicate, reach out, and stay in contact could all be, depending on the man, similar concepts.

Communicate/Reach Out/Stay in Contact

Many men talked specifically about the importance of communication via talking, e-mailing, and letter writing. They stated that men must make an effort to stay in touch, although they differed on whether it had to be consistent contact or could be picked up again after many months—or even years—of no communication. Clearly, men do communicate, although they may not always do it verbally and face-to-face.

We know from research[105] that people who use e-mail can maintain friendships more easily and with less work than by making lengthy phone calls, although the preferred method of communication depends on the people involved. Just as the telephone allowed people to easily maintain friendships when it was first commonly used, so too does the web. Myspace.com and Facebook.com are two examples of online communities that are popular with young men and women because they encourage friends to stay in touch and make new friends. Members of these Web sites post pictures and descriptions of themselves and, most importantly, links to other friends. Some people are purported to be connected with over 1,000 others through these services.

Social media can be a "safe" community for making friends, as new friends have already been vetted by existing friends. Data show that U.S. society has become less connected in physical neighborhoods than previous generations;[106] the younger generation may have become more connected in their cyber neighborhoods.

Ben is one of these electronic communicators. "I maintain friends through e-mail and getting together every now and then. I typically do not talk to male friends on the phone—like chatting. If we're on the phone, it's because we are planning something. 'Do you want to go out tonight?' 'Sure.' 'I'll meet you there.' I can't remember the last time I spent more than a minute on the phone with a male friend."

Casey talks about both the quality and the value of communication and also of providing support. "I keep (*must*) friends by being loyal, honest, supportive, cheerful, and having great communication with them."

Felix jokes about how he maintains friendships. "$50,000 in phone bills! I do e-mails for work, but I need to talk with people, and that is how I stay connected with friends. When I think about how excited I am about my work, I often would rather focus on that than on friends. I had the best time at my last birthday. I was depressed about turning 50 and what I ended up doing was having dinner with good friends who came into New York on their own. I had dinner with them over the course of four to six weeks. There was no party, but I had special time with each of them. But it is the constant communication that keeps these alive, and then doing things with them that we enjoy."

Hal, often chained by his work to his desk and computer, uses both traditional ways and also modern technology to keep friends. He is very methodical in his approach. "I write, I send e-mail, I call. I have one friend who I write a letter to each Christmas and summer. Constancy, I guess—making sure to establish with people how you are going to communicate—if I never sent Christmas cards and [then] started doing that, it would be confusing. No one method fits all. I am pretty central at starting the relationships and keeping them going. I try and be inclusive—if there is a party, I will try and include my friends, like the guy I am mentoring."

Jack is only interested in keeping a certain level of friendship with men, as he has two other best friends in his life already—his son and his wife. "I try and keep in touch. Calls on the cell phone are so cheap these days, drop a dime and say hey. I can go for months without speaking, and we can pick right back up again." These sound like pretty low-maintenance friendships to me, I reply. "Isn't that what everyone wants? Who wants a high-maintenance friend?" Jack responds. Some people want something more intense in their friendships, I counter. Jack is pretty firm on this issue. "If you meet someone and they want that, you are in trouble," he answers back. His wife is his best friend, he says, which reduces his need to make friends.

Do Things Together

Men also like doing things together as a way of reaffirming their affiliation with each other. Activities often provide the structure for maintaining friendships. For Al, however, there has to be something more than just the activity to keep the friendship alive. Al said, "You maintain a friendship by maintaining the activities. Some of those change, but once you find some common interest, you can branch out and do some other things or find other common areas. Sometimes they (the friendships) just don't go anywhere. I've been playing in racquetball tournaments for years and know a lot of players. But they don't belong to my club or live in my area, so there is no association. A lot of people would call them friends, but I would call them associates (*just* friends)."

Be Yourself

Isuko cites a number of ways of maintaining friends, but focuses most on being himself, which is the message he delivers when he talks about giving his opinion and having people to his home. "When you know they greatly value your opinion—the fact they listen to you, will debate with you. Debates can get nasty, but there has to be some commonality and some differences. It's got to be a mixture. You invite them to your home or events that are personal to you. I make time to talk about something outside of work. Keeping in contact is important. It may not be many times or enough, but it may be writing through e-mail, calling them, inviting them to a party, or hanging out with them. You don't worry about it—it just happens. Sharing laughter, humor."

Give Support

To keep the friendship going, David does not need verbal reinforcement from the other man. "Maintaining friendship? Steadiness. There are certain aspects of a friendship that have to remain stable while chaos is going on all around it. The commitment to that person makes it stable, as do dedication and sacrifice. With men, it is not a spoken commitment. Not like, 'Oh girl, I'll do anything for you.' It's nothing like that. It's just a sense that you know they are there for you." "Being there," as mentioned earlier in this chapter, is a key definition of friendship.

Another example comes from Reggie. Reggie is a 40-year-old white small-business owner, who forged a close friendship with another man because he gave support to him by reaching out. They also have something in common—they share a love for making their sons competitive in sports. The interesting value in this story is that Reggie reaches out to maintain his friendships with the *support* of his wife. "The last friend I met, his son and mine were good friends, and we were at Little League. I get in trouble a lot because my wife thinks I ride my son too hard, but I don't, I'm just trying to teach him. I was just sitting there and listening to this guy's wife talk to him about riding their son too hard, and she got upset and got up and left. I walked over, and I sat down and said, 'I can feel your pain, buddy.' He started laughing and said, 'You heard that?' I said, 'Yeah. Kind of hard not to.' And we started a friendship after we found out we lived in the same neighborhood."

Reggie's wife is very supportive of his making friends (perhaps so he won't ride their son so hard). "There are some guys that I know have to go out at least two or three times a week with their buddies. I don't. Because of work, I am rarely home. But when I am, my wife will tell me who called, and she'll encourage me to go see him. I'll want to stay with the family for awhile and the next day I'll call and—cigar, beer, shoot the breeze. It's relaxing. My friendships are my vice."

These guys provide specific details of the work involved in making and maintaining friends. Through these stories we see that, for the most part, effort and willingness to engage with others are underlying ingredients.

How Friendships Are Lost

Losing friendship is difficult—everyone likes to be liked. Sometimes long-standing relationships end for reasons that are easily understood—betrayal, hurt feelings, a perceived injustice, or a shift in power to a point at which the friends are no longer "equal" (such as when one friend receives a promotion and the other does not). Other times, friendships end and one or both of the parties are unsure why. Maybe, with spending more time together, the two friends realize they do not have much in common or do not enjoy each other as much as they once did. Maybe they just stop calling each other, and neither wants to be the first to reach out.

Friendships also wither with age, as sociologist Sarah Matthews points out in her research. In her study of older adults, only a handful of respondents remembered actively ending friendships because of some event. More commonly, these relationships fade out in a way in which, if the circumstances were right, they could be restarted.[107]

In extreme situations, one's friend becomes an enemy because of a perceived or actual incident. A former friend can make a powerful enemy, because the breaking of trust can be so hurtful.

Sometimes, a psychological need exists to have an enemy. In complicated relationships, according to psychiatrist Sigmund Freud, a friend and enemy can exist in the same person, at the same time.[108] Opening up to a friendship makes one vulnerable to being hurt, like falling in love and being jilted. For Freud, a few of his disciples and friends became enemies when they parted ways philosophically or no longer believed in the same things. Freud wanted more friends than he had, but he was uncompromising, setting the bar so high that maintaining friendship was difficult.

Abraham Lincoln also wanted friends, but noted publicly that he would not compromise his own values as a politician to become a friend to someone: "I desire so to conduct the affairs of this administration that, if at the end, when I come to lay down the reins of power, I have lost every other friend on earth, I shall at least have one friend left, and that friend shall be down inside me."[109]

The decision to let a close (*must*) friendship die is a serious one and, hopefully, the one-time friend won't become the life-long enemy. Some men, when a friendship ends, say they don't care why they lost the friend. They are not interested in examining what went wrong. It is not that they are unable to process it, or that they are in denial about the loss of the friend and want to avoid dealing with uncomfortable emotions—rather, they have been raised in a society that allows men to simply let relationships go. As a by-product of this approach, they protect themselves from any possible hurt that may be uncovered through examination of the friendship.

Other men become quite upset about losing friendships and want to understand why they ended. Most of the men interviewed did not mention developing enemies when asked about losing friends but did describe the withering of friendships because of geography, age, and lack of common interests or growing apart.

When asked if they had ever lost a friend, the men in my study said:

- Yes. I lost a friend because of his or my behavior, 50% (one-quarter of this group of men tried to get the friend back; three-quarters did not try to get them back).
- Yes. I have lost a friend from drifting apart or moving away, 30%.
- No. I have never lost a friend, 20%.

A few observations can be made based on the men's responses concerning losing friends:

- Men tend to avoid conflict when it comes to friends.
- Men do not like to work things out interpersonally (some let things drop at the first sign of rejection).

- Men often prefer reestablishing a pseudo-friendship to avoid dealing with conflict or trying to work things out.

Yes, I Lost a Friend Because of His or My Behavior

As we hear from those men who have lost friends, two groups emerge: those who have not tried to get back lost friends because the friendship's ending was too final, and those who have tried to get friendships back, sometimes successfully. Men have different reactions to the end of a friendship, and they may be socialized to the idea that trying to reconcile with a male friend is a sign of weakness.

Al gives a fairly rare reason for the loss of a friend—miscommunication about their sons. Unlike Freud, who seemed to have a need to embody a friend and enemy in the same person, Al's relationship merely ended without the word "enemy" ever entering the discussion. He tells this story: "I lost a male friend within the last year. It was a family association. My son was very close friends with their son, and somehow the whole thing fell apart. It was really painful, as we actually considered them part of the family. We did everything together, from card games to fondue parties. I was running a junior racquetball team and asked this friend of my son to play. He said he wasn't interested. But then I got someone else to play, and all of a sudden the son was upset that he hadn't been asked. They had a different opinion of what happened than we did, but our friendship stopped. Did it hurt? Absolutely. I still harbor bitter feelings about it. Not only was it a male relationship because I got along with the father, but the families got along, too. I tried to say hello from time to time, but he would say he was in a hurry and had to go. They were our best friends, and it failed. It happens in life. We tried to recoup the damaged relationship but it wasn't in the cards."

Al's friendship was very important to him and to his family. When he couldn't resurrect it, he became philosophical (his "it wasn't in the cards" line), and let the relationship go. For most men, a point is reached at which a friendship is decidedly not worth pursuing, no matter how painful the loss. At that point, they move on.

When asked about losing a friend, David cites a crime-ridden past and the sense that it was important for him to cut his losses and not pursue anything further with a particular friend. "I lost a friend that wasn't a 'get back' situation. He moved because he had warrants (for his arrest), and he couldn't contact me because I was being watched and the contact stopped.

The experience was violent, and I've tucked it away in the corner of my mind and didn't try to get it back."

Casey recounted a bad experience he had with a friend he once trusted, one that led to his ending the friendship. "I can count my friends, and I don't have enough male friends. I think I have more female friends. I had a very bad experience with one of my best friends. He betrayed me. He messed up my life. He got involved with my ex-wife. He knew a lot about me, like how much I made, and she used that against me when she took me to divorce court. When I confronted him about it, he wouldn't answer me. I said, 'You don't have to worry, I am not going to fight you. I'm just going to walk away and the next time I see you, I'm just going to think of you like a piece of shit on the floor.' He didn't answer, and to me that means he did it. I just walked away and never want to see him again."

With another friend, the outcome was totally different. Casey got into a political debate about joining the Marines and offended him. Casey was not hurt, but he realized his behavior had pushed away his friend. Casey thought his friend, who was Latino and had family who were Latin-American freedom fighters, had been brainwashed to join the Marines, and he accused him of being disloyal to his family's cause. Running into the friend a year later, they made up. "We came out with a hug, and it meant a lot to me because I had somebody mad at me for a year. Okay, you are mad, but he is still a friend. He's still in my heart. He told me, 'I always think of you,' I think it was very cool we reconciled."

Want an example of a reconciliation approach I wouldn't recommend for everyone? Henry, a 44-year-old white salesman, lost his friend over an argument. "I got my friend back when I called him from my drunken stupor and asked what he'd been up to. He didn't appreciate it at 2 A.M. but that's how we got back in touch. I guess leaving out the drunken stupor part, just calling guys is the way to do it." In essence, he ignored the fact that they hadn't been friends and proceeded as if they had been. In this case, it worked.

But more common are the men, as in Casey's first example, who say that when they are wronged (or have acted poorly), they do not want to re-establish the friendship, especially when trust has been broken. Most of these lost friendships are never restarted, usually because the parties involved don't want the friend back. Louis, a 42-year-old Latino salesman, is philosophical about maintaining friendships. "I do lose male friends. I don't usually make the effort to get them back. I believe in the saying about friends that goes, 'In life for a reason, a season, or for a lifetime.'

If things change, that's okay. If it is a bad break, then I own up to the role that I played in it. Maybe we won't continue to be (*must*) friends, but perhaps stay acquaintances. I do seek closure and try to be as supportive as possible." His response is emblematic of many men who lose a friendship (*must* or *trust*) but still maintain the contact by shifting it to a lower level of intimacy, for example, to an acquaintanceship (*just* friend). This level of re-establishing pseudo- or *just* friendships is typical of men who decide it is easier to have some contact, albeit at an emotional distance, than no contact and have to explain their behavior.

There also are men who are introspective when it comes to their friendship struggles. Jerry, a 55-year-old white lawyer speaks very openly about his own insecurities and how they affect his ability to keep friends. "I could tell you I try and maintain my friendships, but not really. I feel like I don't make as much of an effort as I should. It is the whole trust thing again. Pride gets in the way. Sometimes I reach out to men who are more confident and masculine than I am, hoping it will rub off or I will be more like them." Fear of rejection makes it difficult to reach out because he has to maintain a front. But then he slips in a remark about the kind of men he wants to be around and how he seeks out friends who fill a void he feels. He stated later in the interview that he was taught by his parents to watch out for people who may take advantage of him. Like many people, he was warned against trusting others, so he maintains a distance. But as that distance is maintained, he longs for what is missing, and tries hard to reconnect, leaving him in an ambiguous position with other men.

I Lost Friends from Our Drifting Apart

Almost one-third of the men said they had lost friends from people drifting apart or from geography separating them. In other words, no series of events or single event caused a rift. This is the natural course of many relationships. People who are friends at one point, especially at an early age, grow up and grow apart or move away, and that ends the relationship or shifts it to a *just* or *rust* friendship. Although 30% gave this answer, I think this scenario is probably true of almost every man.

When I asked Hal this question, he used the opportunity to reflect on one of his more difficult friends, from whom he feels he has grown apart. But after airing his feelings, he realized he should reach out to him. "As far as losing friends, one of my friends, Harry, is very needy. He just takes a lot of time. He is fine when he is with me and my wife, but if someone else is around, he will clam up. He's very nice, very smart, he just doesn't communicate much with me or others, and it is hard to keep it up because he is so smart. He's difficult to be with and that friendship has died on the vine." Hal then took a deep breath and said, "I'll probably try and write him again after talking with you to see where he's at. I feel bad about it."

More typical is the response of a 34-year-old white musician, Tyler, who captured what has probably happened to most friendships that end: "Yeah, communication faded, and consequently we stopped contact. Primarily, communication wanes, and you stop doing things together. I have a hard time recalling some friendships from high school or college. I never had a classic breakup though."

I Never Lost a Friend

About one in five men said they had never lost a friend. Some of the men in this group proudly describe themselves as loyal, and say they would not allow such a thing to happen. Ed implies this very thing when he says that, if he trusted someone as a friend, they couldn't let him down. Typical for men in this group is the sense of "once a friend, always a friend." Others in this group dismiss the possibility of losing a friend, saying that they are always open to reconciliation.

Gay Men and Straight Friendships

Many straight men gave testimony to their having gay friends, and gay men talked about their close friendships with straight men. Jammie Price, cited in Chapter 1, talks about these friendships and some of the difficulties that arise in them. According to Isuko, being gay clearly can affect a relationship with a straight man if the boundaries are not clear. He provides some insight into what it is like for him to try to be friends with a straight man, considering he is gay. He lost one friend when he told him he was gay and another when sexual tension emerged. "I lost a friend in college when I came out. He didn't want to deal with my being gay. He was into machismo and assumed I was in it with him. The other friend, whether you are gay or straight, it gets tricky when the level of intensity gets too close, beyond friendship, like you think you might do something more. If that's not mutual, that can screw up a friendship."

Other Endings

There is also the untimely loss of a friend due to suicide that Jeremy, a 40-year-old white man, brought up. He wished that, in friendship, he had reached out to this friend more. In talking about his friend, it is evident that Jeremy feels responsible for his friends, even if he loses contact with them. In this case, what is operating are the normal regrets that often come after the suicide of a friend—the feelings that, "I should have done more" and "If only I had reached out to him one more time."

People often hold to the fantasy that a suicide may have been prevented if only someone had reached out more to the deceased. "In twelfth grade, my friend became reclusive. He was in a college near me the next year. I heard he was doing badly. A few years later, he killed himself. I took it a bit personally because I felt I should have known. But I'd assumed he had other friends." Jeremy approaches all his friendships differently now. He watches his friends more closely and reaches out more frequently, making less assumptions about how connected they are to others. This is one way people cope with death: they change their attitudes toward the living.

I think men feel uncomfortable around needy men because it either becomes a drag on them, or it brings up their own fears of appearing needy. Jeremy may have perceived his friend as too needy (just as Hal did) or believed that he couldn't help his friend. Some men will end relationships if they sense something they do not like in someone else, even if they cannot identify it.

Masculinity and Men's Friendships

"How, if at all, are masculinity and friendships with men connected or related to each other?" This was a tricky question during the interview, the one that left a lot of people scratching their heads, a few intrigued, and a handful put off. To a great extent, masculinity (as well as femininity) is a social construct. Society helps define what is considered masculine behavior, and this definition varies from culture to culture.

For example, competitiveness and toughness are often seen as masculine.[110] This can be true in youth as well as adult gangs, which are often see as the epitome of masculinity and toughness because they provide protection for their members.[111] But what is tough in one setting will be nowhere near tough enough in the next. If I want to be seen as "tough" around a university, I might insist on class attendance, mark students down if they arrive at class five minutes late, and hold students to the highest academic standards—in other words, be a professor from whom it is tough to get an A. That kind of behavior will get me a reputation as being tough. It will not translate into toughness in the military or in prison, where a different set of criteria is used. I would have to rise to a whole new level of toughness to be considered tough in these circumstances. So, when we think about masculinity, it is important to remember that what is masculine behavior for one man (approaching women in a bar, talking sports all the time) may be tame compared to another man's definition.

A few of the men in the study noted that an excess of "masculine" behavior in others is a turn-off to making a friendship. On the other hand, too little masculine behavior can also sour a relationship. Homosexuality was raised as a concern, too, although the consensus was clear—a gay man can be masculine. The bottom line is that these men felt most comfortable with someone whose perceived level of masculinity is similar to theirs.

Casey, who frequently sprinkles his responses with Spanish terms, reflects on his cultural upbringing in answering the question: "I come from a very *machista* society, and sometimes I consider myself a little *machista*, too, even though I am changing. I don't need to be as macho anymore to be masculine, if you know what I mean. For example, if I am out with the guys, I don't like challenge them to drink the most. I don't fit into that. Because of that, some of them call me faggot. Or, if I used to go to the bars or discos with them to meet girls, I don't go with them as much anymore. I like women, don't get me wrong, but sometimes I don't like to meet people in bars or discotheques. For some of my ex-friends, I think they are showing me their machismo by doing that. I avoid these people most of the time now."

David did not initially think about masculinity in relation to men when he was asked the question. "Most men think in physical terms, 'Can you beat me up?' and 'Can you handle the most ladies?' because this is what the majority of men unfortunately think. It's a competition with the other men, but I've removed myself from the game because I used to play it. So, after all of that, I would say that yes: in certain circumstances, there is a connection between masculinity and male friendships because some people are still caught in the trap of trying to impress other men. It's the testosterone battle and back to the homosexual thing, where they say, 'You're not masculine because you're homosexual.' I don't buy into that, because you are a human being and you're doing what you do, and they still have the anatomy of a male unless they had surgery."

Felix, like many other men, took the question to refer to what level of masculinity he liked in a man and linked it to friendships. He referred directly to some of the gay stereotypes. "I don't like effeminate guys. They are a turn-off. I don't feel comfortable with cross-dressers and transvestites."

Greg also agrees that a link exists between masculinity and friendship. In his brief response, he also raises the specter of homosexuality when he thought about the question. If someone is not masculine enough, there are problems. "There has to be a connection. For me, if someone is really prancing—a prancer—I doubt I could form a friendship with him, though we could have a good working relationship. It's not a matter of being gay. You can be gay and masculine."

Isuko answered easily, "I could start with one extreme: if a guy is too 'testosteroney,' I don't like that because I think it is a big power thing. It's a form of elitism I don't like. I never was comfortable with something that extreme. That's the far end of the spectrum. The other end is if you are too weak-minded, whatever that means. You don't want someone who is totally helpless. I like helping people, but you want then to eventually help themselves. So I don't want too little masculinity. I look for masculinity somewhere in the middle, where they are strong, sensitive, and compassionate."

Hal thinks he forms friends with people who are similar to him in the level of masculinity. "Most of the people I know are not super beat-your-chest men. They are not foppish; they are college-educated intellectuals, not-on-sports-scholarships kind of guys. I guess most are middle-of-the-road, not one way or the other. Would I not have a friend if he was effeminate? I don't think so. A lot of people who have gone to college tend to be a little more on the effeminate side but are not flaming . . . and they probably don't know the difference between colors" (laughs).

Ken, a 44-year-old white supervisory technician, raises the issues of affection and friendship. For him, a man has to be his friend before he will feel comfortable with a significant expression of emotions. "When I define masculinity, it is usually who is the most macho, who uses the most bravado. The more masculine, the more ego one seems to have. I wouldn't say that my friends are all that macho, but they aren't that feminine either. You don't have to be masculine to be my friend." I asked Ken if he had purposefully sought out men that were not too macho or too feminine. "I don't see a pattern, but it's partly because I'm in sports and it just happens.

Touching is not a big deal." I pushed it a little more and asked Ken what happens if someone starts crying? "If it was someone that I was a friend with, it wouldn't bother me. If I didn't know the guy, it would bother me. It crosses a line. They would be opening up at a level that I wouldn't just open up at unless my wife was run over by a car or something."

Joe, a 31-year-old white guy who is "in between jobs," gives this colorful response. "A guy likes a man's man. If I met a guy that was into knitting, he would not be a guy that I'd be hanging out with much because I have no interest in knitting. I don't think knitting is masculine. If I meet a guy wearing a Pittsburgh Steeler's hat and sweatshirt, I like him already because I am a Steeler's fan. I may never see him again, but if he is sitting in an airport, I'll go talk with him and when we leave each other, we'll high-five. You can't high-five someone who knits!"

One final quote comes from Norman, a 56-year-old white professor who is unfazed by a man's level of masculinity or his sexual orientation. He looks for commonalities. "There is absolutely zero connection [between masculinity and friendship]. There's a guy at work who is openly gay—is 'queer' the word? He came into my office a year ago and wanted to invite me to a party but he said, 'I want to tell you something first. I'm queer.' I said, 'Well, I'm a Catholic, so we've both got a problem.' For a good part of my life, I played sports, but it wasn't a masculinity thing. It was, 'You like racquetball? Me, too. Let's go.'"

Masculinity, however it is defined, plays a part in friendships. Most men (although definitely not all) feel more comfortable with men who are like themselves in perceived levels of masculinity. If a man feels uncomfortable with acting in a "macho" way, he is likely to not want to hang out with another guy who acts macho. Although common characteristics and interests are the bases for many friendships, friendships also seem to be based on, for many, similar testosterone levels.

Conclusion: Making and Keeping Friends

The men featured in this chapter are men who are connected to other men. They help their friends by providing support and listening to them— communication is important here. They do things together with their friends that include sports and, once again, communication. They make friends through finding commonalities and through other people, another sign of connection. Maintaining friendships also involves communication and spending time together. Finally, these men must feel comfortable with their friends on some level in order to not lose the friendship.

Having friends is possible for anyone willing to make the effort, although it does, in many cases, require a time commitment and the willingness to have fairly frequent communication.

4

What Do Men Learn From Their Fathers About Friendships?

A work colleague stopped me on the street when he heard I was writing this book and started to talk about his experience in a men's group in the 1980s. "We were 10 highly successful guys who were all trying to figure what our roles were now that we were all married to superwomen who were working and making big bucks and taking care of the family. What was our part in this? So, we began meeting as a men's book club that evolved into a support group. We met for eight years. Our wives would meet, and they would talk about mundane topics and drink wine. But we were really trying to push the envelope on this male role thing. One thing that we had in common is that we were all raised by rigid and demanding fathers who thought a woman's place was in the home. We were all trying to break out of the mold and swore that we would raise our children the exact opposite of how we were raised. We were going to connect with men and women in a totally different way than our fathers did."

Most books on men include a chapter that focuses on the father–son relationship. Here, we talk about fathers from a slightly different perspective, from the men's observations of their fathers' friendships with other men.

Mimicking Our Fathers

Growing up, sons constantly observe and monitor their fathers' actions and comings and goings—the way they slouch, talk, and act around others.

Sometimes they try to talk in their father's deep voice or treat others the way he does. One of my closest (*must*) friends from childhood often was admonished by his own father with the words "little man, come here." I was amazed when my friend referred to his own son with the same words and in the same tone of voice.

Sons also observe whether their fathers have friends, what they do with those friends, and whether those friendships are important to their fathers. This is similar to the learning that comes from watching how their fathers treat women, what they say to repairmen (and repairwomen) who come to the house, and whether they show respect to elders. Sons may know if their fathers go off to shoot hoops every Saturday with friends or whether they stop at the corner bar on the way home to have a beer with the guys. Some of those friends may be closely wrapped into the family as a godfather to the son or a stand-in for the father in a crisis. Regardless of the nature of each family, most men who have the opportunity to observe their father will consciously or unconsciously pattern their lives after him—they may try either to be like him or to be the exact opposite of him.

So, if a man was raised in a home in which his father felt comfortable around other men and was always inviting them over for a good time, he will probably have a positive view of his own abilities to make friends. Contrast that with the man who rarely saw his father with other men or observed him acting uncomfortably or defensively around them. That man will most likely have to work harder to make friends, because he has no friendship-making role model to emulate.

Learning from Our Fathers

Sons do not learn only by observing their fathers. From an early age, fathers actively and purposefully teach sons how to interact. Psychologists Dan Kindlon and Michael Thompson, in *Raising Cain: Protecting the Emotional Life of Boys*, describe how boys learn from their fathers in ways that differ from what sons learn from mothers: "A strong father–son relationship may look and sound nothing like its counterpart between a mother and a son. . . . There may not be the exploration of and sharing of feelings or the level of physical contact that we often associate with emotional closeness between women. Between men, the talk may be centered around action instead of reflection."[112]

What Kindlon and Thompson describe is based on working side by side on a task or facing each other across a field and throwing a ball—and, ultimately, how that type of activity builds closeness with others. Sons carry that level of activity sharing into adult interactions with other men. Young boys carry lessons from their fathers about friendships into their own friendships. As a result, they often re-experience their relationship with their father when with their male friends. Boys who go fishing with their fathers grow up to go fishing with their friends and their children. When they fish, they are reconnecting with their fathers.

When I play golf on Saturday with my friends, I remember that my father played golf with his friends on the weekend. He bet with his friends, so I bet with mine and, by doing so, reconnect with him while also building friendships for myself. If my children play golf, they will be connecting with two generations.

From the father's view, teaching also often includes passing down values. Psychologist William Pollack's description of young men in *Real Boys: Rescuing Our Sons from the Myths of Boyhood*[113] talks about the values that a father intentionally or unintentionally conveys. Pollack believes fathers often make the mistake of being so focused on making money for the family, which meets many men's own definition of being male, that they neglect their sons. The children are left to the mother to raise. Another mistake is that fathers try to act "macho" around their sons to toughen them up to survive in the world. When a young man is toughened, he usually is not taught how to interact with other men (or women) in a supportive way.

The great push to toughen up sons is important to many men because the opposite of being tough is being a sissy, something few fathers want for their sons. So, young boys can learn quickly that if they want their fathers' approval, they may not be able to be themselves.

This is not to argue that fathers abandon male values and be like mothers toward their children. For several decades, fathers have been attacked for not being involved enough or interested enough in parenting to provide adequate role models for their sons and daughters.[114] Men can be good fathers without trying to act like mothers. Being available, listening, accepting, understanding, supporting, and warmly encouraging are all things fathers can do while still modeling traditional male characteristics of independence (without isolation), assertion, and action. In addition, men offer a perspective on relationships that is different from and may be more adaptive than the perspective offered by women (see Chapter 5 for men's views on women's friendships).

Coping Without a Father or Positive Role Model

What about a man who grows up without a father or with a father who was not a positive role model for making friends? That man may want to do the opposite of what his father did. Hu, a 49-year-old Chinese man who lives in California told us, "I know I didn't want to be like him as a father or husband. He was violent toward my mother. I knew I wanted to develop friends and not stay as a recluse in my own world and always afraid (as he did)." Hu also told us he does not have enough friends. The father-less man's longing for male friendships (and older male mentors) is often greater than those who had good fathering while growing up.

Not only is Hu struggling to be what his father was not—friendly and nurturing—he has no model for what *to* be. So, he is working against a negative role model (his father) with little clarity for how to set up his male relationships. Men with this gap in their experience are more likely to have difficulty making friends.

And, of course, a man may have had two parents in the house and still be absent a friendship-making role model. A 25-year-old white student, Brady, received a chilling message from both his parents about friendships: "When I was growing up, my parents always said they did not understand how I had so many friends, and I felt I did not have any. My parents conveyed the message that there were other things much more important than friendships, such as immediate gratification, money, gambling, drinking. I am my father's son and, in some ways, I lose sight of how important people are. My father places a higher value on money and achievement and is willing to step on others to climb personally. The fact that my father is that way reminds me to place the people in my life as a priority."

Knowing Our Fathers' Friends

The men in this book were asked whether their fathers (or father figures) had many male friends and, if so, what messages they received from their fathers about friendships. The answers were, at times, rambling, reflecting, I think, the lack of thought most men have given this topic. A few men said their fathers' friendships had changed over time, either increasing or decreasing, so we tried to gain a general impression. The numbers below are thus estimates:[115]

- My father had many friends, 45%
- My father had a few friends, 25%
- My father had no friends, 30%

A handful of the men said they had no significant contact with a father figure and were raised by a mother, grandparent, or an older sibling.

From these interviews, I found great diversity in the way that the lives of the men's fathers were carried out, from the father who grew up and still lives in a small town in the middle of the country to the military man who moved his family constantly. The situation in which the father lived affected that man's friendships. The impressions the men had about their fathers seemed to be similar across race. For example, almost no differences were noted between white and African-American men in the number who said their fathers did or did not have friends.

Fathers with Many Friends

Remembering that, in Chapter 2, 60% of the men responded that they themselves had enough friends, here, we find almost half of the men believing their fathers had many friends and another 25% believing their fathers had some friends. The positive spin on this would be that the majority of men we interviewed said they had enough friends, and the majority of the men said their fathers had at least some friends, with almost half having many friends. But this can be interpreted in another way. The negative spin is that, depending on the generation, one-quarter of the men in this study do not have enough friends and almost one-third believe their fathers were virtually without friends. The interviews suggest that many men believe their fathers' ability to form friendships has influenced their own ability to form friendships. Work is still to be done for this generation and future generations in relation to friendship building.

Al's father came from humble beginnings and has remained in his hometown virtually his whole life. This taught Al the value of long-term relationships that, for his father, waxed and waned over the years. "I always envied my parents because they had lots of really close friends, although some of those friendships deteriorated. My father actually grew up with a little social group. There were a bunch of families that freely associated with each other all the time. It was a small town in Iowa in the 1950s, a different mentality in the small town versus the big urban areas. People are a little more open and a little friendlier although small-town people can also be closed-minded.

"My dad was born in a small shack just outside of a town that had about 1000 people. He was born there, raised there, and he will die there. Everybody knew him. There were five families we were very close with and grew up with. We hunted and fished with the men. He hunted with bow and arrow. My father is 75 now and still hunts that way. While they don't hunt in a group, when someone gets a shot, they call several guys and they drag in the deer and butcher it (examples of *must* friends). I used to have high school friends who I hunted and fished with also. My dad had a lot of good friends, and what I learned from that was the value of friendship. You learn there are people you can depend on, not that you agree with them all the time."

Casey said his father had "thousands" of friends. He learned very specifically how to be a friend to someone. "My dad always gives everything he has. If you need a T-shirt, he just takes it off his back and gives it to you. He's special in that way, and he's very cheerful. Sharing, for him, means giving without asking or expecting anything in exchange. He just gives it to you and says, 'Don't worry. Today it's you; tomorrow it's me.' I heard that from his friends. He always told me I had to be nice with my friends and honest.

"He still has good friends, and they love him so much. They go to his house, and they drink. He drinks a lot. Now he got sick. He was in the hospital with cancer. His friends were at the house when I called. They were drinking, but they don't let him drink. My dad said to me on the phone, 'These sons of bitches won't let me drink. But they bring me food and stuff—they're beautiful.' He always invites people to the house. When he first meets someone, he is very respectful, very playful, but he would never cross the line. He warned me to be respectful because you never know how people will act. They could kick your ass or kill you, he told me. My dad is a peasant who only went to the third grade. He grew up on a farm, and they were all very machismo.

"After he has known someone for a while, he will ask them personal things. Then he will joke with them. That is where I learned that if you joke with me, cool, but you better be able to take my jokes, too. I learned a lot from my dad; he is very cool and a good friend to his sons. When I got into a fight with one of my ex-friends, he asked me what happened and said I didn't need a faggot friend like that. . . . Sometimes my father kisses me on the lips, and I don't feel bad. If somebody saw that and said, 'Something's going on there,' my dad would say, 'Let him think what he wants. He's not perfect.' That's the way he shows love for us. That's a good friendship with my dad. He is my best friend in a way that he can tell me anything."

Casey learned an enormous amount about father–son and peer friendships from his father, whom he respects and loves. To a large extent, it seems that Casey "inhaled" his father and is attempting to lead his emotional life like his father leads his. But, and as with so many other men, an ambivalence about masculinity is expressed when Casey talks about ditching a friend because he was a "faggot." In the next sentence, he talked about his father kissing him on the lips and not feeling bad about it. Although Casey is expressing homophobic feelings, the underlying message from his father may be that it is important to be oneself and to not worry what others think.

Isuko's father had many friends throughout his life. Isuko learned from him very concise messages about friendships, including the notion that, once you have friends, they can confine you. "He taught me to try and stay close with and be there for your friends. Don't ever dismiss them. Always make them feel important because they are. Another thing I learned is that, when your friendship is in the form of a pact, it's like you have to agree with that pact. I don't like that. It's like, if you are on a team, you have to work as a team, which I've had a problem with growing up. There are times when I don't want to be part of a team. But my father sent the message that you have to stick with your friends at all costs. It's like there was no room for disagreements. He said, 'You have to stick with them no matter what.' It was part of a machismo thing, keeping up appearances. You were very *with* the guys. That's how you will be accepted."

Isuko depicts an almost Machiavellian view of friendships that he learned from his father—they can be "played," so that they will benefit you the most. Loyalty is important, but it is loyalty held in the service of being accepted—not for its own intrinsic value.

Jack, like a few other men in the study, was raised more by his older brothers and mother than his father. "My father had close friends. He was close with his brother. But he was an alcoholic and died too young from colon cancer. He died 25 years ago when I was 18 and my mother died seven years ago. I really learned about friendships from my brothers. My parents had divorced before my father died, and I stayed with my mom.

My oldest brother was 12 years older than me. I come from a large family, and my oldest brother was my godfather. He had friends."

Fathers with a Few Friends

In Chapter 2, the majority of the men in the study said that they had enough friends. So, recounting that a father had few or no friends may be a commentary on the plight of the working father of one or two generations ago, when leisure time did not exist to the extent it does today. Fathers, as we hear especially from older men, did not have time for friends—they were too busy working to support the family or too worried about getting ahead. In fact, if union and professional membership is any gauge, being connected to the workplace reached its peak in the middle years of the 20th century, according to Robert Putnam. During those years, about 1950 to 1970, membership participation in collective bargaining and professional groups was at its highest.[116]

Ben, like one of the men quoted earlier whose father was violent, learned from his father not to be like his father. He grew up and charted a different course for himself, something every man has the capacity to do. Ben speaks very powerfully and succinctly of the negative influence his father had on him and others. "My father didn't have very many friends. He had people he worked with and one work friend who was every now and then an occasional friend that he didn't see just at work. I would say my father didn't teach me much about being a friend to males because he is very critical. The closer he is to somebody, the more critical he is of that person. Probably his best work friend was the person he blasted all the time. If I learned *anything*, it was don't do that."

Ben was asked if someone else influenced him as to how to be a friend. "I try to pick up these things from my friends. I try to see what works for people. If my friend has a good quality, why shouldn't I try to make it something of my own as well? If the way they are relating to people is cool, or they show me something I needed, that is good. If I needed someone to listen to me, I learned from them how to do that for others."

Ben has adapted by looking to peers for role models of how to interact. This is a good method for men to use to fill in the gaps they may have from their upbringing.

Ed, the taxi driver, had a father with few friendships. Ed immediately compares himself to his father when answering the question, and makes it clear that he definitely learned about friendships from his father. "Dad didn't have a million friends. He was like me. I am sure this was male 'imprinting.' He had three or four friends for over 60 years. Yet, a lot of people knew my father because when he died I couldn't believe how many showed up at his funeral. With my dad, it was black and white—you either liked him or you didn't. You always knew where my father stood, and that is what I learned. [For me,] it doesn't matter how many friends you have. It matters how much respect you get from the people you know. You need to be straight with your friends. You don't need to be blunt, necessarily. Some time you can give them the truth in a gentle way."

Greg is unsure what he learned from his father. His vagueness may be typical of men who have not given the question of their father's friendships much thought. He feels affected by his father's friendships, however, and they seem to be a combination of friendship categories. "It seems to me he had friends, but I am hedging my bet. He may have lost touch with some of them. How good his friends were, I don't know. (Greg is wondering if they are *must* or *just* friends.) Maybe the messages are just so ingrained, so everything I am saying about friendship is what his [ideas] were. My father wasn't one to talk much about that sort of thing, that I remember. If he did it by example, then one thing I will say is that those names (*rust* friends) I heard about for 25 to 30 years are still in the picture. I'm still hearing about them and finding out about them. So, I wonder if the messages I received were established by my observance of my father."

Hal's father, as mentioned, worked very hard to support the family. Hal's parents only had one child because that was all they could afford. His father had an interesting transition as he aged, though, and he gained more friends. His father's route to friendship has an impact on Hal. "My father had a small amount of friends—he worked very hard and did not have much time for them when I was younger. But he would make time and go out with his buddies and would ride motorcycles with a group of younger guys when he got older. He was able to cross generations to build friendships. So, I guess I learned that, as well as the value of friendships. I've always wanted to take a trip with a bunch of guys like he would do with the motorcycles but I never have. You know, get on a boat and fish off Florida and come back sunburned. . . ."

Fathers Without Friends

Is it an indictment of men in our society that one-third are seen by their sons as having no friends? Maybe . . . but the other side, as mentioned, are the number who believe their fathers had at least some friends. In some of the answers, it is clear that while fathers were *capable* of having friendships, they spent all their time at work or with the family. A few of the men who said their fathers were friendless lamented their commitment to work and family and wished they had been more expansive in their relationships with people outside of the family. Others thought their fathers were incapable or uninterested in friendships with men. In some cases, the fathers were described as downright unhappy.

A sad impression comes from this 60-year-old white man, Hank, "My father was a Colonel in the army and was very controlling and repressive. He wasn't around much, and what friends I would say he had were either family or other high-ranking military officials. But even then, you get the sense that the friendship was as much about hierarchy and the fear of not being sociable to the right people at the right time."

David reminds us, as Ben did, that fathers are not always available as role models for their sons. He describes trying to commune with his father but finding him unavailable. To compensate for this gap, he excelled in sports, which he knew would please *other* fathers. By doing this, he is pleasing his "unavailable" father through this vicarious relationship. I think a lot of men whose fathers are unavailable or impossible to please find ways to please other men (often a coach or teacher) in an attempt to fill this void. "My father had absolutely no friends. My father's father was a gangster in Houston, and he taught me that you don't trust anybody because everybody is out to get you. So, don't trust anybody because it will crumble, and the only person my dad really trusts is my mother because she is a loving and nurturing person. So, part of me talking to you is the loving side of my mother and the street side of my father. He has retired from the military and has no friends. He was away a lot, and I always tried to live up to his expectations though he never told me what they were. I played sports well and that was other fathers' expectations."

The encouraging part of David's story is the change that has occurred in their relationship. "We can now go fishing, and we can sit and talk, and I speak with him about emotions and feelings, and it's not like he questions me and calls me a sissy. He never does that because he has seen the gangster side of me, but he's like, 'I'm proud of you.' He's proud of what I have become as a black man, and we recently spoke about friendships, and I'm trying to get him involved in my fraternity so he can meet some older males."

Their relationship has clearly progressed now that David is an adult, and he has reached a level of resolution with his father. The reference to being a "sissy" is a telling comment about the continued disconnect between masculinity and the expression of feelings. In addition, we see that David has joined a fraternity. Fraternities are an acceptable venue for college-age and adult men to get together with other men to enjoy the camaraderie these groups afford. In fact, on many campuses, fraternities are "masculine" hangouts for men, as much of a fraternity member's time is spent in sports competition and mixers with sororities. Adult fraternities are like clubs— the men get together for community service, socializing, and networking. Thus men feel safe going there for male socialization. David's introduction of his father into this world is a way of showing his father that David is a man.

Despite the rejection Felix has felt from his parents as a gay man, he was able to easily answer what he had learned from his father about friendship—loyalty to those you care about. He also mentions the couple relationships that men form, which will be discussed in Chapter 5. "My father is very loyal, but does not have close friends. My parents have couple friends. He used to have tennis (*just*) buddies, but he did not pal around with them when he was off the court. He can be a Jekyll/Hyde type and can be very difficult. But he is the more caring of my two parents. He will call if I am ill, not my mother. She is wonderful, but he will call. My father did not like Bernard (his former significant other), not so much for the gay issue, but because he feared losing control of me. I think if I had been straight and married someone, it would have been the same problem. But his loyalty to his children is what comes through, and that may be why I value loyalty in my own friendships."

Military Upbringing and Friendships

The military can also serve as a form of parent, both for fathers who were raising sons and for the sons themselves. Numerous men described being raised by fathers who were career military men. Some of the men high-lighted in Part III of this book, in their 60s and older, were profoundly affected by their own time in the military.

Joe, white, 48, and retired, believes his relationships with male friends were strongly influenced by his military-based upbringing. His approach is the classic military philosophy—if one soldier falls, another must be there to pick up after him. This means that, to a large extent, friends are replaceable. "I have always been an outgoing person. My father was in the Marine Corps for 30 years, so we moved around a lot. When you move, you have to be able to make friends. If I had a friend who moved away, I made another one right away, somebody that would fill that void. It might take a while to get it up to the one that had left (a *must* friend), but it would get there." When asked about his father's friendships, he gave the impression that, because of the dangerous nature of the military, friendships were discouraged or kept on a less personal basis. "My father didn't have many friends. I think he felt that it was easier to just have acquaintances (*just* friends) than (*must*) friends, because you always had to pick up and leave. Of course, when you did two tours of Vietnam, you really don't want to make too good a friend because you never know what is going to happen to him while you are there. But now that he's retired, I think he has one close friend of 10 years who lives next door. And, since he has retired, he and I have become very close, which we never had when he was growing up.

"I don't know what I learned about friendships from him except that when you move around a lot, if you want to have friends, you have to go out and make them. The other kids on the military bases were the same way, so we all made friends easily. They all knew what it was like to be the new kid, so everyone was friendly."

The sons of military men seem to have a consistently different impression of their fathers and friendships. Bound by rules and rank, the very real fear of losing friends in combat, and the residential mobility of the career, many men thought their fathers were cut off from their emotions and from possible *must* friendships. The expectation exists that people of the same rank will be treated the same, making it hard to differentiate *must* friends from *just* friends. A friend of mine, also raised by a career military man, recounted recently that his father viewed all his children as equally accomplished, by saying he was equally proud of all of them, even though my friend had clearly achieved much more than his two siblings. My friend resented not being recognized for his accomplishments. Although, of course, the father loved all the children the same, he washed away individual distinctions, in my friend's eyes, in an attempt to be consistent. In so doing, he removed individuality. I wonder if this approach, when applied to friends, is a necessary by-product of military life.

Other Early Influences

Mothers, grandparents, and siblings (note Jack's upbringing with an absent father) were also influential in raising a few of the men we interviewed.

Clearly, lessons about friendships can be learned from any significant adult in one's life. A 39-year-old African-American engineer, Cal was raised by his mother. "She had lots of friends! One thing that I learned from her is that friends should be there for each other . . . just to help each other through life."

Marc, a 37-year-old Asian-American businessman, had a grandfather who was in politics, so there is almost a "genetic disposition" to being social, outgoing, and making personal contacts with others—from grandfather to father to son. "(My grandfather) made everyone a friend. I think he has a lot to do with how I am. I have an ingrained feeling that one is obliged to solve conflict and be the first to help in a crisis and work out problems between groups of people. I think that's where it comes from for me." Although his father was also influential, he credits his grandfather with setting the stage for what he learned about friendships.

Conclusion: Father Wisdom

Whether conveyed intentionally or unintentionally, over the years, men receive varied messages from their fathers about the value of friendships and how friends should be treated. Some said friendships were highly valued; some learned to put friends first, others to put family first; and a few learned not to trust anyone, including their fathers. Among the messages received:

- I learned you don't have to have a ton of friends and that your life revolves around your wife and kids.
- I learned never to get too close to people and don't get dragged into other people's relationships.
- My dad's best friend was my mom, and I learned that everyone needs at least one friend.
- You have to spend time with friends to keep them.
- Friends positively impact marriage and life, and you should work hard at them.
- True friends do not have to be seen on a regular basis.
- It takes time, but once you have established a friendship it is yours for life.
- Friends help friends—you get connections and business from friends.
- I learned from dad that men don't need to communicate verbally.

- I learned from him that patience, respect, and sincerity go a long way, and that everyone deserves that from the beginning.

What we can learn from these quotes is that fathers influence the way their sons think about friendships. In some ways, it is disheartening to think about the bad experiences. Think of the generations of missed opportunities, of all the chances fathers had to convey to their children that friendships are a good thing. Even within the constrictions of economic hardships, where work had to come first for a family to survive, a father could have conveyed to a son that friends are needed in good and bad times and that, along with family, friends are vital to a person's well-being.

But look at the men, like Casey, who said, "My dad gives everything he has" and "He always told me I had to be nice with my friends and honest." David's story points out the hope that men can change, even after they are retired. His father, a military man, does connect with his adult son and is open to making friends. These are the hopeful messages that can be taken from the stories these men offer. Hope also exists that these men will pass on to their own children that friends can fundamentally improve your life and that change is possible. One man even said that he learned from his father he did not want to be like him. That is a powerful message of change—men are not locked into their situations.

II

UNDERSTANDING WOMEN'S FRIENDSHIPS

5

Do Women Influence Men's Friendships?

Having convinced you that men do, in fact, have friendships, let's see what role, if any, women play in men's friendships. Do men learn about friendships from observing women's and wish theirs were similar? Do women help men's friendships by introducing their husbands to their women friends' husbands? Or, do women hinder friendships by discouraging their husbands? And, can men and women be friends without sexual overtones—the "When Harry Met Sally" question?

Can Women's Friendships Be a Model for Men's Friendships?

In answering this question, let's look briefly at the fundamental differences between men and women. Clearly, there are the obvious visible physical differences. As mentioned in Chapter 1, men's and women's brains also differ in that, among other things, spatial imaging, language acquisition, and possibly even emotional response vary. Overall, male brains are larger, even accounting for body size differences, but the part of the brain that deals with memory and emotion is larger in women. This could mean that women are better at expressing emotions as well as remembering emotionally laden details.[1] Boys and girls have different genetic influences that lead, for example, to higher rates of attention deficit hyperactivity disorder as well as oppositional defiant disorder in male as opposed to female children.[2] As early as infancy, differences show up. Infant boys are more apt to focus on mechanical objects within their line of sight, whereas infant girls are more apt to focus on a human face.[3]

Could these early differences in the interest in mechanical objects over faces and higher rates of attention deficit disorder and oppositional defiant disorder cause males to interact differently with people (and their friends) than females do? Yes, these differences start people out on a trajectory. But concluding that these early differences cause men and women to inherently interact in "male" or "female" ways in adulthood is a little tricky. Socialization by family, friends, and the prevailing culture influences behavior.[4] Childhood experiences (a girl playing on the football team and a boy practicing feeding and bathing infants) and adult experiences (a father stays home with his children and a mother works full-time in the factory) can change the early trajectory. How men and women act is not essentially different. A current view of men's and women's behavior is called the *dualistic philosophy*, which is the idea that men's and women's behaviors are based on socialization and not only on biology.[5] The two interact to determine who we are and how we will behave. We have all heard the myths that men aren't built to take care of infants or small children or don't need to share their feelings like women do. If this were true for a particular man, would it be impossible for him to learn how to nurture children or form close friendships with other men? Let's agree that some genetic differences between men and women *may* affect our friendship-related behavior as adults, but these differences do not lock us into behaviors. Men have the capacity to adopt a style of friendship that is similar to women's friendships, if they wish to.[6]

Women's Friendships Could Be Role Models

A boy often learns early on about interactions with others through women—he is typically tended to by his mother, women relatives, female child-care providers, and female teachers. He observes women's ways of relating in their friendships and, if these are positive interactions, he may want to replicate those relationships with his friends. However, interestingly enough, a boy will often not take that route and rather will interact with his friends in typically male ways. As he reaches adulthood, another chance exists to learn about women's friendships. Due to the growing respect and equality between men and women in the workplace, men have increased exposure to women's ways of interacting with each other. The opportunities for learning about women's friendships are increasing. Esther Menaker noted this burgeoning equity 20 years ago, when she wrote about men, "[there is] a decreased fear of the more feminine aspects of their personalities. Despite some prevalence of the 'macho' syndrome, many men permit themselves more softness, tenderness, and enjoyment of aesthetic pleasures than was previously the case."[7] Increased openness to women could signal the opportunity to learn from them and possibly reformulate traditional masculine activities, like friendship building.

Some men have written of their admiration of women's friendships. Terry Kupers, an expert on sex roles, states, "I have learned quite a lot about friendship from women. For instance, I have learned how two friends can be very angry at each other, call each other names, and then when calm returns go on being close friends . . . when my wife has the same kind of argument with a woman friend, I support her and tell her I admire the way she can be so forthright, fierce, and forgiving, and deepen her intimacies in the process."[8] Victor Seidler, a social scientist, also describes his favorable impression of female friendships, "Many men feel envious of the relationships that women seem able to strike up with each other. There is a continuity, a seemingly easy intimacy in women's relationships with each other that allows women to talk about both their personal lives and their work lives, both of which men can find difficult to achieve."[9]

Other reasons that some men might want to emulate women's friendships (and I clearly acknowledge that not all men would want to) are that women's friendships have been described as emotionally closer than men's,[10] more self-revealing,[11] and more oriented toward two-person relationships rather than toward group relationships.[12] In addition, some men often like having women as friends. They feel greater comfort in sharing intimate details about their lives with women than with men,[13] perhaps a throwback to their early socialization by women. They don't compete with women in friendships as they do with men.[14] And, they can be physically close with them (hugging, for example) in ways that they might not feel comfortable doing with men.

Women's Friendships May Not Be Role Models

But not so fast! Despite this exposure to women's ways of interacting, not all men are so enamored of women as friends or women's friendships with each other. For some men, in fact, fostering closeness with men rather than emulating women is highly valued.[15] Author Robert Bly, cited in Chapter 1, advocates male bonding to prevent men from being too strongly influenced by women. He believes women's influence on young boys is the norm in Western culture. To have a more male-oriented environment, some men attempt to build relationships with other men by joining all-male clubs and adult fraternities. They pursue hobbies that are traditional bastions of maleness (like hunting) specifically to be with other men.

It may not be simply an internal drive that presses men to hang out with other men and not model their friendships after women's friendships. Fostering closeness between men and their communities has also taken on a political and social urgency. Men are being called on from the pulpits of most religious organizations, in impoverished as well as wealthy communities, to play a larger part in the rearing of children, particularly sons, or to be "big brothers" to fatherless boys. If this shift toward greater involvement by men in the upbringing of children continues, it will offer a different view of friendships for young boys and the men themselves. If men get together with each other and include their sons, boys will see men interacting with each other as well as benefit from the men's interaction with them. *The Dangerous Book for Boys* offers specific activities that men and boys can pursue, from skipping stones on a pond to building go-carts. These types of activities can foster closeness across generations through noncompetitive activities. Fathers who spend time with other dads or father figures will in turn observe additional ways that men can interact with each other and with children.[16]

Ultimately, men's definitions of friendships *may just be different*, which is why men do not emulate women's friendships. The type of closeness that women have, one that involves verbal sharing, may not be important to men.[17] In fact, John Tognoli, another family specialist, views men as having *more* friendships than women, just less intimate ones. Men may not wish to pursue friendships if they are too emotionally draining or, as we'll see later, too high maintenance.

Can Men Learn About Friendships from Women?

When asked if they had learned about friendships from observing women's friendships, the men in my study gave the following answer (figures are approximate):

- I have learned positive things about women's friendships, 35%
- I have negative impressions of women's friendships, 25%
- I have not learned anything positive or negative about women's friendships, 20%
- Men and women cannot be compared, 20%.

I Have Learned Positive Things

About one-third of the men in the study said they had learned positive things about friendships from observing women's interactions. For example, a 35-year-old married African-American businessman, Samuel, told us, "I learned to talk about things with my friends from watching women, because they are more intimate with each other. Boys don't talk about how they feel, but girls do. Boys talk about sports and how a girl looks, but not about how they feel."

Harris, a 37-year-old, African-American, married, FBI agent, also commented on the closeness he sees in women. His cogent comment about movie-going speaks to the discomfort with public appearances that so many men feel, "Female friendships are different. Females are openly affectionate, and that's a great thing females have over guys. Like, two females can go to the movies, and they will sit beside each other. But I could go to the movies with my best friend, and we would sit with a seat between us. I think it's a space thing with guys. Two females can even go on a trip together, share a room, and sleep in the same bed. Two men wouldn't sleep in the same bed. We would get two beds or one would sleep on the floor."

Casey witnessed what he first thought was an erotic interaction between his sister and one of her female friends. He was at first put off by it, then found it quite informative, "One day I saw my sister talking with her best friend (Casey was nine at the time, and his sister was in early adolescence). I came up behind them. I never intended to listen to what they were saying but they were talking about their intimate body parts, 'Do you have (pubic) hair already?' Maybe I was shocked but they were talking with so much honesty and then they start comparing their boobs. Of course, I was watching her friend, not my sister. They were—'I think mine are bigger.' 'No, I think mine are bigger than yours.' And they started touching. I thought, is she a lesbian? But no, they were, with so much honesty, talking about their bodies. Then my sister said, 'I think you're so beautiful, and I like your body a lot.' And the other girl said, 'Thank you. I like the way you are telling me,' and they hugged. They were almost naked. I thought something else was going to happen and then they just continued studying. I learned you can tell your friends about their bodies. There's nothing wrong about it. You can tell them about their hair and their eyes. So, I'm not afraid to tell anyone about the way they look. It doesn't mean that I like them in the other way. I learned that from her."

Ed was influenced, although subtly it sounds, by the women in his life. "You see your mother make friends with new neighbors—but I don't think I ever made a concerted effort to watch how she made friends. There's less competitiveness between women than men. Every man has to be the cock of the walk so to speak. The man that is putting up the biggest front is the most insecure person. When you break through that eggshell, you can find a pretty decent person. He is just a jerk or idiot on the outside."

Isuko, one of the few openly gay men in the study, said that he has learned a great deal from women's friendships. "The emotional support is great. I've seen when a girl lost a boyfriend or some loved one, they were really there for her. It was almost like a vigil (laughs). But I thought it was neat. They were really supportive and nurturing. Maybe it's the softness, the voice. There is not so much stumbling of egos. They don't need to prove anything about being strong. It goes back to being sensitive. There's a higher level of sensitivity among women."

Jack learned about friendships from his mother, who raised him after his parents divorced. "I learned about communication and keeping in touch as core to friendship."

"Do you think those are more feminine qualities?" I asked.

"Yes, definitely. We used to have Al-Anon meetings at our house as we were dealing with my father's alcoholism. I watched her with her friends there and learned a great deal about how to communicate more openly. I did not learn that from my father."

I Have Negative Impressions

Many of the men who thought women's friendships were problematic were quite open about their feelings. Single men seemed to be more negative than married men. "Hell, no!" Abe, a single 21-year-old African American said, "I don't believe that females can teach me anything about being friends. They keep too much stuff going and too much drama."

Yaz, a 31-year-old Latino salesman who is also single, responded with an adjective (think feline) that was often-heard about women. "Male friendships are much more solid. Males tend to be true, and females seem to be fake. Females are more 'catty.' Females tend to be more surface and superficial by going shoe shopping with someone they call a friend but then talk bad about them. Male friendships seem to be longer lasting. A man may have one good friend his whole life, while females tend to go through friends based on the season or their mood. Some females even hang out with other females based on how they look in comparison to her. I had a single woman tell me she would go out with uglier girls so guys would hit on her, and she would get the attention."

Another white single man in his 20s, Vincent, who owns a restaurant answered, "Women are nuts! They don't talk about anything, especially when something is pissing them off. They just act like nothing is going on, rather than beating the crap out of each other and getting over it. They have disagreements about petty [stuff] and will stay pissed for the end of time."

This belief about women not talking about anything significant was given a different spin by Norris, a 30-year-old, engaged-to-be-married, African-American pharmacist. "I think females seek too many people to call their friends. Female friendship is so open, they believe they have to share everything with their so-called friends, then it is like publishing it in the newspaper."

Ben is one of the few of the 10 men who does not have a particularly favorable view of women's friendships. He believes men are less compli-cated but are capable of closeness with other men—men's closeness just looks different than women's intimacy. "I don't mean to be funny, but there are things that my friends and I have learned *not* to do by watching some female friendships. Males can play off of each other. I don't want to be on tape saying these ridiculously sexist things. . . . I think women can be vali-dating to each other. I just think the nature of male and female friendships is different. Male friendships have a whole different air about them. They're more functional. We're friends because we like to be friends. It's just simpler to be a friend with a male. I've heard women say this, too." When asked to elaborate, Ben said, "Women's friendships are more complicated. They're overanalyzed. There is a lot of emotional intensity. Males can sit in a room and not talk and watch TV and not once think, 'Is he mad at me?' Men are just kind of simple. If something is bothering them, they will say it. You never have to wonder if you're not being told something."

Are men as capable of having intimate relationships as women? Ben responds, "That might not be the nature of a male relationship—to share feelings. If it is about interacting and having a good time together and making each other feel good, I guess that is some intimacy. I just think we might define intimacy differently in male–male friendships. Two guys can go watch a Terminator movie and have wings and beer and talk about chicks and that is intimacy. Any other feelings I would share with my wife—I don't need to share them with everyone else (he chuckles at this).

Same-sex friendships give you the opportunity, whether you are male or female, to be heard and validated on a different level, not on a better level or more intimate level, but a different one than inter-gender friendships. There are just things that women can only understand from women and that men can only truly understand from men. I do think that male friendships can achieve that kind of intimacy. It's just expressed differently. It's not like the typical kind of intimacy. I might be able to complain about my wife and a guy can say, 'Man, that sucks' and that's intimacy. He's not giving me insight, and I am not crying in my beer but only a man can do that."

I Have Not Learned Anything Positive or Negative

The next two examples in this category are both from married men, the first from a 31-year-old white boat repairman, Chris: "I see female friendships, but I don't think about or take them into consideration." The second comes from a 29-year-old white social worker, Brett, whose religious observance affects his view: "No. What I have seen mostly is that my wife's friends are her family. Because I'm an Orthodox Jew, I didn't really grow up with female friends. I went to an all-boys school, and all the girls went to an all-girls school, and friendships between us were discouraged."

Felix, one of the 10 men we have selected to follow in this book, replied, "No. I never looked at women's friendships and thought that I could learn anything from them." When I mentioned that some men said women's friendships are rife with back-stabbing behavior and cattiness, he laughed and said, "Not like gay men! Not as bad as gay men!"

You Can't Compare the Two

Finally, a few men gave answers indicating that comparing men and women was not useful, either because men and women are the same and cannot be compared or because they are fundamentally different, so that observing women would be irrelevant to male friendships. No negative or positive connotation was given in relation to women's friendships. One example of answers in this category comes from a married man, Wylie, a 32-year-old white insurance coordinator who said, "I have a lot of female friendships—I don't think they are different from male friendships."

One trend did emerge once the answers were coded, and variables such as age, race, marital status, and education were explored in relation to the question. Younger men and those who were single were more apt to be negative about the nature of women's friendships than those who were older and married. It may be that younger men and those who are single have less of an understanding of women, having spent less time living with them. Single men, in particular, may be less comfortable with women than are married men, and they may not have developed as favorable a view as a man who has fallen in love and is living with a woman.

Can Men Make Friends Through Their Wives or Significant Others?

Men gain security and companionship through their relationship with their wives or significant others, both as partners with them and in the connections those women help to make with other people. As a result, it could be that some men rely on their wives or significant others for access to friendships with other men.

I recently spoke about male friendships at a suicide prevention conference, where I made the point that perhaps greater communication with other men was one way to prevent the social isolation that can be linked to suicide. One woman said that she did set up her husband with another friend's husband so her husband would have something to do with his free time. She was saying, in essence, that she thought he needed more friends and was going to help him get them. I heard this a lot while talking to people about this book—wives helped their husbands make friends, and husbands left their social lives to their wives.

Wives or significant others may be more comfortable reaching out to others, and this behavior may fit more with the way that men and women are socialized. It may also be, for some men, a form of protection or cover, which we know is a barrier to friendships for some men. First, if the wife is making the arrangements, the man can't fear rejection. Second, a married man can use his marital status to prove to the other man (and vice versa) that he is clearly not gay.

It is important to note in this discussion that many married men identify their wife or significant other as their best friend, so they may not feel a great need to form friendships with other men. I believe that, although this closeness is the sign of a good marriage, it should not preclude a man's making friends with others, because of all the benefits attributed to friendships earlier in this book.

Of the men who were married or living with a significant other, about one-third said they had formed close relationships with men through their wives or significant others. The rest either had made only acquaintances or no friends at all. Although the first group validated my guess that men did make friends through their wives, it is problematic to conclude that this was engineered by their wives—despite the woman who came up to me at the conference and said that she did just that for her husband. A man may not know for certain what his significant other is doing in plotting to get together with another couple or encouraging an introduction with another man; still, the answers the men gave provide further insight into how women can influence men's friendships. Remember that only the men who were married or in a significant long-term relationship answered this question.

Some men, for example, formed friendships—especially *must* and *just* friendships from these introductions. The first quote is from a 44-year-old white, married insurance agent, Marvin, who bonded with other men because of his wife's introduction and a shared problem. The implication is that, without her input, he would have suffered alone: "Sure I have made friends through my wife. Actually some of our closest friends were forged through infertility issues. My wife was a good initiator. She became friends with the wife, and then I'd become friends with the husband."

Another married man of the same age, Kelly, who works as a film production supervisor, acknowledged some influence from his wife. "Not many [friends], but I definitely have made some. I told you about the one guy who I play squash with, that was definitely through my wife. My wife joined this volunteer league here and through that I've met some guys in the neighborhood. I enjoy their company. Now it is just a question of how much time we're able to spend together."

Jack was very clear about the role that his employed wife plays in the friendship department. "My wife thinks I need to make more friends here in Chicago, and we get together at her suggestion so we can find friends for me here. As I mentioned, I have no friends since we moved. It is very isolating doing what I am doing (being a stay-at-home father), and there are no rules. A lot of guys, I find, are 17 years old in their heads and 40 in their bodies. It is hard to enjoy being with them so friends can be hard to make for me."

Of the men who said they had not made close (*must*) friends through their wives, occupational and personal reasons were sometimes at the root. "My wife had friends, and I knew some of their husbands. But none of them were really on the level I was, in the position I had," a 72-year-old retired white administrator, Sal, reported. "So you talk and are friendly, but I never really had good friendships with them. There was a couple we were friendly with, and we would go out together. But he wasn't the kind of guy you could get close to. He was stingy and a womanizer in some ways. He didn't treat his wife in a way that I respected. I felt his wife had a certain regret when she saw how I treated my wife."

One 22-year-old African-American stained glass artist, Jeb, gave a response that is typical of what the men said. "I did not make any close friendships with males but I do talk to my fiancé's best friend's boyfriend when we double date. I don't telephone or see him otherwise because we don't have anything in common." Ben and Hal echoed Jeb's remarks; both said they made their closest friends on their own.

Do Wives Interfere?

As we have heard in previous chapters, the presence of other commitments—wives, children, work—will take men away from friends. Beyond that, the balance that is struck between family, work, and friends is idiosyncratic to any relationship. For example, if a man spends a lot of time with a solitary hobby and away from his family, should he also have time away from his family to be with his friends? If at times he works overtime, does he then miss out on family time or friend time with the free time that he has? This balance must be struck within each individual's life.

Although some women encourage friendships with other men (note Reggie's wife in Chapter 2, who sent him off to his friends when she thought he had been working too hard), others may subtly or overtly oppose them by either demanding time with the husband (this would be a sign of a relationship problem deriving from miscommunication about expectations the man and woman have for each other) or disparaging a particular friend. If the wife or significant other is unsure where she stands with the friend, or has never had a good relationship with a particular male friend, it will be difficult for her to not express her unhappiness when her man announces he is heading out. In a protective way, a wife may not like the way that a friend makes her husband feel about himself. A wife may feel that her husband is being taken advantage of and that his friend is not a "true" friend. In this situation, she may also, for his own "good," attempt to interfere with the friendship.

A man may or may not agree with this perception of his friend. Most men only have so much time, and if they feel they will lose precious time with their wife or children, it will create a problem for the friendship. Loyalty to the friend, however, may pull the man closer to his friend. Regardless of the exact scenario, wives play a key role in supporting or hindering men's relationships with their friends through the messages they send about their own friendships and the value they place on their man getting together with his friends.

So, do wives plot to get a friend for their husbands, and do these husbands find that a safe way to make friends? Clearly, there are men who are aware of and appreciate their wives' assistance in this area, as Jack has indicated. To get a fuller picture, we would have to, of course, ask the wives what their intentions are.

Can Men and Women Be Platonic Friends?

Can men have friendships with women that are nonsexual in nature—the *When Harry Met Sally* question (a reference to the movie raised spontaneously by many of the men interviewed when they were asked this question)? Cross-gender friendships are relatively recent. Before the 20th century, platonic friendships between men and women were rare given the rigidity of gender roles, segregation of the sexes, and religious customs that forbade certain kinds of cross-gender contact. Even today, these friendships can have ambiguous sexual boundaries. [18]

Common sense says that platonic friendships are possible. Men often feel more comfortable disclosing intimacies to women than to men because many were raised, particularly at an early age, primarily by mothers and women teachers and because of the way men are socialized to compete with other men. For a man, talking openly with another man about what is bothering him could be seen as giving the other man a competitive edge, if the speaker feels made vulnerable by what he is discussing.

Three-quarters of the men in this study said that they have platonic friendships with women, and one-quarter said they do not. Take, for example, Barry, a 44-year-old white married electrician, who seeks out women to avoid the world of male competition. "I am more comfortable with women. I don't have to prove anything to them, especially if I am not in a dating situation with them. They give better advice than guys. They are easier to talk to. Guys are always trying to figure out who's the big dog. Whatever it is, the guys are always competing. They compete about how much money you make, what college you went to, what your skills are. They try and 'one up' each other. Women don't do that."

This second quote, from Leland, a 40-year-old married, African-American bank manager, focuses more on the positives of a female friendship, rather than on what he is avoiding in male friendships. "I have a lot of female friends that are nonsexual in nature. To maintain those, I'm open and honest with them. When they want to talk about their relationships, I can tell them from the male perspective about how a man is thinking or how they should be treated, and I'm proud of that because a lot of men don't have platonic relationships."

Casey's observations of his sister have clearly affected his understanding of the possibilities of platonic friendships between women and, ultimately, between women and men. He has a platonic relationship with a female. "I think females are cool. My very best friendship now is with Diane. I go to her house and sometimes I see her boyfriend there. The first time he was mad at me. I said, 'Listen, I've known her for many years. It never crossed my mind to ask her to go to bed with me.' Even my wife thought I was dating her. It's normal for people to think that about a close relationship. I can go to her house, and she is wearing whatever she wants. I don't see her as a woman, but as a friend. She sent me a birthday card that said, 'I never had a friend like you: A man who will hug me as a friend without wanting something.' We laugh, drink. I can stay at her house late. I sleep on her bed. We have no sex. She talks to me about her boyfriend, and I talk about my wife."

David spoke of not being able to be friends with a female when he was younger but that now he has developed the capacity for such a relationship. "By drawing the boundary—and I couldn't until a few years ago—I was never able to have a close friendship with women because I didn't equate them as people, which was horrible. In my early years, it was more like a trophy, more physical of 'I want the hot chick.' They were not really human but actually now I draw healthy boundaries for myself because I want to be able to respect a woman as a person. If you don't make them a friend then, by having sex, you could lose a beautiful relationship. I can do this now because I did all my partying when I was young."

Greg has a nonsexual friendship with a woman but acknowledges the inherent difficulties. "I don't get to see her that often but when we do, we pick it up again. I knew her in high school. We flirted briefly with going out in college but never did. The sexual tension passed years ago. If you act

that out, then what happens to the friendship? Does it make it too complicated, so the friendship can't survive?"

Hal also remarks about how friendships with women can have a sexual
tension but how they also change with age. The second part of his response
shows that he has not adjusted to the new culture of a touch-free workplace. His wife had to clue him in, although he was not happy that she did so.
"I used to have a lot of friends with women—there was a sexual component to it when I was younger. I still have women friends, but there is no
sexual component to it now. I tend to be touchy-feely and, when my wife
came to a party here in the department, she chided me for touching people
on the arm or on the shoulder. She said that level of touching in the workplace was inappropriate."

As a gay man, the question about close nonsexual friendships with
women takes on a different meaning. Isuko does say that commonalities
link him and his female friends—an attraction to men. "In college, it was
weird. I discovered one woman who challenged my sexual orientation. But
we've become friends; we've come to an understanding that it is not going
to happen. There are women who are looking for gay male friends. I don't
want to speak for them, but I think there's a comfort level for them with a
gay man and so I'm open to it. I guess we have something in common
about how hard it is to maintain relationships with guys. So I have nonsexual relationships with women. I invite them because, for me, it's easier.
I don't have to worry about stepping over the boundaries."

What about "friends with benefits"? This term often applies to people
who are friends first and then go on to have sex, although without the
intention of the relationship becoming romantic. One recent study of
125 young people reported that 60% had experienced at least one such
arrangement. One out of ten of those went on to form significant relationships with that friend, one-third stayed friends but dropped the sexual
aspects, one in four lost the friendship altogether (as well as the sex), and the
rest maintained the relationship.[19] Some men in the study mentioned the
loss of friendship when sex got involved and others, like Greg, mentioned
the fear of losing the friendship if sex gets involved.

Men Who Do Not Have Friendships with Women

For those men who do not have nonsexual close friendships with women,
marriage, religion, and the fallout from turning the relationship sexual are
given as the reasons. The first example, from 77-year-old white, married

machinist, Mitch, one of the oldest men in the study, speaks to his marital bond. "My wife is the closest friend I have. I don't go out of my way to establish relationships with other females because I have no need to do that. I already have the best female friend I am going to have."

An engaged 29-year-old lawyer, Phil, also references his relationship as a reason to not have female friends, although from his perspective, this is because of the potential sexual threat it poses. "I have female acquaintances, but not close friends. It could be because it could have an effect on the relationship. I wouldn't want to give my girlfriend the wrong idea if I spent a lot of time with some other girls. Plus my girlfriend fills the role of best friend."

The final example comes from a white teacher in his 30s, who shuns female friendships for religious reasons. "As an Orthodox Jew, there are certain boundaries that exist in order to keep my marriage strong, and one of those is that I don't have friendships with other females. I happen to think it's a good thing because a guy's eyes naturally wander and by not exposing myself to other women, I don't have to worry about wandering eyes."

Marital status was strongly linked to the absence of friendships with women. Single men were much more likely to say they had nonsexual friendships with women than were married men. Some men noted that their wives or girlfriends would not allow such friendships; a few indicated that their wives were their best friends. Age, education, and race do not appear related to whether someone has a female friend (with the interesting exception being that all six Asian-American participants in the study said they had nonsexual friendships with women).

Conclusion: How Women Influence Men's Friendships

So, what have we learned about men and their friendships from asking these questions? First, some men have significant problems with women's friendships. These tend to be younger men, who see such friendships as treacherous and often unkind. Other men would like their friendships to be more like women's—they long for the closeness, intimacy, and physicality that women share.

Second, some men make friends through their wives' friendships. Wives in some marriages do take responsibility for their husbands' friendships and purposefully "fix them up"; other times, such friendships are made as a matter of convenience or chance and are not a planned strategy by the wife.

For a few men, such friendships may provide safety from having to establish their own friendships.

Third, many men, especially younger, single ones, have women friends with whom no sexual intimacy exists. These types of platonic friendships may become easier for younger generations because more women are working side by side with men in the workplace, affording more opportunities than ever before for these relationships to develop.

6

Do Women Feel the Same About Friends as Do Men?

A friendship is a relationship with a woman with whom you have lots of things in common. You tend to be close friends with people who share your same morals and values. The term "friend" means that this other individual is willing to accept me for who I am and not what they want me to be. It is like an unspoken contract—the term of the agreement is unwritten and the time spent on service is indefinite.

—Adele, a 28-year-old female African American social worker

Clearly, men's friendships are different from women's. But how so? I wondered how women would answer the questions that were asked of the men in my study. To find out, we interviewed over 122 women using the same method we used with the men. The women were interviewed to broaden our understanding of friendships in general, with the hope of leading us to greater insight into men's friendships. An entire book could easily have been dedicated to the women's responses to these questions, so forgive me for trying to encapsulate them in just one chapter and maintaining the primary focus of the book on men. Also, this chapter is not meant to be a "he said–she said," in which we conclude that the differences (and similarities) have profound ramifications for humankind. Rather, it is to move along the conversation about men's friendships by reading how women respond to these questions. As I did in the previous chapters on the men, I will use the stories of 10 selected women to illustrate the responses. Due to the by-now familiar nature of the questions and the examples given by the men, I usually limit the case studies to those provided by these 10 women.

Research on Women's Friendships

From the start, I have argued that using a women's perspective to look at men is not the most productive method for understanding men. For example, arguing that men are deficient or inferior in some way because they are less physically affectionate than are women is not helpful. Using a model based on male development to understand women would also be unproductive because, as one family therapist, Monica McGoldrick, wrote, " we have equated maturity [i.e., healthy adulthood] with the capacity for autonomous thinking, rationality, clear decision making, and responsible action, and have devalued the qualities our culture has defined as necessary for feminine identity, such as warmth, expressiveness, and caring for others."[20] In other words, autonomy and action are seen as male strengths, not necessarily female strengths. To understand women's development, McGoldrick believes we should look at how people relate to, not separate from, each other. Taking care of relationships has primacy in women's lives, and the ability to nurture helps form the core of a woman's self-concept.[21] Women's friendships must be considered in this light.

Of course, nurturing is not always a straightforward and uncomplicated process. Author Judith Viorst talks about the ambivalence in women's friendships where "we love and we envy; we love and we compete." In essence, women have mixed feelings when their friends are perceived as doing better than they are because competition and envy are so integral to women's friendships. The difficult test, Viorst notes, is to share a friend's joys when she is doing well. It is easier to be nice to a friend who is *not* doing well than to one who is—the former is not as much of a "threat" as the latter. Viorst also notes that it is common to have sexual feelings for a close same-sex friend and not to act on them.[22] Women are clearly less threatened by hugging and kissing each other than are men.

A down side can exist to the openness and mixed messages being described. Sociologist Lillian Rubin cites one woman as saying that, because women are so expressive and afraid of hurting someone's feelings, compliments are never assumed to be true. "'How can I believe she means I look good when she says it automatically, every time I see her?'"[23] Despite the occasional mixed communication, more women can identify a best friend than can men, according to Rubin.[24]

Women's friendships are important throughout the life cycle, whether playing together in the sandbox, taking significant roles in community organizations and associations,[25] or visiting one another in the nursing home. Women tend to report that other women (not men) are their best friends— it is rare to hear a woman say she feels more comfortable talking to a man, unless it is her husband. The connections that women build sustain them through adolescence, marriage or single adulthood, and into old age (when they need friends, since they are likely to outlive their husbands).

This last point was illustrated when I was talking to a recently widowed 78-year-old about this book. Her husband had been a clinical professor at the university where I teach. She said being a widow has been much less traumatic for her because she is surrounded by female friends. "It is just much easier for women to reach out to others than it is for men." Her implication was that, had her husband survived her, he would have been much more isolated from his friends, because it is harder for men to connect with other men than it is for women to connect with other women, especially in the later years, when fewer men are around with whom to connect.

What do women get from reaching out to other women? Close relationships can foster increased self-disclosure (believed to be good for women), emotional resilience, and a greater range of coping strategies to handle things when times are difficult,[26] as in the example of the widow. Friendships between women can lead to improved mental and physical well-being.[27] But there is another advantage. By forming relationships with a group of women, women escape having their relationships defined by men's way of interacting.[28] By defining relationships for themselves, women are able to construct them in a way that is more consistent with their own beliefs. And those beliefs tend to be more holistic than men's— women are more likely to see their friends as serving general emotional needs for them, while men see their friends as meeting specific, more circumscribed needs.[29]

Communication is key to female friendships. Florence Isaacs, a journalist, writes in her book, *Toxic Friends—True Friends*, that to build friendships, women must be good communicators with each other. That means they must express feelings without attacking, be direct, listen, empathize, and be sensitive. To maintain a friendship, a woman should be trustworthy, reciprocate good deeds, and attempt to see each of her friends often enough to maintain meaningful relationships. Isaacs' words are echoed in what we hear from the women whose stories follow. We can also consider how the classification of friends into *must, trust, rust,* and *just* categories fits women.

My Survey of Women

My students (almost all of whom were women) interviewed 122 women, and I have continued to talk with women over the past few years about friendships. (In fact, when I mention the topic, it seems to spur lengthy conversations about their own, as well as men's, friendships.) The women interviewed have an average age of 38, with half being 31 or younger and one in six being 55 or older. The oldest is 83. The women are divided almost evenly between married (63) and unmarried (59), with most of the unmarried having never married (47), and the rest being divorced (10) or widowed (2). No one self-identified as a lesbian. Almost three-quarters (72%) of the group are white, 18% are African Americans, and the remaining 10% are either Hispanic, Asian, or of mixed ethnicity. Most (about three-quarters) classified themselves in the Protestant/Christian faith, with one in six being Jewish, and the remaining being Hindu, Buddhist, or without formal religious affiliation. At the time of the interviews, one in 10 had a high school education, two in 10 had some college education, three in 10 had graduated from college, and four in 10 had some graduate school education. There were very few blue-collar workers—most women held teaching, counseling, sales, secretarial, or student positions.

By comparison, the men's average age was the same, but they were more apt to be married, slightly less apt to be white, slightly less apt to be Protestant/Christian, and had completed slightly less education. The men were more apt to be working in blue-collar positions.

Study Questions

The questions we asked the women were the same as those asked of the men, although the wording was slightly changed to account for gender:

1. What is a friendship?
2. Are friendships important to you?
3. Do you believe you have enough female friends?
4. How have friends helped you, and how have you helped friends?
5. What are examples of what you do with your female friends?
6. How do you establish friendships with women, and how do you maintain them?
7. Do you ever lose female friends and, if so, how do you get them back (if you do)?

8. Is there a link between femininity and female friendships?[30]
9. Did your mother (or other significant adult female) have many friends and, if so, what messages did you receive about friendships from her?
10. Do you learn about friendships from observing male friendships?
11. Have you made friends through your husband?
12. Do you have friendships with men that are nonsexual in nature?

Because the intention of the book is to focus on men's friendships, the women's answers will be dealt with more briefly.

Study Limits

Similar limitations exist to those discussed for the research on men.[31] This sample is not representative of all women, and the findings should be seen as suggestive of what other women may experience in relation to friendships. The comparisons I draw with the men's responses also should be viewed with caution, because women often gave more responses to the questions than did men.

What Do Friendship and Friend Mean?

The women's answers about defining friends and friendships often were quite involved. Most women focused on the process of friendship (being understood, caring, and sharing) while some described what a friendship had to include (commonality). When asked what is a friendship (the women could give more than one response), they answered:

- Being understood (communicating, sharing, caring, not being judged, and includes having the friend give feedback), 71%
- Trust and loyalty, 43%
- Dependability (having someone to rely on, someone to count on), 33%
- Commonality, 17%
- Doing things with/hanging out with, 14%

Many of these characteristics are also mentioned by the men, although not necessarily with the same frequency. The women gave lengthier responses generally than the men and mentioned more topics. These responses provide a compelling picture of women's and men's need for connections, understanding, and trust. Although there may be differences in the depth in which these characteristics are expressed and the way they manifest in friendships, the mechanics and processes of friendships (what goes into them) are consistent for men and women. We are living in the same "friendship" world and tend to consider friendship the same way.

To better frame the discussion, I selected the answers of 10 women—Alice, Betty, Carol, Diane, Emily, Felice, Grace, Hannah, Iris, and Janet—to illustrate the questions that were asked. These women were chosen for their variation in responses as well as their differences in age, race, and background.

Being Understood

The women answered most frequently that a friend is someone with whom you can talk and share things. Friends give feedback and are nonjudgmental in their acceptance. Betty exemplifies the notion of being herself and being accepted. A 32-year-old African-American, married office manager, she is the mother of two. For her, sisterhood and *must* friendship are similar. "Friendship to me means honesty. You can tell your friend anything and know that your friend is not going to judge what you say. My best friend is really more like a sister. Our bonds go more toward sisters than friends."

Diane is a 33-year-old, white, married mother. She directs a program for teens. She offers a lifespan perspective on friendship that considers youthful as well as adulthood friendships and the importance of being understood as well as hanging out with friends. "Friendship is a mutually beneficial, emotional exchange between two people that includes communication, spending time together, mutual support, sharing of your personal life and having fun. . . . A (*must*) friend is a person to whom I can go whether I am looking just to have fun and relax, whether I'm looking to discuss something that's going on in my life that I may need some help with, or even a place to get advice. I think, especially in adulthood as opposed to when I was younger, your friends are sort of your barometer for what's going on in your life, what's normal and what's not."

Finally, among those who particularly valued being understood, we hear from Iris, the second oldest at 62. A white, single chaplain, she understands the role that her friends fulfill in her life, compared with what a spouse might provide. "They (friends) are extremely important to me as my major support. I probably spend as much time cultivating, supporting, and engaging in relationships with my friends as most people do with a spouse."

Trust and Loyalty

A friend is someone whom you trust with your most significant thoughts and feelings, and they will stand by you when others might not. Carol uses the word "trust" to describe her friendships, and also talks about the balance of being loyal to friends when a husband enters the picture. Carol is a 28-year-old white therapist, who is engaged to be married. She is already weighing how her upcoming marriage could fundamentally affect her friendships with women. She speaks to the fear of many women—that their friends will drop them for a relationship with a man. "Friendships are pretty essential. It is very important to have people to whom you can talk and that you trust. When you get into a committed relationship—whether you are married or engaged, especially if you're a female—friendships have the potential to be pushed to the wayside. Friendships can keep you in touch with the world and get you perspectives other than your partner's, so they are vital."

Grace is a 46-year-old white, divorced mother of three and a community health nurse. In her response, she harkens back to something that the men talked about—friends keeping each other "honest." She also talks about the importance of hanging out with friends as well as having something in common with them. "A (*must*) friend is someone you can be yourself with. It is someone that you can trust, who sees you realistically and can correct you, encourage you, and lift you up. Honesty and trust go hand-in-hand. It is someone to have fun with and who has similar interests."

Dependability

A dependable friend is someone who one can always rely on to be there, no matter what occurs. Alice gives an answer that includes all the categories of responses. I have included her here to give a taste of what dependability sounds like. Alice is a 24-year-old white graduate student who was recently married. "Friendship is a connection between people who share similar interests. It is something that develops over time and has an impact on your life. A friend is someone whom you trust and care about. It is a person whom you have respect for and would do anything for. Most importantly, you are there for each other."

Janet's response also reflects the feeling that a friend is always there when needed. Janet is 73 years old and Asian-American. Divorced, she worked as a school teacher her whole professional career. Having occasional contact with friends is sufficient for her. "Friendship is a relationship with a person with whom you can share your feelings without feeling intimidated and fearing being rejected. There is mutual understanding and trust. We don't expect anything, but we are always there for each other, no give and take, just friends. If they only call once a year, that is okay, but when we talk, we *really* talk."

Commonality

One basis for friendships, as discussed earlier in this book, is commonality or similarity between people. Few people mentioned commonality as a stand-alone category, although with Hannah, the next woman, being in similar circumstances as a friend comes through loud and clear. Hannah, is 56, white, married and in sales. "A (*must*) friend is someone who shares the same perspectives about life. You pick someone who has something in common with you and with whom you have shared interests. When I was younger, they were very important, as they are now—like when you go through hard times or if you are lonely . . . like when I first stopped working, and I was home with two little kids all day, and I was lonely because I was used to being around intelligent people. When I found two friends who were in the same boat as me, the friendships became important. As I have gotten older, I realize I only need a few close friends."

Felice is more typical in that she mentions commonality along with other ingredients of friendships. In her late 30s, Felice is white, married, and a social worker. For her, support and trust are important, too. She brings up the link between friends and family. "A friend is a person you have a relationship with by choice, someone that you enjoy spending time with . . . have common interests . . . be supportive. You'd support them and would want them to support you. A (*must*) friend means someone you can relate to, trust, and fall back on when you need them. It can be a relative or a nonrelative."

Doing Things With/Hanging Out With

Many women also cited the importance of going out with friends and having fun. Emily works as an administrative secretary. She is African-American, married, a mother of two, and 34 years old. Unlike some women, geographic proximity is not essential to maintain a friendship for her. "Friendship is a person who is close to your heart, outside of your immediate family. You don't need to talk to your true (*must*) friends every day. You can go a week or longer and still be friends. Some people are so superficial that they get upset when you don't communicate on a daily basis. Most of my friends I consider to be great and unique in some way. We all feed off each other, whether you need a shoulder to cry on, need a good laugh, or just a girls' night out."

Are Friendships Important to You?

There was some question when researching men as to whether and to what extent friendships were important to them, given their stereotypical difficulties in expressing feelings. We found that for 90% of the men, friends were important. Knowing the importance women place on relationships, asking this question of them seems unnecessary. Still, we did ask it.

With the exception of one woman, every woman interviewed said that friendships are important to them (many with a simple "Very!" or "Yes!"). Some women said that, although friends were important, family took precedent. Felice, although acknowledging the importance of family, also described how friends waxed and waned. "In childhood, friendships are very important. You have more friends, and you have a best friend. Later on, while I was single, friends were important. I had more time for them, too. Then I got married and had less time for friends. Then I had a child and had even less time. I have five or six close friends that I never see. They are important, but I don't stay in contact with them as much."

The one woman who said friends were not important was a South-American 28-year-old single hair stylist named Nora. Nora was "burned" by a friend and will not let women become important to her now. "I lost a friend years ago because she betrayed me by having an affair with my son's father while we were still together. Years later, I had to confront and forgive her so I could move on. We speak now, but I don't trust her, and that experience has had an impact on me trusting a female friend that close again."

Do Women Have Enough Friends?

Before discussing the women's answers, let's recall two points from Chapter 2: First, there is no absolute number of friends that one *should* have; second, what one person considers enough friends, another might think is too few or too many.

When asked if they had enough friends, the women in the study answered:

- I have enough friends, 75%
- I do not have enough friends, 18%
- I am unsure, 7%

In general, most women feel they have enough friends. Three-quarters said they have enough, less than one in five said they did not have enough friends, and a handful was unsure. More women than men felt they had enough friends: 60% of the men said they have enough friends and 25% said they did not have enough, and a larger percentage of men than women, 15%, were unsure.

Yes, I Do

Alice, Betty, and Carol provide three examples of responses to this question. Alice and Betty both feel they have enough friends, but would not object to more, and Carol feels overwhelmed.

Alice laments both the number and the quality of her friendships. "I think that I have an adequate amount of female friendships. However, I wish I had more friends that were closer (*must* friends). It's like, I have a bunch of friends, but I don't get to see them that often, and it bothers me. It is hard with everyone's hectic schedule to make time for one another. I miss the quality time we used to spend together. I also wish I had a couple more close friends because lately, a few of my friendships have been a little high maintenance. I have had to put more into the relationship than the other person. I am the one calling and checking in and trying to schedule time to hang out. The other person always says they want to do something, but things usually fall through."

With Alice, we get the notion of friendships being a burden when she starts to feel that she is giving more than receiving. This theme is echoed by Betty, but for different reasons.

Betty feels she definitely has enough friends, although she does not have very many. "Friendships are not something you need a lot of, personally. Too many female friends are not a good thing. I don't know if it's a cultural thing, but I have heard other female African Americans say the same thing.

Females, you can't trust. They be in your face and behind your back. They be messing with your man. They be talking about you like a dog . . .."

With Betty, we see a second theme that has emerged—whether women can be trusted. She keeps a smaller rather than a larger group of women friends for her own protection and probably maintains a larger number of *just* friends.

Then we hear from Carol, who comes at this question from another direction, "I have too many friends (laughs). I have so many friends that I complain—I can't keep up with all of them. It's been an ongoing problem. When you grow up in one place, then go to school somewhere, then you go to graduate school somewhere else, and then you move somewhere else. In all those places, you leave a trail of (*rust, must,* and *trust*) friends as opposed to someone who grew up somewhere and stayed there and never went off to school. I have five groups of friends in five different cities. It becomes incredibly difficult to keep up with that. There are friends that I go for months without speaking to, and I feel awful about that. I just don't have the time."

No, I Do Not

Of the women who wished they had more friends, most were not friendless—they just wished they had a greater pool of friends to call upon when they were lonely. Diane talks about wanting more friends and about the role that family can play in mitigating some of the need for friends. For Diane, family relationships are highly positive, so they serve as a great source of nurturance for her. "No (I don't have enough friends). I'm the kind of person that has always had a 'best' (*must*) friend as opposed to a large circle of 'medium' (*trust/just*) friends. I've always had one or two very, very close friends that I spend all my time with, but the problem is putting all your eggs in one basket. So, as time goes on, I have kind of traded in one friend for another. I've lost touch with friends when I moved away. I had a very good friend when I first moved here and then that just faded as our lives changed. I had another friend who left where I was working. So, I do wish I had a wider circle of friends—it's always good to have backups (laughs). And, I've tended to use my family; I'm very close with them. I've two sisters, and I have tended to substitute them for friends because they are the people I have the most fun with and can confide in the most."

I Am Unsure

Grace is one of the women who is unsure if she has enough friends. She appears easily hurt when she describes her reaction to a cancelled lunch date and feels she needs more "backup" friends. "I have been transitioning lately. In the last five years, I left the church I was attending. A couple of people that I was friends with went through a divorce and have remarried. We are still friends, but we don't see each other often (no longer *must* friends—now *just* friends). I had a friend who sold her house and was looking for a roommate, but it didn't work out for us. I have friends at work (*just* friends), and I have been dating, which takes time away from friends. I feel like I could have a couple more friends. I was going to have lunch the other day with a friend, and she cancelled that day. I was not shocked that she did this but I wrestle with forgiveness and whether to maintain that relationship. I guess you could say I am in the market for more friends."

As with the men, older women were slightly more apt to say they had enough friends (81% of those ages 60 years and older versus 75% for the entire group). With age may come a greater ability to make friends or a greater acceptance of the number of friends that you have. In addition, 82% of African-American women say they have enough friends. It may be that, as discussed in Chapter 1, members of a racial or ethnic minority group are more apt to rely on each other and form friendships for protection than are members of the majority group. Rarely heard were women saying that they are too wrapped up in work to have time for friends.

How Do Women Help Women?

Earlier in this chapter, I mentioned that relationships are important for women. Helping is one way that relationships are manifested. At the heart of this social support is the give and take that women describe. In my study, when asked how friends have helped them (the women could give more than one response), the women answered:

- Supporting me/encouraging me/being there/taking care of me, 77%
- Listening/talking with me/sharing with me, 47%
- Giving me advice/providing perspective, 21%
- Providing companionship/hanging out, 18%
- Loaning me money, 10%

- Buoying my spirits, 10%
- Helping me move to new residence, 5%
- Helping me with work, 3%

The men were less apt to report that they had been supported and encouraged by their friends (65% for the men versus 77% for the women). They were more apt, however, to say that friends offered advice/provided perspective (32% for the men versus 21% for the women). These are not huge differences between men and women. Given the way that men and women operate in most situations—women being more affectionate and nurturing and men less physical and more problem-solving—some slight differences could be expected. But these answers may be more remarkable for their similarities rather than for their disparities.

As with the men, the women recognize that they help their friends in the same ways that they are helped: 77% said they supported and encouraged their friends; 55% listened and shared; 16% gave advice; 18% provided companionship; 16% loaned money; and 10% buoyed spirits. Help comes through various forms of emotional support, from being there for a friend to listening, giving advice, and hanging out.

Alice discusses how friends have helped her, and she provides examples of many of the responses that were common. "Friends have helped me through stressful times with school and work. They have helped me through tough relationships and, even worse, through breakups. Friends have been there for me as a support system when relatives have passed away or when I have just been down in the dumps and needed someone. They have also been there during the really fun times, like vacation or on a trip. During those times, friends are just there for company and to spend time with. . . . I think I have helped friends in a lot of ways. I have been there to listen to them and loan them money. I have let people move in with me for periods of time until they were able to get on their feet. I have been their shoulder to cry on or their shopping companion. Most important, I feel as though I help (*must*) friends because I am there for them through thick and thin, and they know I wouldn't lie to them. If they want advice, I will give it to them."

Betty also describes unfettered support during trying times in her life. "They listen to me and give me suggestions. It is okay if I don't accept them. They can be supportive with the kids, because some of us have gone through things that others of us have not, and they can support us that way. My best friend was very supportive during my mother's illness and death. She was there just to listen. . . . I help in any way I can. I run across town and get my best (*must*) friend's son when he's locked out of the house. We look for my best friend's other son when he tries to play his little runaway thing. It's just being there. With my best friend, there are no questions. And no matter what the husbands say, we are going be there."

Carol talks about how her family members are her friends, and how her friendships helped her decide her career path. She draws the interesting distinction between going to friends for assistance instead of family when specific issues arise. "The few times in my life when I have had rough situations going on, my friends have largely helped me get through it, and I'm lucky I have a close family. I think a lot of people use their friends as a substitute for family. That's not the case for me. I feel close to my sister and mother. Still, there are many times when you don't want to go to your family member. It's too personal or too close to home, and you want to have a friend help you out. And not just to talk about problems, to have fun, too. . . . How do I help friends? Way before I ever became a professional therapist, I was a therapist for all my friends. I became a therapist because I was good at it. I always had these really messed-up friends with really messed-up problems. I was really doing therapy at the age of 17. I was always the person that everyone came to when they needed things."

Diane covers a lot of territory in her answer. She first talks about needing a friend for her new life stage as a mother. Then, she describes what women provide her that men cannot. Finally, she touches on the self-doubt that she believes some women experience in relation to others. "Your friends are a barometer for you, a validity check. Right now, I'm a new mother. I have a great (*must*) friend who is also a new mother, and she and I will call each other and compare, 'Are you pumping? What can you do to increase milk flow? What have you used with your baby if she's crying?' We talk about marriage, the pregnancy, and deciding when to go back to work. That's a really big support. It's good to have friends outside the family to go to, because it validates a lot of stuff you're going through. Plus, I've experienced in my life when a relationship hasn't worked out, and your friends come over and you watch 'chick flicks,' have popcorn and chocolate. You sit around and cry, which is something women can do for each other that you can't get anywhere else. Men can't do it with each other, and it's hard for a man to do it for a woman. It's that combination of women that can support that sinking into your emotions. Also, just having fun and getting together to go to the spa and being able to indulge in 'girlie' things."

How does Diane help her friends? "I hope that I can give back what I am looking for in my friendships, and it sometimes depends on the friend.

I try to be a resource for them, to share what's going on in their life and to provide unconditional support, to listen and to help validate what they're going through. Sometimes I worry that I am not as good a friend as what I'm hoping to get from others. I think a lot of times, as women, we tend to doubt ourselves, and I try and reinforce the positive qualities that my friends have and what a neat person I think they are and what a good parent or partner that I see them being."

And finally, from Janet, comes a description of a very intense and important relationship characterized by her culture and being a member of a minority group. "Emotional support. I went through a lot, but my friends always supported me emotionally. I was the first Indian woman to get divorced here, but they didn't criticize me. Most of my friends are Indian, but I have one Jewish (*must*) friend in New York. She's an Indian Jew, and she had an arranged marriage. She helped me when I got divorced. I had no job or car. She taught me how to drive. We can't drive to visit each other anymore. Recently, she found she had bone cancer. Still, we talk about it. She is from a big family but is alone here. . . . Most important was my emotional help. Unless you understand and know my pain, I won't tell you mine. My relationship with her was very special."

What Do Women Do with Friends?

It will come as no surprise that the women's answers to what they do with their friends are quite different from the men's responses. The women could give more than one response to the question, "What do women do when they get together?: In the study, they said

- Communicate, 65%
- Shop, 60%
- Go to lunch/dinner/movies/theater, 60%
- Drink/party/go dancing, 33%
- Watch movies/cook (at home), 23%
- Exercise together, 18%
- Travel together, 18%
- Hang out with our children, 2%

About two-thirds of the women specifically mentioned talking with their friends, and a slightly smaller number said they shopped with their friends. Slightly less than half of the men referenced communication—when they did talk, it was often about sports or women. Virtually none of the men said they went shopping with friends, except occasionally to look at cars. Other activities that are common for women are eating out and going to the movies; going out for drinks and dancing; going to each other's homes to watch TV or cook; exercising together (watching or engaging in sports were not mentioned by any woman), and traveling. Laughing and crying together were also mentioned. (Crying together was not mentioned by any men.)

Some of activities listed by the women could be considered shoulder-to-shoulder rather than face-to-face activities (shopping, for example—although trying on clothes and asking for the other's opinion about one's appearance could be considered face-to-face). This typology of men's and women's behavior cannot be seen as absolute but rather as useful for comparisons and understanding potential differences. Women, as these findings bear out, will be *more likely* to participate in activities in which they are looking across the table at each other or communicating directly in some form than are men.

Communication

Betty said, "We talk 'til the sun comes out. Oh my God, we talk all the time. We feed our children together. We eat, we shop. We don't have much money to shop together, but we do at Christmas, spring, and school time. The funny part about it is, you'd think we'd been friends forever but we've only been friends since we were 16 (Betty is now 32)." It is interesting when a friendship of this length is not considered to be especially long.

Shopping

Emily mentions a range of activities that she does with her four closest friends and includes shopping in her answer. "We go to the movies. We go to plays. We go to dinner. We go shopping. We talk on the phone."

Go to Lunch/Dinner/Movies

Carol is struggling to fit in with her friends. "The answer is now very different than it would have been even a year ago, because now I just don't have time to be with friends. When I do get together with my friends, we either have dinner parties at each others' houses or we go out to eat. We also go to festivals, such as arts-and-crafts fairs, those types of things. Once in a while, we'll go to the movies. A lot of friends have children, so there are lots of parties, too."

How Do Women Establish and Maintain Friendships?

Establishing friendships is not a lost art, nor is it a science, according to most of the women. They start at the *just* stage, then may move into a more significant stage. Friendships are started by women if they can find a commonality, are open and friendly to others, and are willing to engage them in conversation. The men's three most frequent responses were the same, showing their similarities in friendship-making actions.

The women could give more than one response to the question: "How do you establish friendships with women?" They said:

- Find commonalities, 48%
- Reach out and be friendly to others, 35%
- Make friends through work, 30%
- Make friends through going to school, religious institutions, armed forces, 28%
- Meet friends through husband and through other friends, 10%
- Spend a long time with people (i.e., friendships take time), 8%
- Be yourself, 8%
- Through sports/activities, 5%

Almost half mentioned that to establish a *just* or *trust* friendship, they have to find a common interest or a similarity with the other person. This could be sharing an activity or being in the same stage of life with another woman (for example, both raising young children). A large number mentioned meeting people through established arenas like work, church, and school. These are safe venues that allow *must* friendships to develop with time and in a context in which people, to some extent, have already been prescreened because of the context. These answers could also be considered as a response in the commonalities category, as people who work together or have the same religion have that in common. They are coded separately here to provide more specific information about the strategies that people use. Examples from the two most frequently mentioned friend-making approaches follow.

Find Commonalities

Alice gives a response that shows that new *just* friendships unfold over time: "It starts by sharing an experience or a common interest or belief with someone. Eventually, you begin talking with that person, and you get to know more about him. Once you have had an opportunity to talk to him for a while, that person's belief system and ideals become more apparent. If my morals and values seem to match theirs, or if we have bonded over a common experience, then we would continue to establish the relationship by talking or e-mailing, maybe even going to dinner together (*trust* stage). Sooner or later, the conversations become less superficial, and you begin to discover more about the person. When you are interested in learning about the other person and spending time with her, then you can say that you have established a friendship (*trust* or *must* stage). Obviously, the relationship has to be both ways, or else it isn't a friendship but more of a stalking." Here she is jokingly referring to how a friendship has to be reciprocal.

Diane is struggling with making friends, and relies on common interests to form friendships. To make new friends, she describes the two most frequently mentioned behaviors—finding commonalities and reaching out. "It's really hard, and I think it gets harder as you get older. In college, you are friends with whoever is in your dorm and in your classes, and you have a lot of free time to cultivate them. I think expectations are looser also. As an adult, you establish friendships by finding common ground in an atmosphere that nurtures it. If you are in a 'Mom and Me' play group, you have a built-in natural connection with the other women in the room, so it's easy to use that as a launching pad. You have to find something in common. But you also seek out people who remind you in a sense of yourself, and then you reach out to those people because you think you have something in common."

Reach Out and Be Friendly to Others

Grace judges the vibes she gets from women she meets, and she wants them to fill in the gaps she feels she has in her own life. "For me, chemistry is important. I am outgoing and try to meet someone at her needs. I like making friends with people who have good self-esteem because mine is not always the best."

How Women Maintain Friends

It is not just important to know how to make friends; they also have to be maintained. The women could give more than one response when asked how women kept their friendships. They said:

- Communicate, 63%
- Stay in frequent contact, 53%
- Do things together, 35%
- Be there to give emotional support, 23%
- Be yourself, 10%
- Reach out, 5%

Women maintain friendships largely through communication and staying in frequent contact. The women describe how they communicate: talking, phoning, and e-mailing are the most common forms. However communication works, most women believe it has to be fairly frequent. In contrast, only 10% of the men maintained friendships through frequent contact. The percentages of men who listed communication and doing things together as ways to maintain friendships were virtually identical. The other notable response, by about one-third of the women, is more related to the process of friendships and the importance of being genuine. These women stated that they maintained their friendships by being there with emotional support and by being themselves. Of the men, only 10% cited giving support and 13% advised "being yourself." When asked the question concerning what they did with their friends, giving emotional support also was more common for women than for men. One woman used a spiritual metaphor and said that to maintain a friendship, she needed to "put God first."

Alice provides an example of the importance of communication in maintaining friendships. "I guess I maintain friendships by calling, e-mailing, or seeing them. When you hang out or maintain contact with someone, then it is easy to keep close with her. It is harder when there are forces against you. That is when you have to put forth extra effort."

Emily is representative of those who believe frequent contact is important to keep a friendship alive. "I try real hard to call my local friends at least once a day, just to say hi and to let them know I am thinking about them and see how they are doing. If they are not too busy, we continue the conversation or they call back. For my long-distance friends, we try and speak three or four times a month."

And there are also the handful who do not find it easy to maintain friendships. Carol was frankly unsure of her ability in this area. "I'm really bad about calling people, keeping in touch, and making plans. If there's a situation with a woman where she's kind of cool and I want to hang out with her, but she wasn't saying to me, 'Hey, let's hang out,' I am not the kind of person who would approach her. Not because of fear of rejection— I just don't have the time for it. The kinds of people whom I like are those who invite me over. They are more outgoing. Maintaining them takes a lot of patience and work. It's a constant thing if you haven't spoken to someone in a while, you need to call her. It takes time to call them. It's like a job requiring care, time, and attention. It may happen that I won't speak to a friend for about a month; then I'll call and find out she's in the hospital. I'll feel really bad that I'm a bad friend who didn't know what was going on. Basically, I try to keep in touch as much as my schedule will allow."

Felice mentions how difficult friendships are to keep now, compared with when she was younger. "I maintain them poorly (laughs). I guess there have been one or two people that I have been getting to know. They have children, and the friendships have been established slowly. We meet occasionally, or get the kids together for a play date. It's not so much when you were a kid, and you meet them, and they are automatically your best friend, and you are hanging out with them all of the time. It's more deliberate. You are much choosier about who you want to spend your time with since you have so little time. The last few friends I have made have come through church, so we see each other on a weekly basis. We don't have to plan it. It's ready made. It's like all the hard stuff is done for you."

How Are Friendships Lost and Found?

Across the sample, approximately five out of every six women said they have lost a friendship. Some of these losses occurred because of the normal processes of moving away or drifting apart that happen over time. But among the women who lost a friendship, three-quarters specifically said they were lost because of some behavior (other than moving away or drifting apart) by them or the other woman. Of those who lost a friend because of some action or behavior, about one in five were successful in "getting the friendship back." Others established a lower-level or *just* friendship. The women agreed to be friends again after a falling out, but were not willing to trust each other in the same way as before. Thus, they became *just* friends, when earlier they may have been *must* or *trust* friends.

When asked if they had ever lost a friend, the women in this study said:

- Yes—I lost a friend because of her or my behavior, 65% (three-fifths did try to get them back; two-fifths did not try to get them back)
- Yes—I lost a friend from drifting apart or moving away, 20%
- No—I never lost a friend, 15%

Women were more apt to lose a friend because of their or the other woman's behavior and more apt to try and get the friendship back than were men. In the responses, women seem to be more upset about the loss of a friendship and more prone to try to understand what went wrong with the friendship. Men have a "simpler" (for lack of a better term) reaction—a man will have a falling out with a friend, reclaim it or not, but not try as hard as a woman to process where it went wrong.

Women have a greater need to communicate about the friendship dissolution and to understand what happened. Men are often at the root of the loss of friendship—either a woman married and no longer had time for a friend, or there was competition for a man that caused the breakup. Another reason that was heard was that the female friend was too emotionally draining.

Someone's Behavior

Alice, in a story that sounds typical of a made-for-TV movie with a happy ending, lost a friend initially because she told her the guy she was dating wasn't any good for her. The friend ended up very angry at Alice and ignored her for six months. But when she broke up with the guy, Alice and the friend got back together (the friend apologized), and they have a stronger relationship now.

Men were also involved in Diane's and Hannah's situations. For Diane, a close friend clashed with her future husband because it seemed as if they were competing for Diane. It became an uncomfortable relationship that has now assumed a much more casual, "pseudo friendship" feel to it. Hannah, like Diane, also had a friend who did not get along with her husband, which caused a rift for years. "But time moved on, and you let things go, and we became friends again," Hannah reported. "It happened very slowly and took a lot of effort on both our parts. We eventually realized how much we were missing."

Drifting Apart/Moving Away

Carol has lost friends because of geography or because the "vibes" didn't feel right. She did not try to get them back. Felice described people who have drifted away or moved away from her, and specifically cited two roommates from college who were "crazy" and whom she came to dislike.

No Lost Friends

Iris has lost no close friends, although she does say that the intensity of friendships lessens with time, so that friends are easier to maintain. Janet is forgiving and will try to let time heal whatever wound has occurred; she is willing to make the first move and apologize. She has not lost friends, she reports.

What Do Women Learn About Friendships from Their Mothers?

Volumes have been written about the relationships between women and their mothers.[32] In my study, the question was, "Did your mother (or other significant adult female who raised you) have many friends and, if so, what messages did you receive about friendships from her?"

A few women said their mothers' friendships had increased or decreased over time, so we tried to gain a general impression. Thus, the numbers here are estimates:[33]

- My mother had many friends, 42%
- My mother had a few friends, 40%
- My mother had no friends, 18%

A handful of the women said they had no significant contact with a mother figure and were raised by a grandparent or an older sibling. Also, some remarked that their mothers only had a couple of friends or were only friends with their sisters.

Although the answers to the first part of the question were not always easy to categorize, an approximation is that slightly less than half said their mothers had a lot of friends, one-third thought their mothers had some friends, and the remainder, a little fewer than one-fifth, thought their mothers had no friends. One respondent, for example, said her mother was embarrassed by her husband's alcoholism and never wanted to have people over. By comparison, the men perceived their fathers as being more apt to have no friends (30% of the men gave this response).

Regardless of how many friends mothers were purported to have, do mothers serve as role models for building friendships? Yes. Mothers do serve as role models, although the learning process can be complicated. Sometimes, the mother had many friendships and showed the daughter how to build social support. Other times, the mother's lack of friendships motivated the daughter to build more and better friendships.

My Mother Had Many Friends

Carol's mother had many friends, but it seems they were always in need. "Everybody was always pursuing her; she was the therapist, like me. Everybody always wanted advice from her, and my dad would call her the 'friend of the friendless.' Every person who has no friends and who is down and out somehow finds my mother. She would call them her projects—she helps them out, finds them friends, gets them jobs, and that kind of thing. I definitely got that from her. She's also the type that can't be bothered to pursue a friendship. The only friendships she has are the people who come after her and try to maintain their relationship."

Emily's memory of her mother's friendships is a bitter one, and it has affected her to this day. Getting from a *just* to a *trust* or *must* friend takes a long time for her. She keeps her guard up. "My mother had many friends. When you're young, they look like friends at least. She taught me that you're supposed to be there for your friends no matter what. But, when she was diagnosed with her mental illness, the friends went away. So, I became harder than she was. I have a harder shell; it takes a lot to break me because I feel now that that lesson was a good one—I screen people a little longer before I let them in. I say that because my mom was the nicest, kindest, and most generous person/friend I knew. And her friends took her for granted. So, I don't want to be in the same position."

Hannah understands that her mother grew up in an era when people often had many friends yet had no one with whom to share highly intimate things. Hannah wants something different for herself. "I think she had a lot of friends. She was friends with Joan, and Rose, and Aunt Peggy. At work, she had a lot of friends who sustained her when Dad got sick. Growing up and seeing how important that was to her allowed us to grow up and become more amenable to that. Some people are afraid to form friendships and be soulfully honest. Mom seemed to be more private than me, though that might be the generation she grew up in. People weren't expected to share their emotions, and people looked at you a certain way. I grew up in a whole other generation. I really didn't care what people thought."

For Janet, learning about friendships from her mother was straight-forward. "My mother was very popular. She used to help the ladies. She gave us the impression you should always help those in need. She was very popular and generous. She never cared for herself but for her friends and family. She was very selfless, with a great deal of tolerance and patience. Maybe we got our patience from her? Until she died, she never neglected her family. My four brothers died very young, and my mother took in their wives and children. She paid for them to go to school and other finances. That's why my family is so close, so united. She was very courageous."

My Mother Had a Few Friends

Alice falls within the group raised by a mother with few friends. In her answer, she focuses on the lack of time her mother had available to be with friends, similar to what we heard from some men about their fathers. Although Alice says she did not learn much from her mother about friend-ships, she did learn important lessons about how to treat other people. "My mother did not have many friends while I was growing up. My parents divorced when I was very young, so she raised me alone. I honestly don't think she had much time for friends. Once I got older and started making friends, she became friends with my friends' parents." She pauses and then adds, "But I still don't think that I learned any significant messages from her, through her relationships. I will say that growing up, she made sure that I was always kind to my friends and made me share belongings all the time. She also encouraged me to try new things and make new friends, which allowed me the opportunity to have many different types of friends."

Although Betty's mother also had only a few friends, she too left a distinct impression on Betty about kindness. "She was kind of like me, she had a few female friends but not a whole lot. That's where I learned about the female friend thing. My mother was just generally a kind and caring person as far as friends were concerned. She was the kind of person who would do anything for a friend. I learned that from her. We never had a lot of money, but were financially stable so we gave what we could. If my mother could help out by doing the cooking for a friend's party or watch the kids, she would. It wasn't about the financial situation, but about being there and helping. People don't understand that these are important things."

My Mother had no Friends

Diane observed her mother drifting away from friends as an adult and getting closer with her family. She sees a bit of herself in her mother. "My mom had really, really tight (*must*) friends in high school and into college. She lost touch with them, and then she got married and, I think, that together she and my father had (*just* or *trust*) friends. But then they got divorced, and she remarried. I've never known her to have a close female friend since then. She is very tight with her sisters, so I guess I am repeating that pattern a little bit. She has some (*just*) friends from work, but they don't socialize that much after work. She has no friends in her personal life. She kind of spends time with her family."

And, for an example of the role that sisters can play as friends, we hear from Iris. She received very distinct messages about friendships from her mother in relation to extended family and how to act in order to make friends. "My mother was a member of a big family, and she maintained relationships with her sisters, even with a great geographic distance as an issue. I consider my own sisters to be friends, also. In our neighborhood, my mother had several close relationships with neighbors that she still maintains today at 84. She doesn't have anything like the extent of friendships that I have. But then, I don't have the nuclear family that she had to absorb my time. I have many more friendships than my mother did at my age. As a girl, I remember her talking to me about maintaining friendships. As I was moving into adolescence, the girls were making fun of me because I was different. I remember my mother telling me that if you want to have friends, you have to do things to fit in. I was smart, and she told me to not use big words. Isn't it interesting, as I look back, that that was the message she gave me about friendships?"

Mother Wisdom

The wisdom these women gained from their mothers was positively toned, cautionary, and often conflicting with other messages:

- Sometimes one or two close friendships are all that you need.
- Let your friends be who they are, and love them no matter what.

- Reciprocate quickly, and don't always be honest with your friends. Edit yourself so people won't see your negative side.
- Get what you can from each other.
- Friends at work don't translate to friends at home; mother's place was with her husband and children.
- Celebrate friendships, and be friends with lots of different people.
- It is important to maintain friends, and your sisters can be your friends.
- Your life is long and changing, and you need to maintain friends.
- Female friendships are important, as is involvement in the community.
- Friendships cannot be trusted, and not everyone is worthy of your friendship. However, family will always be there.

Many of these are testimonies to the benefits of friendship and the unbridled love and respect that one needs to give a friend. But also mentioned here is the importance of family and community. These messages, coupled with the women's impressions of their mothers, also further confirm the issues discussed at the beginning of the chapter: that women also have complicated friendships, and that previous generations of women were not necessarily surrounded by female friends either.

What Do Women Learn from Men's Friendships?

Three questions asked of the men about women were also asked of the women about men: Do you learn about female friendships from observing men's? Have you made friends with women through your husband or significant other? Do you have platonic relationships with men? As with the men, the answers are hard to categorize and should be viewed only as suggestions of possible trends.

About one-quarter of the women had good things to say about male friendships, but one in five thought male friendships were a mess. The others either said they had not learned anything, or that women and men are different and hard to compare. The women, however, were neither as admiring of (35% of the men said they have learned positive things from women's friendships) nor as negative about male friendships (25% of the men have negative impressions of women's friendships) as the men were of women's. Their answers were more balanced, with fewer extremes.

Can Women Learn About Friendships from Men?

When asked if they had learned about friendships from observing men's friendships, the women in the study gave the following answers (figures are approximate):

- I have learned positive things from men's friendships, 25%
- I have negative impressions of men's friendships, 21%
- I have not learned anything positive or negative about men's friendships, 39%
- Men and women cannot be compared, 15%

I Have Learned Positive Things

What kinds of things did women say they learned from men? To take themselves less seriously, get over things more quickly and don't hold grudges, be less catty, and learn to have fun. Diane praised men, but also pointed out shortcomings. "I learned there are aspects of male friendships that I would like to see more of in my female friendships, and then there are aspects that are lacking. I think they can last longer because they are not as emotionally volatile. I think women have a tendency to get things heated, and sometimes these emotions can escalate and ruin a friendship. Guys never really get that close emotionally, they just enjoy each other's company and don't put emotion into it, so nothing ever gets complicated. It is fun, lighter, and sillier, and their friendships tend to last longer."

I Have Negative Impressions of Men's Friendships

Women describe men as being emotionally unavailable, selfish, and noncommunicative in their friendships. One divorced 33-year-old, Sara, offers this wry comment on men's friendships. "I've not learned anything from them. I don't go up and smack my friend on the butt or have a spitting contest."

Alice told us, "I don't think that women strive to be guarded, closed off, and cold when it comes to their friendships." Betty adds, "In my lifetime I have never really seen a deep friendship among men." Carol's impressions are similar. "It's really hard for men to sit down and have a serious conversation about anything. If they have a problem, they joke about it, and physical affection makes them uncomfortable."

I Have Not Learned Anything

Some women gave a brief, "No" to this question. Others offered further explanations by saying that women's are more emotional and have more depth, without explicitly stating that men's relationships with one another are inferior. Felice answered "no" and, when pressed, went on to explain, "From watching my husband, it's funny because he and his friends can spend all day together and not one thought or feeling will pass between them. His friend will ask me if anything is wrong with my husband but won't ask him."

Hannah observed her husband spending his time much differently from the ways in which she spends hers. "My husband has very little need for friends, which is amazing for me. It was probably good that he has always had a job where he worked 65 hours a week, because he doesn't like to do things with other people."

Men and Women Can't Be Compared

The answers here indicate that the differences are very basic, so no learning can occur. Grace responded, "They are two different relationships. Male friends do not seem to spend as much time together. They also need to do something, and seem to be action-oriented. Female friends mostly get together and talk. Women need to do these things. I think you need to respect the differences in the friendships."

Have You Made Friends Through Your Husband?

Surprising to me, women may be slightly more prone to make friends with others through their husbands than men do through their wives. Over two-fifths of the women said they had made friends that way, compared with about one-third of the men. I asked this question of the men, thinking that men were not skilled at making friends. Now, it seems that women use their husbands (or boyfriends) even more. It could be that women use every opportunity to make friends, and that the wife of their husband's friend offers another opportunity for the husband's wife to do things as a couple. It could also be that men are more reluctant to avail themselves of opportunities to make friends.

Diane describes how this plays out. "My husband has a ton of friends, both girl and guy friends. When we get together, we hang out with his friends more than mine, and I ended up developing friendships with the girls in his group. These are the ones I joined the Junior League with, and I actually spend time with them without him."

And, yes, husbands do interfere with their wives ability to make friends, just as women interfere with their husbands. Men can greenlight a relationship with a friend or try and hinder it in many the same ways that women apparently interfere with men—speak ill of the friend, ask that the woman spend more time with the family, or ask the woman to choose between time at work or with a solitary hobby and the friend.

Karen, a 56-year-old white social worker, had this to say about a friend's husband: "I had this one friend that I really loved. She was born and raised in the South, and her husband was really dominant. He and I did not like each other, though he got along well with my husband. It was okay if the four of us went out. But her husband thought I filled her head with ideas. The two of us went to D.C. one time while her husband was away on business, and when he found out he had a fit. She had to report to him all the time. They moved back to Texas, and he discouraged her from having contact with me. It was easier on her if we didn't have contact."

Do You Have Nonsexual Friendships with Men?

Not quite as many women said that they have platonic friendships as do men, about 65% of the women versus 75% of the men. Given the variations in the answers, and the dynamics of such changing relationships, it is safe to conclude that, although perceptions of friendships between the sexes can differ, the percentage of men and women reporting such friendships is about equal.

How do these friendships play out? Janet, divorced and the oldest of the 10 women we have been following, does have friends. "I have a lot of male friends. We are just like brothers and sisters. They help me when I need them, and I help them. They treat me like their older sister."

Iris, also single, describes her male friendship: "I have a very close friendship with a man whom I have known for years. I maintain the relationship with phone calls. I suppose it is a little like my female friendships in that we talk about a whole range of topics, but we don't really do the social types of things that I do with my female friends."

Carol, who is engaged, talks about the transition from being single to being in a couples relationship and the impact on friendships. She also alludes to the sexual tension that can be beneath the surface. "I've had many close male friends, but I don't have any right now. I don't know if that comes from having a significant other. As an adult, I have had a couple of really close male friends, either people I have lived with, not in a sexual way, or ones I have worked with. I have found the men I have been friends with have been very understanding, validating, supportive, and very antistereotype. Maybe that's just the type of guy I am attracted to as a friend. The difference is that the physical aspect is very different—you are not afraid to hug your girlfriends."

Is There a Link Between Femininity and Female Friendships?

This question was designed specifically for the men, to test the link between friendships and masculinity. We asked the women the same question about femininity. The majority thought there was a link, and gave answers that talked about the common bond that women have with each other, which is expressed through issues like feminine hygiene, the ability to be themselves with other women, and the nurturing and emotional connection that women have with each other. Not mentioned, except by a handful of women, was the feeling of finding friends who were at the same level of femininity. Remember that the men, when asked this question, talked about looking for other men friends who were equally as masculine as they were. Although this appears to be a significant concern for a number of men, only a few women mentioned this as a concern.

Carol believes a connection exists between femininity and friendships. "There is a quality to the relationship that a woman has with another woman, or even that a woman has with a male friend, that is very different than the kinds of friendships that men have with each other. Any relationship where there is a female involved has a lot less rules and more open boundaries than male friendships do. I think you are allowed to be more open and show more affection and those kinds of things in female friendships."

Alice was in the group that did not see a connection. "I think that femininity is a term that describes female characteristics, like the way they act, dress, think, or present themselves. Quite honestly, I have a few female friends that are more masculine than feminine. So, no, I really don't think that there has to be a connection."

Conclusion: So What Have We Learned from Women?

We must be careful about making sweeping generalizations about women's friendships, just as we must be careful about making generalizations about men's. Great diversity exists in these women's takes on friendships, and interpreting their responses can be difficult in some cases. Yet, we can see that some differences—as well as similarities—exist between how the men and women interviewed answer the questions and how their friendships operate. For example, in this study:

- Women were more apt to say they feel they have enough friends and that friends are important. From the responses, it appears women were less apt to say they did not have time for friends. Although the majority (60%) of men say they have enough friends, 40% do not have enough or are unsure, a greater number than the women. It may be that some men are pulled by work and cannot find the time to balance friends, work, and family. Or, it could be as we have heard from some men that they have a hard time connecting with other men in a way that is satisfying to them on a friendship level. They may feel they do not have enough *must* friends.
- Women were more apt to help each other than were men, by being supportive, encouraging, and "being there." Men, on the other hand, were more apt to give their friends advice and offer their perspectives. Both mentioned the importance of listening and talking. Men tend to be fixers, and see getting something concrete accomplished as a way of helping, whereas women are more comfortable with emotional support, which sometimes involves listening without giving specific advice. This could account for the differences in their responses.
- When with friends, women spend more time shopping, going out to dine with them and going to the movies, as well as staying home with friends to cook or watch movies. Communication, as part of the relationship, is frequent for both women and men. Men, who gave fewer distinct responses to this question, are much more apt to be involved in sports-related activities, either as a participant or viewer. This comparison further confirms the importance that sports play in a man's life (as well as the lack of interest they show in shopping with their buddies).

- To make friends, women may reach out to others a bit more than men, and they are less concerned with finding commonalities as a basis for friendships. Men mention sports more often than women as a basis for making friends. To feel comfortable, men may be slightly more apt to need a socially acceptable arena for having a friendship begin, like a similar hobby or sports. This would be a shoulder-to-shoulder approach to friendships, as opposed to women perhaps feeling slightly more comfortable making friends without a specific activity or commonality being at the center of the friendship.

- To maintain a friendship, women put a much greater value on frequent contact than men. Men often mentioned being able to pick up again with a friend after little contact, whereas women placed a greater value on staying in touch. The differing levels in the need for frequent contact could be a result of the differing socialization of men and women. Women appear to need more communication in general than men, according to many of the men and women we interviewed. Emotional connection is important to them, and it is often manifested by staying in frequent contact. Men also are in the workforce to a greater extent than women, and may have less time for friends. The result is that men may feel less need to stay in frequent contact, although they acknowledge the importance of communication to maintain the friendship.

- Women were more apt to lose friends and more apt to try to get them back than were men. We have learned already that men are often less concerned about slights than women and so may be slightly less apt to lose a friend because of someone's behavior. Given women's interest in maintaining connections and relationships, this difference in response rates in trying to recover the friendship also makes sense.

- Women viewed their mothers as having more friends than the men viewed their fathers as having. The reasons discussed in Chapter 1 for men having difficulty establishing friendships could be at play here. Early socialization, work pressures, and wanting time with family when not at work could all coalesce to make it more difficult for previous generations of men, when compared with women, to have as many friendships.

- Women were much less apt to raise issues related to homosexuality and fears of appearing lesbian. This does not seem to be an issue for women to the extent that it is for men.

- Women spoke much more about the need for emotional connection with their friends than did men. (At this point, this difference should not surprise anyone.)

Similarities also appeared in women's and men's answers. For example:

- The words used to define friendships are similar. Being understood, trust, dependability, and loyalty are key features of women's and men's friendships.
- The percentage of people who said they had a friend of the opposite sex is similar.
- The importance of friends, although slightly higher for women, is very high for both men and women.
- Women and men both make friends through their spouses and significant others.
- Both women and men acknowledge the positive and negative aspects of the others' friendships, with men being more apt to believe they could learn something positive from women's friendships.
- Women's friendships can also be effectively grouped using the *must*, *trust*, *just*, and *rust* categories.

The bottom line? Although we can tease out potential differences, it is more useful to focus on the similarities. Women and men both have their closest—*must* friends—people with whom they share their greatest joys and greatest concerns. Without them, lives would be less rich. Women verbalize and behave in a way that would indicate they need their friends more, as well as more frequent contact with their friends. Women often take primary responsibility for the emotional life of the family, making phone calls for arrangements around the children and plans with other couples. But this is changing, and has always been a matter of degree. Sometimes men initiate these social contacts or encourage their wives to do it for the family. Men may not *show* they need their friends as much as women do but they may, in fact, need them as much.

With the interview responses from the women, we learn how involved, complicated, and rewarding their female friendships are. Friendships are important to all these women. Everyone has a story, and each story defines the character of the woman as well as her circles of *must* and *trust* friends, who are a reflection of her. A greater understanding of these friendships can enable women to connect better with friends as well as build more connected communities.

III

MEN'S FRIENDSHIPS ACROSS THE DECADES

7

Marty in His 20s: Needing Friends and Family

I'm honored to meet people every day. Some people are just acquaintances, and some are true friends and people that you can rely on. A true friend is someone who you have known for five years and knows you on a more intimate level.

Men in their 20s rely a great deal on their male friends until they partner with someone. Many students take an average of six years to finish college, not graduating until their mid-20s. Although they lose their teenage awkwardness and continue their emotional separation from their parents, college allows them to extend their adolescence a few more years. By their mid-20s, these young men may be working hard to get their career off the ground or further their education. They may have their own place, shared with a roommate, or they are saving money by living at home with their parents, as many men do in Western society.[1] Toys are still fun for young men at this age—think video games—as are other childhood-related things like sports memorabilia and gag gifts related to sex.

These guys get together to watch sports, hit the bars as a group (men tend to go alone or with one buddy when they are older), and they may even vacation together. Regardless of the exact situation, for many, this is the time to "sow their oats" before they settle down. Marriage usually comes later for these guys. Even if married, a 20-something will still try to carve out time for his friends. His wife is unlikely to object at this early point in the marriage, as she often wants to spend time with her close friends, also.

Some men in their 20s are able to run on all cylinders—they can hang with friends and work long hours. Others face financial and even physical

constraints on their time. Ultimately, friendships are forged by the character of the people involved and the contexts in which the friendships unfold,
as is the case with Marty, highlighted in this chapter.

Marty, age 27 and white, is single and lives with his mother in suburban
Philadelphia. He works in criminal justice and as a part-time local government employee. He has a 24-year-old brother and two older step-sisters
from his father's first marriage. His parents are divorced.

Marty recently graduated from a local college and is interested in legal
research and public affairs. He is drawn to these areas because he is, by his
own description, disabled. Due to a mistake at birth (for which his family
received a substantial financial settlement), he was born with cerebral palsy
and uses a wheelchair. He lived in Philadelphia until he was 14, then
moved to a suburb of the city, before moving 10 years later to his current
residence. In their one-floor apartment, he travels by himself by electric
wheelchair from his computer-laden room to the kitchen for our interview. His mother hovers nearby as we talk and comes in and out of the
room, but I don't get the sense that this affects his answers. Some people
with cerebral palsy can be difficult for me to understand. Marty is not and,
when heard over the phone, does not sound disabled. I raise this issue
because, according to Marty, his is a visible disability in some contexts and
an invisible disability in others. I met him through a friend outside a government office building, and he eagerly agreed when I asked if I could
interview him for the book.

Friendships in the form of a Buddy System whereby he figures out what
his friends mean to him are especially important to Marty because he has
a greater reliance on people for his physical well-being than others do. He
may also have a greater emotional reliance, as he seeks out people as friends
who are able to validate him as a person by looking past his initial appearance. As Marty responded to the questions that frame the book, his disability was almost always present as he emphasized the importance of
being accepted, regardless of appearance.

Is Marty typical of most guys in their 20s? In one obvious way, no, but
in many other ways, yes. He, like many young people, searches for acceptance and defines himself through his friendships. Maybe also like many
young people, he has doubts about himself and his abilities. Although his
are obvious, many other young men, emerging from an unsettled adolescence, also have doubts. Marty has the support of his family, unlike other
young men who are actively separating from their own families without

such a high level of support. Compared to young women in their 20s, young men can seem immature in their outlook and their behavior. Marty strikes me as being mature—he is insightful and thoughtful with his responses, paying tribute to those who have supported him over the years.

How Does He Define *Friendship* and *Friend*?

In his descriptions, Marty emphasized the need for a broad definition of friendship, most likely as a way to ensure that he will be accepted for who he is. "A friend is someone you can rely on no matter what the circumstance. He should be there for you to rely on for emotional support, as well as being there for discussing all the trials and tribulations, and also for the positive moments. A friend you can rely on through thick and thin and take you for face value and what your attributes are, not just your particular aspects. A friend looks at the whole picture."

When I asked if friends are important to him, Marty immediately referred to the importance of his family. This could be a reflection of his living with his family and not having to face some of the challenges he would on his own. But living with family is also quite typical, as noted earlier, of people in their 20s, who save on rent (and doing their laundry) by living with parents. "Friends are most definitely important, along with your family as people you can talk to—friends are supposed to be there for you as an avenue for you to discuss your successes and weaknesses and to offer you all sorts of encouragement with all your endeavors. A friend will not sugar-coat the truth, and will make you a better person for the future."

Does He Have Enough Friends?

Marty believes he has enough friends, and mentioned having friends that are in different categories—the *must* friends and the *just* friends: "I have more than enough. If you have five true friends you can count on, that will be enough, as there will always be the select few you can count on no matter the circumstances. You can never have enough friends. There is a difference between a friendship and an association. A lot of us have associates from our work who are just, like, 9-to-5 friends. But those are different than people who you know outside of work. The guys who you play ball with down the street are few and far between, and there is a differentiation between the true friends (*must*) and everyday associations (*just* friends)." Although Marty counts five to seven people, including women, as his closest friends, he believes the number can vary as things change in his life.

Does a person with a disability need friends more than others? Marty never said he does, but what he does seem to need is a different type of friend—someone who will be more accepting than the average person. Marty believes he can find that in a woman more easily than in a man.

How Have Friends Helped Him?

I asked Marty how friends have helped him and how he, in turn, has helped his friends. "Obviously, my close friends have been there through thick and thin. It is always difficult growing up—when you are a young adolescent or even a young child, and you have this problem, and you don't understand why you can't throw a ball as hard or run as fast or why people are looking at you or why you look strange. Obviously, you have less control when you are young, and you look strange and can't control your muscles. When you are young, you don't have fine motor control. There was incessant drooling. People look at you like you are different, and sometimes young children don't know how to react to you. It was hard to make friends when your buddy can run after a ball or run out the door to someone else's house and you can't."

Marty paused and moved on to talk about growing older and interacting with friends who are slightly more mature: "When I got to middle school, there were still kids who were cruel, but there were one or two others who could look past that and see me. There were people who said they wanted to find out more about me. I think, in some way, I have helped them as they have helped me. We have each learned more about each other."

I wondered to Marty if perhaps he attracts special people to him, people who are capable of looking past outward appearances. "Maybe. They are people who can look more deeply, and who maybe are looking for something different in a friendship. They have certain traits and qualities, and I have been an inspiration to some of them." What I take from his answer was that not only has he been helped by friends but that his presence in their lives has enriched them as they observe how he deals with his disability. Friendships should be reciprocal and give something to both parties.

What Does He Do with Friends?

The next question on my list led me to inquire how he and his friends spend time together, and I got a typical male response: "With my friends, I go on road trips, get together with them, and go out. Sometimes we get together and watch sports. The Super Bowl is a big thing, and we are big into college football." He also added, "We don't get together just to talk, but we will talk about things that are personal when we get together."

Men are rarely comfortable getting together *to* talk but they will talk about personal things (sometimes) when they are together. The more personal discussions often have to arise spontaneously to be less threatening. This is a hallmark of the type of male "shoulder-to-shoulder" relationship that opens to the door to communication.

How Does He Make Friends?

Commonality is the basis of friendship for Marty. "To make friends with others, you have to look for common interests. Always take advantage of meeting other people; find characteristics or traits that you can relate to—dependability, leadership, honesty, hard-working, persistence, things like that." These are qualities that also speak to character, something that Marty holds in high esteem, as shown in his remarks throughout.

How Does He Maintain Friends?

What, I asked, about maintaining friends? "Maintaining your friends will be different from one person to the next. And, going back to the last question, making friends may not be as easy for one person as it is for another. When I was younger, it was extremely difficult for me to make friends because of my condition and my circumstances, but to maintain them you just keep a healthy dialogue going with them. If you haven't heard from them in a couple of weeks, give them a call or drop them an e-mail. If you have a family function coming up, and you know they are close with the family, invite them to it. Or invite them to a play or a ball game because you know it is one of their common interests."

What Has He Learned from His Father?

Marty's father, who divorced Marty's mother, has been a big influence on his friendships, particularly with people from older generations. Most men tend to make friends within their own age group, but having friendships with people from different generations can open up opportunity for change and growth. "I learned a whole lot from my father—that is where most of my rapport from my friendships comes from. My dad was in law enforcement, and I watched how he got along with everyone. That is why I love that type of work—law and politics—and that is why I met so many older men in my life. He understood people. I learned how to pick out a true friend versus somebody who is a fake. Most of my dad's friends have also been friends with the family and have stayed close with the family and my mom over the years."

When someone grows up with divorced parents, it is difficult to know whether his connecting with older men is a way of compensating for absences in his own family or a true appreciation of what an older mentor can offer. I took Marty at his word on this.

What Has He Learned from Women?

Has Marty learned about friendships from watching women interact with each other? His answer centered more on the quality of women than on their friendship patterns. "There are a couple of women who I have had as friends, and I have also thought that I would like to have a friendship with someone that has that level of tenacity or integrity, but I see nothing out of the ordinary in terms of my admiring their friendships with each other." He then added that a woman is his best friend, next to his brother.

"I would say that I have a female who is a good friend, and I think she is above and beyond anyone else I know outside of my family. She is all-knowing, humble, high integrity." Marty differentiates male from female friendships, and speaks to the core values that he perceives women possess in relation to acceptance that men do not have. "You can find some of those same qualities in a male, but I would say the difference between a male friendship and a female friendship with me is the fact that I have been able to develop a closer camaraderie with women because they have a more caring side and a more devoted side when it comes to individuals like myself, partly because of the disability and their willingness to rise above imperfections they see. Women are more accepting than men."

In turn, something about his relationship with women, he believes, makes him more acceptable to them. He feels, in a way, that he is less threatening to them. "From my perspective, I get along much better with females. I am better able to get along with them than other men because I can talk things out and dig at the core with them in ways that other men can't. Women are used to male-dominant relationships but, because of the way I am perceived, I get along better with them. This is not to say I don't have good male friendships but, because of women's greater generosity and interest, they want to know more about me. Women are more apt to be open to me than are men. For me, it's an entirely different playing field in this day and age, when you are trying to make a friendship and you have a disability, because they have to look past your imperfections. I may meet a guy who has been sheltered and has a hard time looking past my appearance—he will be embarrassed to be seen with me. He will meet me and won't ask what is going on with me. A woman will."

Is There a Link Between Masculinity and Friendship?

I came back to Marty a few months later and asked him this question. He thought about it for a while and replied in a way that reiterated his statements about his relationships with women. "I am not sure I can relate to the question. But in society, you are supposed to be rough and tough if you are a guy, but I actually have a lot of women friends. I find they are more understanding of my situation, my physical disability. If the woman has a child with a physical challenge or is working with kids—I have always seemed to get along better with females than males because of my disability and their sensitivity. I don't see a connection there in relation to masculinity, and [I] just typically relate better to women."

Conclusion

Marty serves as an advocate for the disabled and gives speeches through an organization he is a member of. For his own needs as well as for others, he wants to change the way that people relate to the disabled. Open about his disability, he is also open about his feelings about friends. True (*must*) friends must be of long standing, as his beginning quote attests. Women are more apt to have the qualities he is looking for in a friend because he perceives them as more sensitive.

Marty's story is instructive for other men as a cautionary tale. To some extent, he is everyman—only he wears his disability as a badge of courage. He says—here I am! Get to know me. Men in their 20s are finding out who they are for the first time through their work, through their living situations, and through their friendships. To a greater extent than the men interviewed next, these young men are in flux in all these areas. Many men in their 20s believe they have shortcomings, although they may not be as obvious, and they may not know exactly what they are.

For young men in their 20s, the first task of growing is to find out who you are and become comfortable with your identity. It also means becoming comfortable with the changes that are going to occur at this stage in life. Marty is comfortable with his identity and believes that many of his male peers may be uncomfortable with theirs and so may not be as accepting of him as they could be. Comfort with oneself leads to acceptance of others.

8

Zach in His 30s: Balancing Family, Friends, and Work

I am pulled. The pressure is there, but I am pretty firm in my commitment that my wife and children come first. And then, if I have time, it is for my friends, which is increasingly rare.

Perhaps the men most struggling with balancing friends, family, and work are those in their 30s. In their 20s, men still feel they can come and go as they please with their friends. As these men find partners, launch careers, and have children, responsibility for family and career increases. At this stage, men begin to feel pulled in various directions. Life becomes more routine and predictable, and there is less opportunity to pick up spontaneously with friends.

Must friends can be a significant part of life, but, by necessity, many men forego intense relationships with their friends as they shift their lives to accommodate their families. Also, single men find their married friends less available to them.

Zach, age 34 and white, has a Ph.D. in sociology and works for a West Coast think-tank. He has been married for six years and has two children, aged two and four. Like many successful men, he is on a career track that has brought him to many different cities as he climbs the professional ladder. We played e-mail tag for two months before we were able to arrange a time when I could interview him. A tall man, he believes his physical appearance sometimes makes him come across as more intimidating than he views himself. He, like other younger men, relies heavily on e-mail to stay in touch. He doesn't like talking on the telephone, never did, preferring face-to-face interaction, then e-mail.

Zach had a rather unique upbringing. His father worked for a large U.S.-based chemical company that required the family to relocate a great deal. In addition to moving around the United States, when young, he spent four years in London and three years in New Delhi. He had to learn to make friends fast. At some point near the end of these moves, his parents divorced.

But the most important part of his upbringing in relation to friendships is that he has an identical twin. This close relationship with a brother offers the possibility of gaining an understanding about the intersection of brotherhood and friendship, particularly a brotherhood as intense as a twin relationship. Do identical twins need friends if they have each other? Do they relate to other men in the same way? The way the brothers relied on each other when young and the way they rely on each other now is quite instructive about the nature of brothers who are also close friends.

Zach may be one of the more social people I interviewed. He takes great joy in being with people. Although the transition to parenthood and married life has come with some costs to his friendships, he is adapting because of his extreme sociability. I began by asking how he manages the competing demands on his time.

"I am pulled [between them]. The pressure is there, but I am pretty firm in my commitment that my wife and children come first. And then, if I have time, it is for my friends, which is increasingly rare."

Before you had kids, did you have time for friends? I ask. "Yes. But with getting married, that dynamic really changed. The amount of time that was appropriate for me to spend at happy hour with my friends wasn't there. I really enjoy socializing and am a very social person, and I'd be at happy hour every day until 10 at night if it was acceptable to my wife, which it is not."

Did that change Zach's relationship with friends? "Yes, it did." For many men, the shift away from friends toward family is a reality they readily accept. However, for those whose home life is not as exciting as their friendships, it can be a tough transition.

How Does He Define *Friendship* and *Friend*?

I asked how he defines friendship to learn how he views the differences between a *must* and a *just* friendship. "A friend is first and foremost someone I can count on. I have a lot of friends that come from a variety of backgrounds. I expect them to be loyal and responsive to things that I need. A friend is a person I can call for a favor and that I would happily do a favor for. Someone who would cover my back (a *must* friend). Apart from that, I have (*just*) friends that I have reciprocal kinds of friendships with, like my neighbor, where I would help him with a ladder at his house or he would help me but I wouldn't necessarily sit down with him and have a deep conversation with him."

Just to clarify, I said that his neighbor sounds like a very different kind of friend to me, but a friend nonetheless—you would help him out, and you enjoy his company, but he is not in your immediate circle of friends. "Right. People who I am tight with, those are people who I would want to continue talking with or be around the rest of my life. That would be how I would define my inner circle." If Zach felt closer to his neighbor, he could also be a *trust* friend.

Does He Have Enough Friends?

I asked him how many friends he had. "I am very social and require contact with friends and family. The more the merrier. My wife thinks I collect too many of them! She is not social. She will have three to four close friends and that is enough. . . . I try and keep contact by e-mail with a pretty wide circle. Maybe 20. Enough that I care about to say hey, we should get together, that I make an effort to see even if they don't make an effort back. Maybe 30." Pretty big circle!, I comment. "Yeah, as big as I can manage."

Thirty close friends is a lot of friends. I wondered if he is at the limit, or if an upper limit of friends exists, so I asked if he has enough friends. "I keep collecting them so don't know if that concept even applies. Those who become too difficult to maintain, I might drop off. But the number has stayed pretty stable. It may be more limited to my willingness to extend the energy, so I may be at the threshold of how many I can maintain. It is hard work keeping up with all of them."

I was intrigued by the notion of trying to maintain friends and asked what would cause him to drop someone as a friend. "Apathy on their part or on mine would cause me to let them go. Disagreements would not—I actually like disagreements. So, it would most likely be difficulty connecting with someone. Time. A lot of my friends travel a lot, so that is what would cause the friendship to stop, as maintaining it from a logistical standpoint becomes tough."

How Have Friends Helped Him?

I asked Zach how friends have helped him and whether they are a source of social support. Notice in his answer how he has given up the notion of the single man's friends for the married man's friends. "Absolutely, they are a source of support. Male friends with kids have been a great resource in dealing with children, either in terms of what to expect or what you are going through; making you feel you are not the only one going through these feelings. Coping with stress, though I don't tend to call my friends when I have had a tough day. I am not the kind that unloads on people. I would be more likely to want to share experiences, like 'Has this ever happened to you?' then I would be to say this is what happened to me, and I just want to talk about my experience. That's kind of my therapeutic approach with friends."

It is not uncommon for men to make friends at work as a way to advance their career. These friendships may be a means to an end—*just* but not *trust* friends. "In work, friends are very important in terms of opportunities and networking. Friends are a key survival mechanism as far as psychologically and as far as career are concerned and as far as if I need help around the house and it's a three-man job—can you lift this? Those kind of things."

It turns out Zach's wife is the most central person in his life and his best friend, as confirmed by his answer when I ask whether he would go to his wife with a problem rather than to his friends. "Yes. She is my best friend. We have been together a long time, and we are like brother and sister but more like friends."

Given his description of his relationship with his wife, I was especially interested to know about his relationship with his twin brother. "It might be unique, as my brother and I grew up overseas, and my father worked for a chemical company and lived in two foreign countries and then moved back to the U.S. and to a new town every two years. Early on, we were dressed alike and everything was the same, and then we made an issue of our each having our own friends and our own reality. That ended really fast when we moved, and we had to rely on each other for friends and for entertainment because, when you moved to a new town, you didn't know anybody. We started to realize we were really good friends with each other, and we started to not care it was your friend or my friend, and we would just include the other brother in each other's activities. So, it was conscious. It was apparent to us that it was the new arrangement."

As Zach explained, once he and his brother began to rely on each other in adolescence, the level of trust greatly increased. "My parents were pretty permissive and, in high school, they knew we were going to drink and that we would do it responsibly and that we shouldn't drive, so it got to a point in high school where one of us would agree in advance to drive and not drink and watch the other guy's back. That set the tone for one of us being in charge, and we always have covered each other's back. We've been very close friends since then. Having moved so often, you lose your network, and your network goes down to one. This is the person you are always with."

It's interesting that Zach has such a wide circle of friends, far more than most men. It may be that having so few friends when young and being part of a twin relationship made him want many more friends when older. At the same time, his brother took a different friendship route.

"The obligation is to back up your brother, and that is the same attitude I take to close friends. If you call me at 4 in the morning—and this has happened—I am going to be there because that is what I expect a friend to do for me. Over time, and as with many friendships, my relationship with my brother has really grown. We left high school planning to go to different colleges—we didn't even discuss it as an option. I guess we wanted to have our own identity in college, and [we] have been living in other cities until recently, when he went through a messy divorce and I convinced him to move out here. We have reconnected, and it has been good for him as well as for me. I don't think the closeness ever ended, even though we are terrible with each other on the phone—like, we talk to each other once or twice a month. We aren't accustomed to sitting and catching up with each other on the phone."

I wondered if his identical twin maintained a friendship style different from his own. "I think we are different," Zach responded. "First of all, the type of people that he seeks out. My group of friends is a constantly evolving circle, and he seems to hang on to a few tight (*must*) friends a lot closer than I would. I have lived all around, and every few years I am moving. So, when I move it is, 'yeah, so long, we'll stay in touch.' I maybe have a few friends from childhood and college that I really care to keep up with." Earlier he had described having a wide circle of 20 to 30 friends with whom he keeps up. These might qualify more as *trust* than *must* friends given this description. "If they are not part of my interactions on at least a yearly cycle I don't keep them," whereas he does put a lot of effort into keeping in contact. "My friendships are always changing and mutating. What I would consider close friendships have to be relevant to my life now. People who I was close to in grad school probably wouldn't recognize me now because I have two kids and I go to work everyday and am not in grad school, and I don't think I could connect with them anymore, so I don't even try to maintain those friendships."

I commented to Zach that his brother has tended to stick with a few close (*rust*) friends, but Zach's circle is always evolving. I asked if that is a result of his education and what he brings to the workplace, where there is a constant atmosphere of inquiry. "I think it is a reflection of my childhood, of constantly changing and moving and being disconnected from my old network and trying to build a new one. I can't keep up with the kids in those places that I have lived, so I have a much easier time saying, 'Okay, if we run into each other again that's cool,' but I have no expectations of maintaining this friendship after I move on. I don't feel nostalgic or any kind of loss in moving on to a new relationship. I feel confident in my abilities, in a new town or job, that I can build a new social network and friendships as I had before. I see no reason to keep up contacts with those old friends if I have no chance of seeing them again.

"I talk to my wife who has three old friends from high school, and I am amazed because I can't even remember who I went to high school with. I have one guy's number from then, but I don't know what I would talk with him about if I called him. We were close, but I don't think my friendships are any less significant because of their duration. I think they are more significant because of the frequency of contact."

I commented that his ease in making friends is characteristic of many children whose parent or parents were in the military and moved around often. He did not think this characterization of his relationships applies— he believes that he has very intense relationships during the time they exist, more intense than a typical "army brat's." He compared himself with his wife with his childhood friends. He thought that his relationships with past friends were even more intense than hers are today. "I am more than happy to let people in, but I don't feel this obligation to keep in touch once they move out of my sphere. My wife will ask me why I haven't written to Frank and I'll ask, 'Why? He's moved on and I've moved on.' I still have a social network here I am trying to maintain.

"My brother may have been affected differently by the moving around. His situation is a little different. He makes friends easily, and has a good group of friends but he also puts a lot of effort into keeping his old buddies. That's not for me. . . . I am more of a here-and-now [person] than he is."

What Does He Do with Friends?

When I asked Zach what he does with friends, he explained how he tries to balance family and "the guys": "Routinely? I used to go out and drink.

Now, if I go out, it is with the wife and kids and their wife and kids. If it is a guys' night out thing, we will go to the bars, hear music, maybe a ball game—your typical things. I do have friends where I will go a buddy's place, and we'll brew some beer, keg some beer, and watch the game. We'll go hiking, most often in groups and with the family. Having kids definitely changes the dynamic and it is no longer 'See you folks later, I am going out with the guys.' So, I tend to gravitate and pick my moments when it is appropriate to bring the family along. Like last weekend, we went to a festival with two friends and my wife and kids and had a great time. So, we always include our kids."

But if the wife and kids are not around, I ask, do you and your male friends have conversations in which feelings are shared? Here, Zach described how feelings are rarely shared directly, either one-on-one or in a group. When feelings are shared, it is in a roundabout way: he won't say that something has happened to him and he is concerned about it. Rather, he mentions the topic and then checks the response without actually admitting that it is his situation that is being described, even though it clearly is. He is only willing to risk so much, and definitely will not risk much on a personal level when a group of guys is present. "It is very loose and light—if it is one-on-one with a friend, it will be more of a question than as a statement, like 'Hey—has this ever happened to you?' That will be over a happy hour kind of thing. If there is more than one guy, we don't discuss feelings that much."

It is much riskier for some men to open up to a group, because it is harder to gauge what the reaction might be. For others, the group may be safer to open up to, because it is less intense than a one-to-one conversation.

How Does He Make Friends?

Given the large circle of friends Zach was maintaining, I asked for his advice to other men on how to make friends. For Zach a certain vibe must be present. "I wouldn't bother to make a connection with a guy unless he's on my wavelength. . . . I have friends from all different stripes in terms of religious, racial, nationalities, though I don't have any gay male friends; I do have gay female friends. How to make friends? It's an intangible—you have to be very outgoing. Find someone you feel comfortable with, find common ground, and, if you find them interesting, you set up and go out for drinks. It can be tough—I just happen to be able to accumulate people around me without being conscious of it."

I thought Zach was going to say something about character. "Yeah—he has to be laid back and easy-going, but not too easy-going. My wife always kids me that I pretend to be type B but I am really Type A. I look for that in other people, interesting, a little motivated, but not ornery. Some people are just born that way, and I tend to screen them out. But you can get a sense for people after talking to them for 5 or 10 minutes. I look for interesting people with interesting experiences who I can learn from. If someone is just a very conventional person, I probably would not make them my friend. I would prefer someone who is unique in some aspects that could add to my life. I don't mean to sound like I am taking advantage of people. But that is what I consider important in people. There is something in what I would look for in a male friend. What I wouldn't want to do is hang out with someone who did not want to get loose every so often and have a drink. I don't know what it is. But most of my friends are drinkers because there is something honest about sharing thoughts over a drink, when inhibitions go away."

Drinking in the service of opening up may be a middle ground between the classic shoulder-to-shoulder way of interacting—with little direct communication—and the more direct face-to-face interacting that women typically engage in. "I do make friends when I make an effort. I would certainly approach [friend making] in a conscious manner. This is someone I would want to hang out with. It is similar to picking up a girl. You work out a plan, and you go for it. Not that I have—I am way out of practice. But you approach it from the same way."

How Does He Maintain Friends?

For Zach, maintaining friends is a very conscious process. It is a balancing act, with a sincere attempt to keep everyone close. "I see it is Tuesday night and we have nothing going on Saturday night, and I wonder who I haven't seen that I want to connect with to keep the friendship going. Some friend I will think, well I saw him three weeks ago, so I will call the guy I have not seen in four weeks first. And I will select for parties people who I do not want to neglect, and I will keep track of who I owe socially and who owes me."

How does that play into whether he has ever lost a friend? Zach remembered an event between a very good friend of his and his wife. Laughing he said, "He was being a jerk to her, and she was being a jerk to him and we all got kind of pissed off and did not talk to him for about a year, and then we just picked up again and started the friendship. I think guys can get over things like that pretty quickly." Okay. This is not that unusual. Men have a fight, don't talk for a while, forget about it, and start taking again.

"I have another good friend that I went to Utah with in the summer. It was supposed to be a six-week trip and, about two weeks into it, he just said he was missing his girlfriend too much and wanted to go home. It was his car, so we just turned around and drove back east, barely talking on the way. I then got out at my house, and we did not talk for eight years. And this guy was as close to being a brother as you can get. His wife, the girl-friend, now his wife, has been trying for every year to get us to talk, and she will call and put him on, and we'll each mumble something, and that's it. We don't see any reason to keep in touch. I think apathy is the biggest threat to ending my friendship, not conflict. If it is conflict, it is over pretty fast."

I was laughing at this point and asked if he ever started to call this friend and then backed off? "Nope. Never occurred to me. I don't know what I would say to him. I don't pick up the phone to catch up. I have to be with them." I told Zach that I think a lot of guys, like me, would have done the same thing. "Yeah. I didn't want to get into a pissing match with him about it, and I would much rather just let it go. No resolution or explanation needed. I was angry about the trip being cut short, but I ended up going to visit my girlfriend at the time. And she is now my wife, so it worked out okay. But we should have taken my truck instead of his (laughs)."

What Has He Learned from His Father?

When asked, Zach said "My dad is an interesting character. He is very socially adept, but I don't think very interested in friends. It's hard to speak about your father when you only know him as a father. My take is that, even in later life, he is not that interested in keeping up with friends. He does have a small group, but they are not very close. He is much happier to be with his wife, now my step-mom. He is not the kind of guy who needs to accumulate friends, like I am. And not the kind of guy who needs to go have a drink with the guys or have them over. My dad never sought out that male companionship, whereas now I will try and have over other families, and we will be in the backyard—the guys—and women will be in a different room, and the kids someplace else. That's my world now, aside from a few single friends. My dad wasn't like that. He didn't seek it out, and he never took much of an interest in my friends, and never gave me any guidance on that. Never a role model on how I should handle my friends."

Zach and his twin brother, in fact, model their outgoing and friend-making behavior after their mother. "She is quite adept. She can go into a room and want to know everyone's name. I am the same way. I got that from her. I am not shy at all. My dad would be the cool cat in the corner that may be considered aloof."

What Has He Learned from Women?

Despite his mother's influence in socializing, when I asked Zach if he had learned about friendships from observing female friendships, he said no. "I have talked about this with my wife. Her mother and sister are very close, and they talk about five times a day and, even with her friends, the types of things they talk about are very different and are about other people, and observing other people. Guys don't talk about that stuff very much. I would never ask a friend about his relationship with another woman. I don't care. But the women always want to know about the relationships. It doesn't even occur to me—it's 'how's the old lady?' 'Okay?' 'Fine.' So, I don't think about my friends in that way. My wife is more like my brother, in trying to maintain a few close friends with a great deal of intensity, whereas I can trade one friend for another."

Zach does not need his wife to help him make friends. His situation is more the reverse of the stereotypical view of the wife as the social center of the family. "I'm the more social of the two of us, so it has happened, but not in the way that she is helping me make friends. I want her to have friends, so I will try not to do anything to screw it up when she meets people. Some of her friends are pains in the ass, but I will try and be nice to keep those going because they are important to her. I am as pleasant and as nice and engaging as I can be, because she needs friends. And my zeitgeist is that people need friends, so if she only has a few, she has to keep those."

Zach has few female friends, "because there is a tension there for my wife that I don't want to deal with. My wife might feel this is not a friendship—it is something else. I have women friends at work, but if it is an attractive woman, it would be really hard to be a friend, not from my perspective, but from my wife's. I do have gay women friends because they are safe."

This answer is a further confirmation of what we have heard from other men. Marriage can interfere with these types of friendships because of the potential jealousy that could arise.

How Does Masculinity Affect His Friendships?

When I asked about masculinity and his friendships, he said that he looks for friends with a level of masculinity similar to his own. "All of my friends are M.D.s or Ph.D.s, and I think these types have stereotypical behavior. These are not the guys who are slamming tequila shots and watching hockey. We like watching ball games and doing male-type things, music, etcetera, but we are not talking about the NASCAR race. The discussions can get pretty intellectual or talk about women in a pretty base way but none of my friends are out to prove that they are a tough guy.

"I don't have any friends that are gay males that I know of. Not for not trying. My wife has some gay male friends but, for some reason, they treat me very differently. Maybe I come across as Alpha Male too much. But it is hard for me to get a sincere discussion on with a gay male. Female gay is no problem. But there is a lot of tension with gay males that I don't understand. Some people said to me it may be that they think I am kind of your bully jock."

Conclusion

As the interview ended, I asked again about the conflicting pulls among the roles of family, work, and friends. "I think the tension is with single male friends. If the guy is married, we both have a wife and maybe kids, and we understand the pulls. But it is hard to bring the single friends into the loop. I don't get that many opportunities to go out with the guys and tear it up. The tension is with the single guys alone going out and enjoying a night with just guys, which is different than going out with guys with the family, and are the kids about to jump off the staircase. I think a lot about what it was like being single. But it is just as much fun now with the family and kids. But you have to realize it is very different. There is that tension. The work comes in only when I travel, and it pulls me from the family, not from the friends. The biggest thing is that kids change your relationships with other people in dramatic ways."

The task for many of the men in their 30s is to accept the changing circumstances of their lives and try to figure out who they are in relation to their family, career, and their *must* friends. They are apt to be balancing career moves, family obligations, and the loss of the freedom to pick up spontaneously and run off with friends to Vegas. The sadness associated with the loss of that freedom should not be underestimated—it is inevitable. The strength of the pulls between these three distinct parts of a man's life will vary, and the pulls cannot always be balanced equally. Something will have to shift. It is not just that youth and freedom are being given up for adult responsibilities. It is that youth has hopefully given way to loving relationships with other people (wife/significant other and possibly children) as well as to satisfying work. Men must navigate these competing worlds through conversations with wives and friends. It is only when people are not clear about availability, obligations, and expectations that feelings get hurt.

Zach has it figured out. This does not mean he still does not long for more time with his friends. But he realizes that, for the time being, his obligations have turned elsewhere. And, Zach does have his twin brother as his closest male (*must*) friend. To some extent, despite the changes in his relationships with his other friends, he maintains this as his primary friendship, one that does not compete with his immediate family (wife and children) responsibilities. Because his association with his brother has always been understood as a given, he automatically maintains it despite what other family pulls occur. In this way, he may have the best of both worlds.

9

Mal in His 40s: Continuing the Balancing Act

I can call them on anything they do. For instance, if someone does something I think is wrong, I can just tell them about it without us getting all worked up about it. That is part of what a friend can do.

Because very young children have not developed distinct personalities yet and still follow their parents' leads, most men in their 30s may see their young children as needing constant supervision, so that they don't get into harm's way. Fathers with young children are likely to have the children adapt to their interests. But the children of most men in their 40s have, by this age, developed more distinct personalities and needs, which affect how these men form friendships. These men are more likely to adapt to their children's needs, rather than having the children adapt to them.

Although old friendships may not be affected, the potential for new ones certainly will be. For example, a man with a 12-year-old son with a musical talent is going to become engaged in musically related activities. The father will drive the son to music lessons, attend concerts, and shop for musical equipment. That father may make friends with other fathers with musically inclined children.

Unlike men in their 50s, 60s, and older for whom friends are companions who exist largely outside of child rearing, in their 40s, men who are fathers are often trying to combine parenting responsibilities with their male friendships. Children, of course, provide a way for men to get closer to men (just as sports do), as men can share unique parenting experiences together—watching winning and losing sports teams, taking school camping trips, monitoring the middle school dance, and so on.

When children are involved, it becomes the ultimate shoulder-to-shoulder relationship.

Mal is 42, African-American, Protestant, and married with two sons, 12 and 15. He works as an engineer/entrepreneur. We met while he and I were sitting next to each other during a five-hour cross-country flight. We struck up a conversation, the topic of friends emerged, and he agreed to be interviewed for the book.

How does Mal balance his children, his marriage, and his friendships? One challenge in balancing everything is that he is not home as much as he would like. He travels out of his home base of St. Louis about one week per month, leaving his sons alone with his wife of 20 years. He is aware that she has a hard time managing them when he is away, and he feels guilty about it, not only because they can be a handful but because they are sons, and he believes they need a male hand. As an African-American, he feels his responsibility to be with his sons more acutely because, he says, he is aware of the lack of male role models in his community. His wife's experiences trying to parent sons while the father is away are replicated in many homes in which the man can best control the children. Everyone who has ever heard the phrase, "Wait until your father gets home," knows that fathers are often the stricter disciplinarians, particularly with sons. At the same time, Mal is aware that by working so many hours he is providing for his family in ways that he and his siblings were never provided for when they were young.

I sensed as we began talking that he is the kind of person who is initially wary of strangers. But once trust was established, he became open and, when he learned I had been trained as a family therapist, he asked me for advice on raising his oldest son.

How Does He Define *Friendship* and *Friend*?

Mal started with many of the friendship-related issues identified in Chapter 2: trust, dependability, and being understood. "Friendships, to me, are my whole thing. They are incredibly important. I don't know what I would do without them. I have three very close (*must*) friends. One I have known since high school, and the other two I have known for about 10 years through work. One is the godfather of one of my boys, and I am his son's godfather also. We can talk about anything, and we can get real emotional.

People don't think men get emotional, but we do." These *must* friends are all African Americans.

His relationship with them is very honest. Like other men who were interviewed, there is pride in the sense that Mal can be so upfront with his friends. "I can call them on anything they do. For instance, if someone does something I think is wrong, I can just tell them about it without us getting all worked up about it. That is part of what a friend can do—just tell a friend what he is doing and be called on it also. We help each other out in many ways, and whenever they call I'll drop whatever I'm doing. They do the same for me. We help out with money, or I help one of them with money sometimes, and we help with our kids." These are some of the common ingredients of friendships identified in earlier chapters—it is a complete letting down of one's guard; friends can give it to each other straight, and friends will come to the rescue in the middle of the night.

Does He Have Enough Friends?

I asked Mal if three friends are enough (most of the men interviewed had a handful of *must* friends). They are enough, he says, but then tells me about a new (*trust*) friend he was making in South Africa, where he sometimes travels on business. "I met this guy through work, and we would get together at his house and bonded over cooking and music. He had a get-together, and I came with one of my special recipes and put on some of the music that I like and taught him about my culture and my life. He's been to my house and done the same thing. He's met my wife, and I've met his and the four of us have bonded."

Not only is this friend South-African, he is also white. Mal's cross-racial friendship seems exciting to him because of the opportunities for new learning it provides. My impression from talking to men in other countries, as well as in the United States, is that cross-national friendships such as these are relatively common, whereas cross-racial friendships between people born in the same country are less common. For example, immigrants to a host country will often befriend other immigrants from different countries of origin. They have their immigration status in common, and they are seeking friendships. If both men are born in the same country, often inherent impediments to the friendship exist, based on the history of the race relations in that country.

Although Mal has enough friends, he is open to making new ones. His may be the ideal perspective to have—the belief that you have enough friends but are open to making new ones. I asked Mal how he was building that new friendship and how he maintained the other friendships he has. His answer is: "E-mail. I can drop him and the other guys a quick line and stay in touch, and I don't have to worry about the time difference between us and Cape Town." I asked if he would ever call the new friend in South Africa just to chat. "Occasionally, sure, but I'd have to time it right." E-mail is an inexpensive and convenient way to show someone you are thinking of them without getting into a long discussion. He keeps in touch with his American friends by seeing them a lot and talking with them on the phone.

What Does He Do with Friends?

Mal is strengthening his relationships with friends both through their own activities together as well as through their children's activities. "I hang out with the other three guys in St. Louis a lot. We do things together like dinner or, with one of my friends, with the kids, and I play basketball with one of the others. Through our kids, I really have gotten closer to one of them. We are coaches of my younger son's soccer team. His boy is on the team, too, so we get to spend a lot of time doing that together and being with our sons. It is through coaching that we have gotten even closer. I'm telling his son what to do and he's telling mine."

How Does He Make Friends?

The conversation segued into male competition on the playground and whether boys who are less skilled at sports have trouble making friends, as I suggested in Chapter 1. He talked more about how young men can make friends than he did about himself, as he generally makes friends from work or his sons' activities. Mal says that a boy today can always find a team to play on, whether it is school or in an after-school program, and that sports are not as important in the building of friendships as when he was young. According to Mal, American society (whether it is the school, religious institution, family, or television) is doing a much better job of making the child who sits on the bench feel accepted, and this goes a long way toward building better, less competitive relationships.

This is one of the few positive comments I have heard from anyone interviewed for the book about the direction society is taking in building a better sense of community, one of the goals of this book. When children can make friends through the performing arts or through scholastic achievement, their options for finding a niche for themselves, and then making friends within that niche, increase.

Raising Sons

Mal expressed concern about his sons' values, which are related to the friends they hang out with. He believed that they could become too centered on material goods and only want to be with friends who have nice things. "When I was young, I would get a good pair of sneakers and take really good care of them. I would brush them after I used them and make sure they lasted. Today, kids don't take care of anything. They get one pair, and then they want the next more expensive pair of shoes. We really spoil them."

I asked Mal what he is doing about his concerns. "I make my kids work. We have a contract with a school where we cut the grass. So, every Saturday, we spend a few hours doing that, and I pay them. So, when one of them comes to me and says he wants a new pair of shoes I say, 'Fine, you can get them when you have earned the money.' That stops them for a while."

He worried that if his boys don't take care of their things, they will not take care of each other. Mal's philosophy is similar to another parent, who I heard say that, even though he could afford to give his children the things they wanted, he was not going to give them those things. He wanted his children to learn that "privilege is not a birth right but a blessing." This comment is also related to the broader sense of community-building that Mal holds to be so important: every child should have a place, and every child should learn how to take care of the next guy.

Mal also shared a concern about his boys not listening to their mother when he is out of town and how he feels conflicted when he travels. "I can control them when I am home, and she can't. I wonder if she shouldn't be at home more and working less. My oldest is having trouble with his grades and has developed a rep of being a class clown. He should be more serious in his work." Does Mal talk about these concerns with his friends? Yes. And he thinks he has gotten closer to his friends through talking to them about what keeps him awake at night.

Has He Ever Lost Friends?

Mal then confirmed my initial impression about his reticence with me: "Maybe I learned from my parents that you have to be careful who you trust. I lost a friend because of something he did. It takes a lot to get me off but, when it happens, that's it, it's over. In business, it can be tricky. Once something happened to me in business, and I never hung out with him again in the same way. We stayed close, if you know what I mean, but it was never the same."

Mal described the shifts from one category of friendship to the next, when the *must* or the *trust* friend becomes the *just* friend, which happens a lot in a competitive workplace. He decided it was better to maintain a different relationship with the male friend (note Mal saying, "I never hang out with him in the same way"), rather than break it off or attempt to rebuild it at the same level of intimacy. This is the kind of pseudo-relationship that men sometimes choose to maintain, rather than end a friendship altogether or work to resolve it and make it a *must* or *trust* friendship again.

What Has He Learned from His Father?

I asked him if he had learned about friendships from his own father. He told a story that many other men have told me about fathers who grew up in tougher economic times. "Not really. My parents were more concerned with surviving than with friendships. They were just trying to get by, and I didn't see him spend time with friends. My older brothers were more my friends and maybe my role models for making friends. I learned about loyalty and trust from them."

What Has He Learned from Women?

The conversation turned to the role of women in men's lives. Like many men, Mal thinks that women's friendships are too high-maintenance. "Women's friendships are very different than men's. They can't get it out and then have it be over. Men can just say what's bothering them and go from there (although Mal did not do this with the relationship just referred to). They are much more emotional and backbiting than men are. I wouldn't want a friendship like my wife has with some of her friends. Too much stuff."

Mal has a lot to say about whether he had platonic friendships with women. Lowering his voice as he talked to me, even though his wife was not within 1,000 miles of us, he told me that he had a friend at work who was very attractive and with whom he flirted, but who was only a platonic friend. They will sometimes flirt through e-mails but never in person. He described something that I believe is common—the workplace flirtation that neither party takes seriously and that neither party would ever act on, but which provides an element of excitement to a friendship that does not exist in heterosexual, male-to-male friendships.

Many of the men who were interviewed talked about having friendships that contained an element of sexual fantasizing but that were still considered platonic. Mal has worked hard to not let his wife know about this particular friendship. "One time, we were at a gas station, and I saw her there, and I was staring at her. My wife, who is extremely jealous, asked what I was doing. I lied and said I didn't know her because, if my wife knew I worked with this woman, it would really upset her."

How Does Masculinity Affect His Friendships?

Mal sees a clear relationship between masculinity and friendship and, like other men interviewed, thinks his friends have the same level of masculinity as he does. For Mal, this translates into their enjoying the same activities. He tells a story about going to a bar with a friend. "We're sitting there drinking and talking, and these two women sit down. Now, we knew they were hitting on us, and we could have gone with that, but we were really more interested in catching up with each other than getting into anything like that. I didn't feel we were not being masculine because we didn't go there, but someone else watching us might have wondered what was going on with us. But we didn't care. We wanted to talk with each other."

This could be considered the ultimate expression of masculinity: men who are comfortable with themselves—and each other—regardless of appearances. Mal acknowledged that this could make him look less masculine, but he was unconcerned by appearances—he wanted to spend time with his friend.

Conclusion

Mal lives for his family, his work, and his friendships. Like many men in their 40s, the responsibilities of a husband and father come first, and he has never forgotten his role as breadwinner and provider. Although he wants to provide for his family what he didn't have growing up, he also wants to maintain the friendships that his father never had the time to pursue. Because one of his closest (*must*) friends also has a son his son's age, he may be able to maintain a high level of meaningful friendships better than most men his age. His model of how to do it is certainly instructive.

Mal offered the only opinion I have heard about friendships and child-drearing practices growing beyond the immediate one-on-one relationship and the impact they can have on the broader community. By talking about the inclusion of the child who sits on the bench and raising children to take care of others, he is illustrating how communities can be more supportive and inclusive by modeling a nurturing environment. His beliefs may be particularly reflective of the African-American community, where a great emphasis is placed on community responsibility and where family and friends often look out for each other. If fathers are only looking out for their own sons and not for *all* sons, this outlook implies, the community will suffer. What if adult men in all communities looked for ways to include each other in activities that were not as concerned with outcome but more concerned with connection?

The challenge for men in their 40s, in relation to friendships, is to weave them in at a time when work responsibilities are often increasing, children continue to need them, and wives (or significant others) may also be on career trajectories that pull them away from home. Overlaying these forces is the first hint of aging. That hint, sometimes brought on by peers dying unexpectedly or parents aging, spurs some men to try to find time with friends who can engage in youthful activities. Finding time for basketball, running, golf, or going out to sports bars are all ways men use to reassure themselves that they can still have fun. Fitting in these outings requires juggling but, in some ways, fitting them in takes on increased importance because of aging.

Simultaneous to this development, new friends are being made through children, and these friends may reflect more the personality of those children than their parents. As mentioned, the son who is good at guitar will hang out with other guitarists; so, fathers of musicians may meet each other based on their children's interests, even though the fathers had no prior musical background. These adult friendships will further concretize the man's identity as a father, a more fleshed-out identity than he may have had when his children were younger and he could still shape their activities and time around his own interests. He gives up part of the identity he grew up with for one shared by his children's (as well as his wife's) interests and influences. He may lose old friends along the way, and he may add new ones. Being open to meeting new friends through children or through one's wife becomes particularly important at this stage and can serve as a way to bridge the competing demands on a guy's time.

10

Mick in His 50s: Needing Friends More Than Ever

*While I'm sure I took almost all friendships for granted earlier in life,
now I am ever reminded and so much more grateful for how lucky
I am and have been in my relationships with my friends.*

By the time a man reaches his 50s, his children are often gone from the
house (or need little daily input from a parent). Time dedicated to Little
League and helping with science projects is freed up. Work and career are
more settled, and few new career mountains are left to scale. With luck,
more disposable income is available and more weekends are free for travel.
Talk begins about retirement. Concerns about mortality are no longer
a glimmer—more friends have died at too young an age, and parents and
older relatives may also have died or become incapacitated. Men become
concerned with their health, and take pride in what they can continue to
do physically. Communities grow in importance as men begin to explore
connections beyond the immediate—they begin to wonder what will
happen to them as they age, and they may begin to feel lonely, with less
activity in their home. Men become more philosophical about their lives
and seek out others to combat being alone. Connections with old friends
are reignited, and new friendships may be initiated around activities that
are possible to pursue with increased time.

Mick, age 55 and white, lives in small-town America, where people help
raise each other's kids by coaching them in sports, teaching them in school,
and providing summer employment for them. Born in Philadelphia, Mick
went to college in central Ohio at age 18 and has lived there ever since. He
teaches 9th grade history in an even smaller town, a 25-minute drive away.

He is married and the father of four adopted children, all of whom are now out of the home. His wife is also a school teacher and volunteers in their church as a youth leader.

In Mick's "other" life, he is an outstanding musician, having co-written a top-ten hit for a country singer in the 1970s. The royalty checks helped pay for his house. He performs with local rock groups, as well as with his wife, as part of a singing trio. He buys and sells guitars on eBay. The guy even looks like a musician. He is tall, thin, with shoulder-length graying hair and a mustache. In addition, he is an exceptional teacher. When one of his former students won an award for outstanding scholarship during his senior year of high school, he was able to invite one of his teachers for an all-expense-paid trip to the White House. The student remembered and honored his 9th grade teacher, Mick, with the invitation. Here, we hear from a guy (the interview was conducted partly in person and partly by e-mail) who is able to make remarkable connections with people on many levels. Because some of his answers were written, and he is an English teacher, they are often quite articulate.

How Does He Define *Friendship* and *Friend*?

"Friendship starts with a shared experience: people thrown together in school, at work, social activities, worship, etcetera. Then, through casual, superficial interaction, common interests, opinions, likes, and dislikes are discovered. In subsequent deeper conversations, shared values, triumphs, struggles, joys, and fears come to light. Over time, these shared experiences, interactions, and conversations lead to opportunities for mutual support, validation, encouragement, guidance, and appreciation. Being a (*must*) friend is not a function of who you are, being a friend is all a matter of what you do. To me, a friend is, in no particular order, a playmate, consultant, sibling, mentor, motivator, advocate, assistant, comrade, regulator, confidant, therapist, tour guide, team mate, confessor, follower, partner, cheerleader, audience, coach, fellow pilgrim, entertainer, and source of light."

Mick links friendship to what two people have done for and with each other. But the character of the friend is also important, given how central shared values are. Note that Mick mentions many of the friend attributes from Chapter 2: trust (confidant), support system (therapist), someone who has your back (team mate), and someone who will tell you like it is (regulator). The extent that all or some of these characteristics appear in any one individual would help Mick build his Buddy System: a confidant might be a *must* friend while an entertainer might be a *just* friend.

Does He Have Enough Friends?

Mick then reflected on how he began developing a positive sense of self as a young adult, and he connects that with his ability to make friends, "I believe that I have enough friends. With my wife, my children, my parents, and my siblings, I'm already so far ahead in the friendship game that it's ridiculous! Given my understanding of friendship as per your previous question, I naturally feel that I have been so very blessed with these many wonderful friends within my own family. Therefore, the mile-thick icing on the cake made up of the friends that I have outside of my family qualifies as sort of an embarrassment of riches. Interestingly enough, outside of my family, I really do not have any close friends from before college. Perhaps this is a function of the fact that I do not think that I really became myself until I was given the opportunity to redefine myself that going away to school affords one."

This last statement confirms my belief about why some men (and women) stay in close touch with high school or elementary school friends—they liked themselves at that stage of their life. Mick is saying that he did not like who he was in high school as much as he likes who he became in college and afterward. These later-made friends have become his touchstones.

How Does He Make Friends?

Mick returns to the discussion to detail how, at each developmental stage or marker of adulthood (college, marriage, work, parenthood), he has made friends. "I have been incredibly fortunate to make a small number, six to ten, wonderfully close (*must*) friends, most of whom are men. Some of these are people I met in college, some through work, some through raising our family in a small town, and some through my wife, her work, and her friends. Quality of friendship is very important to me, in that I feel like I let very few people get close enough to me to be welcomed inside a sort of circle of trust within which I can feel safe to truly be myself with them. Outside of that circle are plenty of neighbors, colleagues, associates, and acquaintances (*just* friends) with whom I may enjoy lots of delightful experiences.

But I do not feel about them the incredible sense of family significance that I feel toward those inside the circle. I treasure those on the inside just as if they are family to me, which is saying a lot in my lexicon. Do I have enough of these people in my life? Oh yes—far more than I could ever deserve! It makes me feel extraordinarily lucky!"

Also, like many men, Mick believes in finding a common bond to establish friendships with men, "Here I must return to the idea of 'experience shared.' The only way I ever encounter a potential friend is through a shared experience—at work, musically, athletically, socially, or working together on some social-service project. Then, if we discover that we have a shared interest or interests, perhaps we can set up some kind of get-together—after work, with families, a dinner, etcetera. Then, if a greater depth of commonality is discovered, more social get-togethers or shared experiences could lead to friendship."

How Have Friends Helped Him?

Mick was one of the few men to comment on the notion of friendships as a guard against loneliness. He also hinted at how connections with others enhance his own experiences. "The real number one way in which friends have helped me *is* through social support. First of all, friends have given me the priceless gift of letting me know that I'm not alone in all that I experience—the struggles, frustrations, confusions, and fears as well as the delights, dreams, hopes, and aspirations. In reality, life will most likely prove to be a pretty solitary venture, but I'm not the kind of person who wants to make a home for that sorrowful notion in my soul. Perhaps this is because my experiences lead me to believe that everything in life is much better—deeper, richer, more fun, and far more delightful—when it is shared with those I love, my friends. Friends also have been an extremely important source of inspiration, encouragement, and education in my life. Without friends, I think I would become the poster child for the expression 'A stick in the mud.'"

From talking with Mick, it was hard for me to envision him as a stick in the mud, which I told him. "It has been my friends who have encouraged and inspired me to go to interesting new places; try fascinating new things; and broaden, deepen, and expand my experiences, understandings, and appreciations of so many marvelous things that I'm quite certain I would have missed completely had it not have been for my bold companions."

To some extent, Mick might sound like a naïve child pressing his face against a store window filled with puppies when he describes his relationships, but his eagerness is infectious. When I ask Mick how he helps friends, he says "I believe that the greatest gift that I can give to these wonderful people is the gift of *enthusiastic delight*. I think that because the business of living in the world today can be so demanding, so often my friends either can't or don't take the time to step back and truly appreciate how really delightful they are as people, as creations, as spirits. I'm very much enamored of the word 'delight' as in 'from The Light.' Somehow I think that I have an ability to pick up and reflect back some of this 'light' to these magnificently luminous people, and I think that they sense and appreciate this. Other than that, I try to return the gift of letting my friends know that they are not alone either."

Mick reported that he enjoys his friends in the moment. "What I usually do [with my friends] is play, play, play, and then go somewhere and perhaps play some more. As far back as I can remember, this has always been the case. This is probably a product of my relationship with my older brother, who was already there and ready to play whatever I wanted to play, right from the first time I was able to climb out of my crib. I do not believe that what I've played over the years has been all that important to me compared to who I was able to be with, laugh with, talk with, and share the experience with." Mick brings this attitude to everything he does, although is able to be more serious if necessary. His ability to go back and forth separates him from adult men with adolescent relationships who are unable to switch to more appropriate behavior when a crisis emerges. "Even when I am working with friends, it's play for me. Play music, play cards, play tennis or Frisbee, go out on the town, go fishing, go shopping for guitars or tools or books or food. Work at school, if I'm with friends, is play. Working to build, rebuild, or repair someone's home, if I'm with friends, is play. I guess it all comes across as play to me because if I'm with friends, I'm having fun; and if I'm having fun, it must be play. Of course, if one of us is severely down in the dumps, under the gun, or really stressed out about something, then that's a whole different ball game. If I'm the one in a jam, and I don't want to escape into play mode, then what I do is talk, listen, and look to my friend for some understanding, some support, and maybe some good, useful advice as well. If it's my friend who's struggling, and play doesn't seem to be a helpful path to follow, then I'll do my best at listening, understanding, supporting, comforting, letting him know that he is not alone."

Unlike many men who need to be in a position of control, Mick does not have to be in charge of the relationship and enjoys a self-mocking tone. "I'm far more comfortable receiving advice than giving it. . . . My initial default setting is usually close to, 'Anyone looking to me for advice is probably in way too much trouble for me to be of any help!'"

Mick went on to describe a new friendship he has developed—an online relationship with a guitar buyer and seller who he met through eBay but who he has never met face-to-face. "We did some deals, and I liked his humor, and we just began e-mailing back and forth. He's my buddy."

I asked more about it: "Do you talk about problems, children, work, your relationships, physical illnesses, or just guitars? And does calling him a friend diminish your other friendships you have just described?" Frankly, I am skeptical about on-line relationships that are called friendships. To me they fly in the face of everything else I have been hearing about trust and dependability. "And what about knowing someone for years?"

But Mick replied that he essentially considers this a *must* friendship. "My buddy Jorge definitely seems like a friend to me. At first it was very similar to the kind of friendship that one might strike up with a fellow chance traveler, someone at work, or a neighbor with whom one might share similar interests (*just* friends). But, in a way, it seems much deeper than that now, perhaps because we have discovered that we have an awful lot in common or perhaps because the unusual environment created by the Internet might make it easier to bypass a lot of 'small talk' and get into deeper conversations once a level of comfort and/or trust has been established. We have written to one another quite a bit about family, aging parents, wives, and kids. I recently received a photo of his son, who as a high school junior decided to quit the marching band to play linebacker on the football team. We've discovered that we are both not only crazy about guitars, but we're also pretty nutty about baseball and old prop-driven airplanes."

Mick goes on to describe the relationship, "As an only child, Jorge remarked once that being able to talk with me was like having the brother that he never had as a kid. Since then, we often refer to each other as 'Brother Jorge' and 'Brother Mick.' I sent him a copy of a CD I recorded, and he sent me some delightful biographical stories. I even got incredibly delicious Mexican wedding cookies from one of his aunts one Christmas. My wife and I have promised to meet up with him one of these days in Texas, so he can take us across the border for some serious Mexican food. Jorge and I have spent way too much time conversing about food."

This communication made me reconsider that maybe, in today's world, these friendships can develop. Journalist Bill Adler, in his book *Boys and Their Toys: Understanding Men by Understanding Their Relationship with Gadgets*, when writing about Myspace and other online social networks, believes that the whole definition of friendship is being reshaped by such venues. "Many people think of people they've never met or spoken with as their friends, and indeed many of these friendships seem to have strong emotional bonds . . . people tend to talk to each other much more frequently and much more intimately than they do in the real world." The Internet allows for the beginning of a relationship, and continued e-mail can test out whether it is worth pursuing. This relationship spans more than two years, so it has stood the test of time and is, according to Mick, a friendship. The anonymity of it, Mick's reference to the fellow traveler, is also a salve for someone who may want to talk to someone about highly personal matters and never have to face them. It is cathartic to open oneself up to an interested stranger. The flow of communication has been such that both Mick and Jorge want to pursue this friendship further. Whether it is a *must* or *trust* friendship is hard to tell at this point. It certainly appears on the way to being a *must* friendship. Perhaps after the face-to-face visit, it will become further cemented.

How Does Masculinity Affect His Friendships?

When I asked Mick about masculinity and male friendships, he said that masculinity does not hold much meaning for him, "I don't know whether or not I ever think of anything in terms of masculinity. Certainly, I share a point of view, humor, topics of interest, and many activities with the male friends in my life that I do not share with any women, with the exception of my wife, who at least feigns an interest in guitars, the Phillies, and fantasy baseball. And, while I definitely value this apparently uniquely male set of interests, activities, etcetera, I cannot honestly say that an awareness of any 'masculine' connection ever gains much purchase in my mind."

How Does He Maintain Friendships?

Maintaining friendships is not difficult for Mick, "Inclusion. I continue to deliberately include people in activities, experiences, communications, and other forms of social and personal interactions. I like to do things with other people rather than just work alone all the time, and by including others in these activities, I think that helps to maintain and strengthen our friendship. I also like to ask friends for help when I need it and offer help when I think I can be of assistance. Finally, just staying in touch by communicating somewhat regularly seems to be a healthy thing to do."

As far as losing friends, Mick does not remember any single precipitating event that cost him a friend. Rather, he has the sense that something went sour in relation to someone because of issues of personal integrity. "I cannot recall ever losing a friend, but I can definitely recall a couple of times when I was quite young when a disagreement or conflict over something seemed to let all of the magic run out of a relationship that had seemed to be so perfect prior to that. I cannot recall what kind of rift caused this change to take place. Looking back, it was probably just reality setting in, letting me know that no two people will agree about everything all of the time. The best that I can remember is this sense that I felt let down or somehow betrayed by the fact that someone hadn't said or done or felt what I had assumed they would, and I was not at all prepared for their independent thoughts or actions. My guess is that, for most of us, it can be hard to learn that not everything will always go as we expect it to."

What Has He Learned from His Father?

Mick has learned a great deal about friendships from his father, who is still alive in his 80s, although struggling following a stroke that affected his speech. What he learned mirrors what has been said about men having friends who they *do* something with, rather than friends who they just get together with— there has to be a shoulder-to-shoulder activity or reason to get together. "It always seemed to me that my father's friends were people with whom he played tennis, and that was pretty much his only reason to have any friends at all. However, upon further thought, I realized that he actually socialized with these men, their wives, and their families. Would he have anything at all to do with them if they weren't tennis players? I tend to doubt it! On the other hand, he may have had plenty of friends from work that I never got to know, but what I observed as I grew up was the model that suggested that friends were the people with whom you shared the activities which were most important to you as an individual. This probably contributed to the fact that most of my closest friends are guitar players."

What Has He Learned from Women?

Like some of the other men, Mick has not learned a great deal from women about how to positively construct friendships with others. His response surprises me, given how close he is with his wife and how many friends she has. I would have thought that his closeness with her would mean he admires her friendships. The terms he uses to describe women's friendships turn out to be fairly typical. "Have I learned anything about friendships from observing females relationships? I don't think I look at women and their relationships with each other in any attempt to learn something useful about relationships. I suppose it could be said that I might have picked up a few pointers on what not to do. I think that perhaps women take some little things much too seriously—comments, gestures, trivial acts, or omissions—in their relationships with each other, while men either don't notice or don't care about such trivial things. Plus, I think that men are much less likely to be 'catty,' and much more likely to be out-front with another man if they are bothered about something. The big question that remains in my mind is, did I really learn any of these things or are they all just stereotypes that I've come to accept and subscribe to along the way?"

As for platonic friendships with women, he described an honest awareness about their sexuality without feeling that the friendship is tilted in a sexual direction. "Definitely (I have female friends). Of course, I cannot honestly say that my relationship to any woman is 100% nonsexual. Although I have several close friends who are women, I am still at least aware of the fact that they are women and they are sexual beings. Do I lust after any of them? Nope, not in the least, but do I sense and appreciate everything about them that is female and attractive, you bet!"

Conclusion

As we ended the interview, I wanted to know whether Mick's friendships were different from those he had when he was younger: "As far as I can tell, the big difference in my life now, that colors every aspect of my life, including my friendships with others, is that now I appreciate everything so much more—deeper, wider, stronger, more present in my conscious mind. While I'm sure I took almost all friendships for granted earlier in life, now I am ever reminded and so much more grateful for how lucky I am and have been in my relationships with my friends. Now what I need to do is let 'em all know it!'"

Mick talked almost exclusively of *must* friendships, although he did mention his *just* friends, those who are not inside his "circle," and his online friend. In his 50s, he is at an age when he is starting to appreciate the role that friends can play (even those he only knows online) once the children are no longer the central focus of his life. And he has turned friendships into a life preserver, a guard against loneliness. He appreciates them now more than before. He hints at the understanding that life is not going to go on forever and that he better appreciate the good things he has, which include his friends.

Men in their 50s can no longer ignore the aging process and everything that goes with it. Retirement looms, especially for men in their late 50s, the daily demands of children are diminishing, and talk turns to what to do with free time. The arc of life that pulled men away from friends is now shifting to a point at which men have more time for friends. This is a great period in a man's life, when he can reach out to others to rebuild friendships or seek out new ones. But, unlike the man in his 40s, these new friends can be made based on the man's interests and not on his children's pursuits. Wives, often the emotional caretakers of the family, may also be encouraging friendship-building activities, possibly through relationships with other couples, and children may also be prodding their father to explore new vistas. In their 50s, men's comfort and satisfaction with themselves can often be high, making it a wonderful time to connect with others.

11

Michael in His 60s: Friendships Shaped by Early Experiences

I think the most important thing is not to try very hard [to make friends]. The older you get, I think people get suspicious of people who are trying too hard to do anything.

Men in their 60s are less apt to retire than their fathers were at this age but retirement is still the norm, with about one out of three men retired by the end of this 10-year age range, according to the U.S. Bureau of Labor Statistics (2006). Even for men who are working, employment is not as all-consuming as it was. There is more time for friends. At the same time, with retirement may come relocation, as is evidenced by the retirement community boom. Old neighborhoods are left behind, and new ones are entered as people move to smaller residences requiring less upkeep. Many residential shifts are to southern climes and are centered on lifestyle interests— people want to live on golf courses, near the beach, or where it is warm, so that they can spend more time outside and escape the vagaries of winter. Such moves require efforts to both make new friends and maintain the old ones.

What is the meaning of friendship at this age? The drive to find ways to keep busy, although stronger in the later years, begins to pick up momentum for the man with time on his hands who is in sound health. Wives become more frequent companions for the men as shared activities play a great part in their lives. Friends are a primary source of satisfaction on a daily basis, particularly if children do not live nearby. Men appreciate still having friends, and friendships become less competitive. Rivalries of old, sometimes sprouting from work or jockeying for women, are laid to rest.

Michael, age 64 and white, is a highly successful architect in a Virginia suburb of Washington, D.C. He has achieved a great deal and feels appropriately comfortable with himself. Married, and the father of a 25-year-old son, he is a graduate of the Naval Academy and served one tour of duty in Vietnam during that war. A star athlete in high school and college, he speaks with a thoughtful air, occasionally punctuated by bursts of laughter. Much of his adult life is shaped by his early military training and war experience.

Our conversation took place in his office, which is filled with mementoes from his many travels. Like many men who were interviewed, he views himself as unique compared with others his age and explained why.

How Does He Define *Friendship* and *Friend*?

"I think friendships for me are a little different than how I would perceive others' friendships, and I think friendships really are a product of my history. I've managed to make my way through the last 60 years, I think largely influenced by my military experience. I compartmentalize my life from my early years, growing up and going through high school, participating in sports, and I suppose there are friendships that evolved at different levels. They were different friendships, and they had relative degrees of importance to me but I think having experienced Vietnam, and that is a very personal thing, that you get to truly understand the value of a relationship. A friendship is a kind of relationship that does not require any personal overhead. It is a frictionless relationship that I am not sure I can characterize, but it is a relationship that goes beyond the pure interpersonal contacts and actually bores down into the family relationships and everything else. A wonderful (*must*) friend is family, and is there for you. True friendships are ones where you understand what you expect of yourself in supporting that relationship."

Michael considers integrity central to a friendship and differentiates (*must*) friends from acquaintances (*just* friends) by what is asked of him. "None of my friends has ever asked me to do something that I honestly felt I didn't want to do—so they have never had to ask. There are others who make demands and somehow that diminishes the relationship." For Michael and the other older men, the idea that friends do not ask for anything unnecessary will be a theme that emerges again and again.

When I pressed him further about friendship, he returned to the bond formed by the military and how it affects more than just the immediate generation. "When I think about it, we are formed because of Vietnam and because I have as much fondness for the children of classmates who died in Vietnam as I had for them. I just visited the daughter of one of my classmates who died, and we have set up an educational foundation to provide scholarships, which she was one of the early recipients of. It is interesting when these kids come and ask you what their dad was like. . . . It's tough. Being a midshipman, this notion of friendships is quite extraordinary when you consider the classmate system (members of the same class are treated in a certain, predefined way by upperclassmen—this builds an enormous bond between classmates). Whether you knew the individual or not, it is a matter of shared experiences, shared losses. There is a lot in it, which is quite interesting with respect to the direction that the Naval Academy is taking today, where it is finding that, by virtue of wanting to look more like a university, it has de-emphasized the classmate system in part because, when we went, everyone had the same experience." In de-emphasizing the class experience, according to Michael, the experience became more individualized and the notion of community was diminished.

Michael downplayed the war part of the experience, although he had previously emphasized the shared nature of serving together. "Yeah, but the sharing is no different in many ways than playing sports in high school."

Wasn't Vietnam more intense than high school sports?

"It's all the same. A team sport is a lot different than an individual sport. A team sport, you subordinate your interests to the group, and I think that is how good relationships are nurtured. It is a constant subordination of your own interests in the interests of those around you whose values you share. All those things I learned about leadership at the Academy could somehow be boiled down to the fact that most people operate in their own self-interests, and friendships fall into that part of the thing where you are willing to forego your own self-interests. In business, it doesn't work that way. In friendships, it does.

"It is not painful for a true friend to do something for someone else. By example, one of my closest friends went to visit my mother who was in a nursing home when I was out of town. He didn't do it for any other reason other than he wanted to. Those are things you don't talk about, you just do it. You are not trying to get points."

Does He Have Enough Friends?

Michael has no doubt that he has enough friends. "I don't seek friends. It is not something I suppose I even think about in a quantitative sense—I think

I have some quality friends. I enjoy meeting people, and there are certain friends that I view differently. I have a few (*must*) friends that are like a narcotic fix—you just have to be around them because they are crazy, fun, and interesting people. I have some friends who are just so smart. They remember everything they read. They are so much fun. These are relationships that you enjoy."

How Does He Help Friends?

Like many men, he is able to pick up with a friend after months of no contact and will dedicate himself to helping him. And, like men who served together in the military, they will come to an old buddy's aid at the drop of the hat. He gives the following example of such a reunification, which ultimately left him dissatisfied: "I had a friend, a roommate in Vietnam, who was seriously messed up in combat. Saw some serious, bad stuff. I hadn't seen him in a while and, on top of that, his wife was killed while he was over there. He was seriously scrambled. He called me a while ago out of the blue from across the globe, and he said he was just thinking of me, and wanted to call. Then he became the head of a European major business operation and was posted in London with the corporation. One day he called me, again out of the blue, and he said he was desperate. He had remarried, and his wife had just walked out on him. I thought he was suicidal. I said, I will be there tomorrow morning. So, I booked a flight, gave him my flight information. I got over there, was met by his driver, taken to his huge manor house, and he arrives a little later from the office and I found out over the next three days that things weren't as I had thought. It turns out his wife left him because he was having an affair with the nanny. I was scared to death, concerned about him. Here I am thinking, I have gone out on a mission of mercy, and he had every opportunity to stop me from coming. I stopped my life for him."

Like many other men who were interviewed, having your feelings abused in that way would have killed the relationship for me, and I said that to him.

"Do you know how much airline tickets are when you buy them at the gate? (laughs). Well, it did change things. I took a slightly different view toward the relationship with him after that," Michael admitted. His friend asked him for help when, in Michael's judgment, he did not need it. In his opening statement, Michael said that friends did not abuse other friends by asking for assistance needlessly. This friend crossed that line, and Michael never forgave him.

I asked Michael if he thought that he is unique in the kind of significant, long-term friendships he maintains. His answer implies that he feels less connected with his peers because of his personality makeup and his subsequent military training and experiences. "I think I am in the average range in that way. There are people who, because of their experiences, some negative, really kind of disassociated themselves with the whole war thing. But I always associated myself with being adventuresome. It is not always that Jewish guys go to the Academy and like it and are risk takers in the same way. So, I really thrived at that and thought I was good at what I did. My friends from high school grew up and were cut out of the same mold as their parents. I was the exact opposite. I enjoyed going off on my own and never felt I needed a support system. That individualism that one develops, the certainty in oneself, is something they try and develop as a central element of command in the military. Command is a very solitary kind of thing. This philosophy has served me, and may have changed the nature of my relationships because you come to feel, through commanding, that you don't need people as much as others."

How Does Masculinity Affect His Friendships?

In many ways, Michael displays masculine characteristics through his military service and the way the military shaped him to be independent and not in need of others. He connects with men from a masculine position. He is loyal, as military men are taught to be. He also gives no hint of vulnerability. The interviews with the men in their 20s to 50s did not elicit references to rugged individualism in the same way as Michael's does. The older men lived through harsher times, and often wars, and their stories reflect it in terms of the reliance on themselves more than others.

In Michael's observation about masculinity, he believes it is a retro thing—men bonding together to do things that their fathers did. They are recapturing or unconsciously honoring their fathers. "Some of my friends think they should go on hunting or fishing trips together because that is something guys can do or something their fathers did. Pull out the beer, pass gas, and be guys. They have their duck hunting trip every fall and whatever. If I look at those guys, I would tend to think those relationships are ones that may be the last generation to do that. In some instances,

I know where the guys came from, but their kids may not know that as important. I've done these weekend sailing deals, and they're fun. But when I talk to the guys who go, they say their fathers went on these trips. They are being their fathers."

What Has He Learned from His Father?

Like many who grew up during the Depression, Michael's father worked long hours and, although friends were in the picture, his father did not serve as a role model for friendships. "My dad had his own business, and all he did was work. He had some friends, and, as it turned out, they were friends who were customers and became friends, and they would come in and chew the fat. He had some good friends but never had time because all he did was work. Got us through school. . . . My sister was two years older and she was quite introverted. I was the outgoing one, played sports successfully, was in a fraternity and socially connected, so I never really learned about friends from either of them. I never really thought about friends. In high school, there were six of us who were very good (*rust*) friends and, when we graduated from high school, we posed for a picture. Well, 22 years after that, when we turned 40, we got together and posed again in the same pose."

What Does He Do with Friends?

Michael pursues a range of activities with his friends. What is noteworthy and rare is that all the events revolve around activities that promote communication, rather than fostering a shoulder-to-shoulder relationship in which communication is a by-product. "Mark and I try to have lunch once a week, and we just talk. Mark is very proud of his wife's work (she is an author). Also, I love to cook, so we will have dinner parties. A lot of my friends, I just enjoy being around because the conversation is so interesting. Many of my friends have done a variety of things, including public service, so just hearing them talk, and these are all accomplished people, especially my Academy friends. The one thing that kind of distinguishes us is that many of these guys have been in a lot of different places and are very interesting. The ones (*rust* friends) from my old home town are more interested in talking about vacations and sports. A lot of my really interesting (*trust* or *must*) friends and I have all read the same books. We share similar interests. One of my friends, I'll call up—his name is Will—and I will say I need a "Will Fix" because he is so interesting to talk to."

Although Michael is close to his high school friends, it is clear that the friends he made at the Academy and later are more intriguing to him. They may also represent, as with Mick in the previous chapter, a clearer separation from friends he had while growing up. "I will go back to the Academy for some reunion and meet people who were in school with me who I never really knew, and I come to talk with them and they are fantastic people, and I say to myself, 'I wish I had known them when we were in school together because they are such great people.' With my friends and with these people I've been meeting, you can spend time with them and, if they call me at the last minute and say 'Can you help me out?,' we would be there for each other. The bonds you make through the Academy are incredible. One of my classmate's remains were found in Vietnam recently, and a number of us went to the service. His grown children were there and wanted to know about him, and we could talk about him in ways that they never knew their father, all the idiosyncrasies."

How Does He Maintain Friends?

In terms of maintaining as well as losing friendships, Michael is a doer. He likes to help others as well as reach out to them when he has not seen them enough. "It is so infrequent that I ever ask anyone for anything. It is always, you see a need and you just try and be there for someone and provide some validation. I enjoy doing things for people and do not enjoy being taken advantage of." He has withdrawn himself from friendship, as with the friend in London. "I don't think I have lost a friend, but when you perceive someone is using your relationship, that it is one-sided, the only time I hear from you is when you want something, you become naturally a little bit [cautious] . . . and I guess that's fine, but it is just part of my makeup." He alludes again to the importance of his not being needy, although it is okay if a friend intuits that he has a need. That is how a friendship is maintained. The definition of a friend for him is someone who realizes a friend needs help and provides it without his asking for it, without the friendship being abused, and without too much vulnerability being shown.

What Has He Learned from Women?

Women are not role models for Michael's male friendships, "I would have no interest at all in having the kinds of relationships that women have because they are constructed, in my view, so totally differently than the relationships that I have. They become so overly personalized that at some level there is a total loss of objectivity between the parties, so it is almost a boom or bust and there's a constant 'Don't talk to me for another year' and then they get back together and you'd think they're cemented. There appear to be unrealistic expectations as to what a relationship should bring to the respective parties. . . . In my relationships with men, there are no expectations. You just enjoy it. You enjoy giving, you enjoy receiving. They are just frictionless."

For some men, friendships are nurturing but the nurturance is not talked about—it is just provided. Also, it is clear from Michael's perspective that communication just for the sake of communicating is unneeded. A man only talks when he has something important to say. He explains, "There is just so much stuff that goes on in women's relationships, they are just overcommunicated, too much communication. If I had to talk to Mark every day, I don't think our relationship would ever last because what we talk about we think is meaningful, and there are just not that many new and interesting things to talk about all the time."

Then Michael segues into a comment about the roles that women now play in men's lives, which their mothers did not play in their fathers' lives. Because men and women do more things together, less separation exists between husbands and wives. He also comments on where he sees the husband–wife relationships going. "Women play a far more important role. There has been a change. People have so little time today, and I personally did not realize how little time we had to enjoy family until a few months ago when I sold off another business I had. I didn't realize how much time it consumed, and I am now trying to catch up for the last 30 years of working my buns off. And, while I do think about taking a vacation with the guys sometimes, it would be just to be with the guys to screw around. I know if I went with my wife, it would be shopping. With guys, there would be no shopping. Do you want to call it a guy thing? It is not shopping. But society is changing. Guy things won't disappear but they will be a little different and softer because there are just some things that guys like to do that women don't, so it will never disappear, but it won't be one of these secret handshake type of things.

"Women are partners completely in families today. And the young adults today, it scares me, are living always at the edge, so consumed. When I was in my 20s, we were doing things that our parents who lived through the Depression couldn't do. Wives made dinner . . . and then you go to this nuclear family with air conditioning and then frozen dinner. [Then] the father is working later and the mother has to work as a necessity to the lifestyle. When mom is making money, it changes how money is being spent and rightfully so."

Conclusion

Michael's advice on how to make friends reflects his age—he is laid back and believes people need to be true to themselves. "I think the most important thing is not try very hard. I think the older you get, I think people get suspicious of people who are trying too hard to do anything. The question is, 'What do I want to get out of a friendship?' and try to be that friend. I think people want to be friends with people who share interests as well as experiences, so that friends are not someone to be around, they are someone to share other experiences with."

Michael grew up in the 1950s and '60s, when social conventions began to shift. Yet, he had a Depression-era father and an early experience in Vietnam. Men's roles and masculinity were still clearly defined when he was coming of age, but, as he observes, they have changed markedly since. A complex man, he has had to adapt to enormous social changes during his formative years. He has been able to bridge the new and old cultures by forging and maintaining *must* friendships that are characterized by loyalty born of war experiences. The friends he most enjoys being with are not from his childhood, but from later in life and include his wife. Yet, despite the masculine stereotypes he describes, he also has a good deal of face-to-face conversations and feels comfortable in these situations.

Showing vulnerability is not something that could be afforded during the year's of Michael's youth—a guy can give help, but he cannot ask for it. Friends have to anticipate it—that is how he is taken care of. For men in their 60s, vulnerabilities are creeping in to their everyday thoughts. Understanding that feelings of vulnerability are normal at this age can help men to relate to each other. Definitions of friendship may have to change so that men can ask for help, although not all men will want to talk about frailties or self-doubt. Friendships should be largely about fun, companionship, and a shared perspective on life. But they can be deeper and more satisfying when all topics can be discussed.

12

Donald in His 70s: Going Strong

Most of my buddies that I had close relationships with have died.

According to Australian sociologist Bob Pease, when a man retires, he often loses his workplace colleagues, the chance to be competitive in the workplace, his income, and the level of independence that comes with earning power and going to a worksite every day. This can threaten a man's sense of masculinity.[2] Gail Sheehy, a popular psychology writer, states that "men who define their manliness by expecting themselves to be eternally strong and able to overcome any obstacle alone" are often unprepared for what happens with aging, when physical and psychological problems begin to add up.[3] Some men seem to compensate for the loss of workplace competition, physical strength, self-reliance, and a possibly threatened sense of masculinity by remaining highly involved in contact sports. This allows them to stay actively involved with peers, compete in some way with peers, and forestall aging. Despite the changes that men have gone through by the time they reach their 70s, they often are still interacting with their friends in the same ways they always have. For retired friends at this age, it is important that [according to data from the U.S. Bureau of Labor Statistics, less than 10% of men over age 75 are still working] they can still hang out together. Donald, the man featured in this chapter, is no exception. He offers a divorced man's perspective on friendships at this stage of life.

I met Donald, age 70 and white, at a senior citizen center in a suburb of Baltimore. The Center, for people 60 and over, was hopping. It is a hub of activity for this age group, with activities including woodworking, basketball, shooting pool, and day and evening outings. Lunch is provided five days a week. It is part of the Department of Aging's outreach to the local community. Women were working out in the gym, others were cleaning up after lunch, and a group of men were watching a Humphrey Bogart movie on a big-screen television. Donald knew many of the lines from the movie and was anticipating a lot of the action. Some of the men sitting with him looked a little annoyed as he kept on calling out the lines from the movie—they would have preferred he kept quiet, so that the story line could unfold at its own pace.

Donald had been going to the Center for 10 years, since he turned 60, when he retired as a construction engineer. He does play sports but is also content with reading and discussions of politics.

At the peak of his responsibilities in business, Donald had 120 people working for him. A big man in good physical shape who appears quite vigorous, he has lived in Baltimore his whole life. His family grew up in a very close-knit Hungarian neighborhood. He has one surviving sister and another has died. Both his parents are dead, his father having died of alcoholism at the age of 61.

Donald was married 25 years and has been divorced for 25 years. He is the father of four children, ranging in age from 30 to 43. He is at a point in his life where his friends play a significant role, and his time with his children has diminished. It's unclear if he is not overly engaged with his children because of their wishes, his wishes, or a combination of the two. He apparently had an acrimonious divorce, and the children may have sided with their mother during the break-up. They are not mentioned during the course of the interview.

Donald's answers are often tied specifically to relationships he has built while attending the Center. These are relatively short-term friendships, given his age, and they vary in intensity from *just* to *trust* friendships. By his own description, he does not have a current *must* friendship. He uses the Center as his reference point, and it is now the greatest source of his friendships. In some of his answers, he reveals an independent side of himself that borders on the emotionally inaccessible. He may use that edge to keep people at a distance.

How Does He Define *Friendship* and *Friend*?

"A friend is someone who you can relate to age-wise, with similar experiences that you have had," Donald replied to the first question.

So, I asked, how do you decide who to befriend? "We have a lot of people here who play tennis together, so we have a similar sport that we both enjoy. I don't have really close friends anywhere."

To me, this was quite an admission so soon into the interview. I don't think younger men are as willing to make this statement, even if they believe it to be true. Maybe as a way of diverting attention from his admission about his lack of close friends, Donald immediately shifted the conversation and seemed to blame the management of the Center for hindering his friendship formation. He also revealed his view of women in his response, a view perhaps affected by his divorce. "You know, this Center is predominately run by women, and you have to change your perspective in life when you go from working where males have taken over to here where the women run it—they have never worked, they have stayed home, and then they come here and put down all sorts of rules. They are completely rule-oriented."

He then drew a distinction between his friends who are married and those who are single at the Center. It may be that he is acting a little defensively about his admission about his lack of friendships and is retreating from it. "The single men are friendlier than the married men, who still think of themselves as more family-oriented. The widowers and the divorced men and I can relate to each other because we are alone so much. We can identify with each other and relate because we don't have anyone at home telling us what to do—that's good and bad. Married men have totally different concepts because they are not out on their own. We single guys can go to dances and a lot of functions here where we can have a lot of fun."

Does He Have Enough Friends?

I asked whether, even if he does not have close friends, he has enough friends. His response touches on the changes that friendships go through over time and apply to *just* friends. "Yes—the main object here [at the Center] is to have lunch and come to meet people. People have sports friends, where they are up here just to play sports—we have a pool hall here where that is all they do. These people are also totally involved in tennis and get upset by a mistake. There are also TV friends, the guys you met. We know each other to kid around with, and the banter goes back and forth as it did when we were kids. (These are all *just* friend characteristics.) We don't hit below the belt, though. As you get older, you better get adjusted to the fact that life has limitations and what you did before with your friends, you probably can't do anymore—friendships are not as intense as when you are young and you are first married and things are more one-on-one than with groups." The admission in this statement is that limitations come with age.

Unlike many of the men interviewed, who often give up friendships when they are young and first married, Donald's friendships remained untouched early on. Most likely, when he got married in the 1950s, it was just assumed he would still be able to keep the group of pals he had developed as a youngster. Men and women led more compartmentalized lives then than now. "Marriage did not affect my friendships—we'd still play cards on Friday, go hunting, fishing. These were all classmates from high school, and I just kept up with them. I kept all those friendships for years."

But many of those old ties are gone, and he has built new relationships, although not necessarily *must* friendships. "I do have enough friends, even though many friends have died. (He did not recant his earlier statement about not having "really close" friends.) When someone new comes here, I can become their friend if the other guy is open to it. You do not have to be friends with someone for many years to be their (*just*) friend." Donald is not looking for, nor does he expect to find, a *must* friend at this point. He is looking for a guy to hang out with, although I don't get the sense that he believes a deeper friendship is impossible at this age. Some men believe that close friends need to be formed over years. This can be a healthy perspective, as it allows for the formation of new friendships when old friends move on or die.

How Have Friends Helped Him?

"It is hard to know how I have helped them, but I think it has been as a sounding board. What would you do *if* this happened to me or, now that this *did* happen to me, what would you do? We might have similar illnesses, male illnesses, that come up, and you would ask a friend what he has done about it. Illnesses are on the radio all the time." This is an example of how friendships (or even contact with others) can enhance one's health through an exchange of information and why people with friendships live longer and healthier lives.

Aside from health, I asked, how else do you and your friends help each other? His answer implies that most people are independent of each other. "In the pool room back here, we kick things around in terms of politics.

You might give them a ride home, but most of the time there is no money given as people here are in a pretty good financial position."

What Does He Do with Friends?

Talking about feelings is not a common activity for Donald and his friends. "Usually, we fish, hunt, tennis." I asked him if they ever get together just to talk, a typical face-to-face activity. "Very seldom." I wanted to pursue this because Donald seemed pretty gregarious and, if he wasn't doing much talking, I figured most men in their 70s were not. So, I posed the question a different way.

"Would you go for a walk with someone just for a chat?"

Donald replied, "I have dogs, and we will go for a walk with our dogs. We will talk about politics, what is happening in the neighborhood that is affecting things. Are you selling your house, moving?"

Anything about feelings? I asked. "No—men will shy away from that. We won't get into that." Donald is then engaging in a shoulder-to-shoulder activity, walking the dogs, as a forum for communicating. Also, this generation is not apt to easily share vulnerabilities.

How Does He Make Friends?

I asked what advice he would give other men on how to form friendships. Donald answered, "I sit at the right table. I am outgoing, so I will engage men by asking them questions about themselves. Where are you from? Can you believe how bad the food is here? Half of my friends here are women. But I avoid the table where people have a negative outlook as opposed to staying with a happy table. We can have a pleasant, funny, or serious conversation. I would also avoid people who are not capable of carrying on a conversation and some are [cognitively] handicapped in that way."

That is how a friendship can be formed, I reflected, but how would you keep a friendship alive? I asked.

He gave what I think is a typically masculine response, which may also reflect how he would want to be treated by others. "Don't push the other guy too much. If they are not feeling well, if they are quiet, then I try and recognize that they would rather be left alone." So, I offered, the notion of being able to read somebody is very important to you. This reminded me of Michael's description of a friend, in which he said a friend knows your needs without those needs having to be voiced.

"Right, Donald said. "The friend may be effusive one day and quiet the next day."

If you want to communicate with friends, do you call them, e-mail, or knock on their door? I asked.

He answered, "I don't do e-mail, and I do not contact the men, only the women. It is contact through activities. I would not call the guy just to chat except on extreme occasions. Most of my original buddies that I had close relationships with have died."

With the death of longstanding *must* friends, Donald has been forced to form new relationships and is open to these being significant, activity-based friendships. Also, as with Michael and the older two men whose stories follow, Donald does not use e-mail— part of the technology gap that exists for older men, and one that makes communication more difficult.

I asked if Donald had ever lost a friend for some reason other than death. His answer revealed something very fundamental about what he expects from a friend—support even if he is wrong. This is something many other men have said: men want someone to stand up for them to others, to be by their side if things get tough. Donald was hurt by a friend and deeply resented his lack of support. "Funny you should ask that— something happened with me recently, with my tennis playing buddy, where I felt he didn't back me up. Essentially, I felt he rejected me. (This is the first hint of vulnerability he has expressed since he said he has no close friends, although in this case he faults his friend and not himself.) I don't want honest feedback from a friend. I want him to back me up. I didn't think he backed me up in this one situation. So, I put him off. And we didn't talk for about a month. Then I told another buddy that I thought my tennis buddy was getting senile for not supporting me. That got back to him, and he came to me and broke the ice and said, 'Let's be friends again.'"

This sounded interesting, so I pressed Donald for more specifics but that was all he wanted to say about it. What was revealed, however, was a perspective on friendship: some men want honest feedback, others want backup, some want both. Donald is rare in saying he does not want honest feedback from a friend. Many men interviewed took a certain masculine pride in saying that their friends could tell them the truth, and they could stand up and take it.

How Does Masculinity Affect His Friendships?

When I asked Donald the question about masculinity and friendship, the first association out of his mouth was about sports. Regardless of age, sports is how men engage. "We have basketball teams here. Men are bonded through basketball. They play a tough game, and guys are always getting bruised and hurt. These guys are from 80 down to 60. There are serious games going on. I have never been a contact-sports person. I was never into football, basketball, or wrestling. I did not want to get injured."

Are you saying a notion of masculinity comes off the basketball court? "Yes—they get into this thing. It is real heavy masculinity. And I noticed that back in high school. Those athletes would come in unbelievably banged up, and that is how they made their friends." I ask if he agrees that men hang out together with men who have the same level of masculinity. His answer revealed a different side of him than the guy whose tennis buddy doesn't back him up. "I see it, but it does not apply to me. I prefer to see a male as an understanding, kind, thoughtful person. And, since I read a lot, I keep up on a lot of things that are happening in the world, like this crazy Iraq thing. I do see a more politically conservative view as a masculine thing. In order to accomplish something, you have to provide a basis for a goal, and the only way they saw they could prevent a problem there [in Iraq] was to take it over. They realized they would lose people and needed to sell it to the general public. Conservatives are more willing to take action and that is more masculine. Maybe they are just militaristic maniacs." He laughs, with a twinkle in his eye.

Here, he intentionally set himself apart from the traditional views of masculinity and the connection to sports. This was never him, he says. His is a more thoughtful and caring type of masculinity. The discussion of politics, which he mentioned initially, is one way he connects with other men.

What Has He Learned from His Father?

The conversation moved on to his father and his friendships. Donald paused, and I got the feeling he was about to reveal something highly personal—a secret. He speaks with a hint of shame. "Okay. This is good. My mother played the predominant role in the family. She was the breadwinner. My father was ill quite often and had an erratic work schedule, so she went to work and he took over a lot of the home duties, the cooking, and so on. So, the friendships my father had were mainly with relatives, his brothers. Other relatives would stop at the house, and we were part of a close-knit ethnic neighborhood. We all came over (from Hungary) at the same time, and everyone knew everyone. My father had friends when he was young, and they used to play cards. That was during the Depression, when people would get together who did not have much money."

I asked if his father was close with his brothers. "No, not that much. He was an alcoholic who died at 61." This revelation helped me understand his reticence and perhaps embarrassment about the role his mother played in his upbringing and his father's illness. Fathers were supposed to be the breadwinners in his neighborhood, and his father was impaired. Seeing a mother in the role of head of household, more so than a father, might affect some men's views of what masculinity means, and it may explain Donald's affiliation for caring and thoughtful behavior.

What Has He Learned from Women?

I ask if he learned about friendships by observing his ex-wife's friendships. Donald sees clear differentiations between how women and men interact with their friends and does not see women's friendships as a model for him. "My ex-wife maintained her friendships from the beginning—but I never thought I wanted that kind of intense relationship with my male friends. I still had my own male friends, and I was busy. I was preoccupied with two jobs, four kids, making ends meet, but I still had time for male friends. We were always able to get together for a few hours to fish. The costs [of fishing] weren't anything like they are today."

Conclusion

Donald's shoulder-to-shoulder friendships (his version of *must* friendships) were the standard of his day when he was young—get together, fish, but keep the conversation simple. Life was about working hard to make ends meet, and friendships did not involve sharing intense emotions. But Donald, despite his potentially difficult upbringing with an alcoholic father, has adapted to his current situation. Old friends have gone, but he has figured out how to stay active and involved. His philosophy, which reflects how he has adapted, came out when I asked him for advice for other men: "When you are older, you need to have a friend because you realize you should reach out, and the other person should bend, too." He is willing to meet someone half way, although he is not especially interested in an intense level of friendship—he never was. It was always about companionship. He may not want to share feelings but, like many men his age who grew up in difficult circumstances and during harsh times, he is willing to share his time.

As we see from Donald's level of activity, the 70s does not have to be a time to slow down. Although many friends are dying off (it is no longer just a few who have died), a man must begin to build new relationships if he is going to have male friends and stay engaged with others in meaningful ways. This is especially true for a single man, and it requires actively reaching out to others and perhaps compromising on long-held beliefs about what a *must* or *trust* friend is. For example, no longer can a man define a close friend as someone he has known for years—if he wants to have someone to pal around with who he likes and trusts, he will have to open himself up to men he has known for shorter periods of time. He will also have to be more tolerant in his friendships as the pool of available friends narrows—the politically moderate, Boston Red Sox fan who likes tennis may no longer be around. The hiker who keeps his political views close to his chest may be. It may be that, by forging friendships with new and different people, a man may expand his own horizons and continue to learn and grow.

According to psychologist Erik Erikson, who has written a great deal about development across the lifespan, the wise man maintains hope as he ages. He makes the most of his past memories as he opens himself up to new people. In so doing, he fights off the sense of general deterioration that comes with age. For those in their 70s and older, this requires active engagement with others, a letting go of past resentments, and a deep appreciation for playfulness.[4]

13

Tom in His 80s: Realizing All His Friends Are Gone

She is my only friend . . . she is my best friend.

Most people, by the time they reach their 70s and 80s, are clearly slowing down in all their activities. For example, my father retired from professional photography at 84, but his best work was years behind him. He found that, by the time he retired, it hurt too much to move from behind the camera to adjust a light to better flatter a subject. Working into one's later years is no guarantee that one is as effective as when younger. Although the average American lifespan keeps creeping upward, and health is better than ever, as one ages, fewer of your own generation are still alive, thus fewer long-term friends are still around. The trick is to adapt to these changing circumstances. Research suggests that people with friendships live longer and healthier lives.[5] Some people are better at adapting to their longevity than others, and sometimes that is the result of their earlier experiences with friendships. If they had trouble making friends when they were younger, they will have to work harder at it in their later years. At the same time, as sociologist Sarah Matthews notes, in writing about friendships in old age, physical and mental changes that come with old age can also make friendships, particularly longstanding ones, difficult to maintain at the same level:[6] a man sees his friend aging and becoming infirm, and he is faced with the loss of the friendship and the realization that he, too, can become infirm.

I met Tom in Arizona, at a family member's funeral. After the ceremony, I found myself in a corner with this man I didn't know, and I began the usual casual conversation. How did you know the deceased? Were you close?

I then asked him about his friendships and learned that all of his friends have died. "When you get to be my age, there isn't anyone left." This was not said with a twinkle or any hint of irony. It was a straightforward statement from a man who appeared lonely.

Tom retired to Arizona 15 years ago, following the death of his wife from emphysema. He is an attractive man, tan, trim, and looking younger than his 85 years. He exuded energy and good health. Although he (like Donald in Chapter 12) is single, he has a significant other who is the focus of his friendships.

Tom grew up in New York, on the Upper East Side. His father died when he was five and he, his mother, and three older siblings moved downtown to what he described as the ghetto, a neighborhood of immigrants from Eastern Europe and Italy. The family was very poor, and his mother was what Tom called a "char" woman, a cleaning lady. Over the years, their fortunes slowly improved and, like many families, they became upwardly mobile, helped, in part, by his older siblings contributing to the household income. "We followed the American dream," Tom told me. "We moved every few years from one apartment to the next. I went to school in Brooklyn and never finished high school, because I had to go to work at menial jobs to help support the family."

Tom was drafted into the Air Force in 1942, as a 21-year-old. "I was an instrument flying instructor for the Air Force during the war," he recounted with some pride. "After two years going around the country and training, I became a celestial navigation instructor for another year, and then left the service in December, 1945."

Life was not easy for him after the war. "I went back and had a tough time adjusting because my life in the service was orderly. I needed regimentation. My brothers and sister all got married, and I lived with my mother and took a job as a shipping clerk, and then my brother persuaded me to start a small appliance store with a minimal amount of money in Brooklyn. I finally got married and moved out, later than most of my friends. My wife came from a stable family situation with a house in Brooklyn. We kept on moving up to nicer and nicer apartments from 1953 to 1966, and then bought a house in Long Island and lived there until 1988. We had a happy home life with no problems. My son was born in 1955. He now has four children and is a salesman." Like many men, he marks off his life by what he was doing in terms of work and upward mobility. It is also characteristic of men and women who grew up during harsher times—the Depression and World War II—and had to adjust to the new realities of the 1950s, when the world was becoming a safer place in which to live.

"I pursued the business until 1957 and then sold it and went to work as a salesman for a series of larger and larger stores in Manhattan, until I retired in 1986. When my wife died, I moved to Arizona. This is where I met my significant other, as they call it nowadays. In the old days, she would have been my girlfriend. We have a fairly active social life but no sexual life because I can't do it anymore."

How Does He Describe *Friendships* and *Friends?*

Tom appeared depressed when I first interviewed him. As he talked about friendships, I sensed that he kept hidden more pain than he revealed, both as he talked about the present and as he reflected on his past. "I did not have many friends when I was young. I never made them easily. I was a street kid and, whenever my friends were busy, I would go to the library and read."

Why the library? I asked.

"It is a great place to hide from life. We moved a lot, and that made it tough. The friends that I developed, I developed in my mid to late teens. Those with whom I maintained a relationship over my life are all dead. They are gone."

Like Donald, in the previous chapter, Tom has outlived his old friends. When someone has no friends in the present, I ask about past friendships. I asked him what his male friends meant to him when he had them.

"A (*must*) friend is someone you can empathize with, you can rejoice in his triumphs and not rejoice in his difficulties. You can talk with him easily without difficulty in getting expression out, and [he is] someone who would come to your aid and you could go to with your help. I don't have that now." Tom's response again reminded me that he is lonely, a recurring theme throughout the interview. He also revealed a hint of vulnerability, in that a friend should come to his aid, without his flat out saying that he would need help or had needed it in the past. Like Michael and Donald, Tom danced around actually saying that he had asked for help.

"Friends are important—very much so. As a single man, life can be very lonely. I don't live with my lady friend but am with her on weekends and Wednesday night—I like my freedom, and I like to have my apartment. I wouldn't contemplate moving in; we are together, yet we are not together."

Is she your best friend? I ask.

"She [Edith] is my only friend."

His girlfriend is his one consistent contact with people outside of his relationship with his son (which is problematic). He appears to have always fended for himself in terms of relationships, and now finds himself extremely reliant on his girlfriend. They maintain a certain distance, however, which is increasingly common among older people who, for legal and financial, as well as personal, reasons see no reason to move in together or get married. But this relationship is also representative of what happens to a lot of men—their female "friends" outlive their male friends. Unless men develop younger friends, men who live long enough increasingly rely on women, who are the only ones left in their age range.

Does He Have Enough Friends?

I always ask people if they have enough friends, but it is clear at this point in the conversation that Tom does not. So, I modified the question to ask whether he had enough friends 20 years ago, when his wife was still alive. He had a few, but not many, a probable result of his particular upbringing. "I had three close (*must*) friends, but they are gone. I would call up and have a conversation with them; we had couple friends, too. I had one friend who moved down here but then he developed a problem with cancer and died." Couple friends are common among most married people, and these friendships sometimes wither when the marriage breaks up or a spouse dies.

What Tom *does* have is a number of acquaintances, or what Sarah Matthews might describe as "friendly relationships," rather than friend-ships.[7] These are men he knows from his condominium community, men met while exercising or going to various activities in the community.

How Have Friends Helped Him?

Tom's independent streak and pride in his accomplishments came out in his reply to my questions about how he helped friends and how they helped him. (I knew that Edith was his best and "only" friend, but apparently he does have *just* friends.) "First let's talk about money. They did not need it, and I am rather independent, though not necessarily financially as comfortable as my friends were. I don't like to ask for help if I don't need it, and I really haven't needed anyone's help." Here he is reluctant to acknowledge vulnerability. "The only time people came to visit me is when I was ill. It is not that I needed help—it is just the type of relationship that we had when people would visit—I was ill three years ago with pneumonia, and 12 years ago I had a heart bypass."

As people age, the notion of help often revolves around illness and infirmities. Not only did Tom's friends visit him when he was ill, but he helped one of them in a similar fashion—not emotionally, but through the provision of a service. "I was able to help my friend by driving him to the doctor. He never helped me, because my lady friend would help me when I needed it. My lady friend has stuck with me through all my problems. She is my best friend."

How Has He Maintained Friends?

He then segued into a discussion of friends further in the past and again reminded me of his losses, "I made friends in the Air Force and kept in contact with those people, but over time they disappeared. I was in a base in Idaho, and I became friendly with one of the families there, and I retained the relationship for years afterwards but eventually people went their own way. We had five to six close friends as couples. And unfortunately, they are all gone—this is one of the penalties of living too long. For one thing, all of my friends have all died, they are all gone."

I asked Tom about friends from his childhood. His answers devolved into the loss of friendships rather than the maintenance of them. "During my teen years, I went to school and then worked, so the only time I had free was weekends. We would go to the park, pick up girls, typical teenage things. Later on, when my friends went to college, I lost contact with them. They were busy, and I was working. I saw them on weekends. I was the first one to go into service. The others went into service, but they met some girls and then they became engaged and that's when the symbiotic relationship had ended. It was now a relationship of couples, and I was no longer included. They were married, and I was not—I was not married until I was in my 30s."

Why were you single so long when all your friends were getting married? I asked. "I was living with my mother, and I had dates, but I was working hard. I was sitting in a park in Brooklyn one evening, and a woman who I know walks by and gives me a piece of paper to call this girl, and it stayed on my bureau for two weeks. One evening, I called her and that is how I met my wife."

How Does He Make Friends?

Tom's response on how to make friends was quite blunt. "I don't know how to make new friends. It has always eluded me—I just don't know how to make friends. When you sit down and talk to people, it may be I rub people the wrong way. If I did not have my lady friend, I would be lonely. Things keep me busy—I like to read, be active physically—it is not easy to make a friend. Maybe I don't know how."

I did not believe Tom would easily "rub people the wrong way," at least at first meeting him at the funeral. He interacted easily with me and seemed to interact well with other people at the funeral. His distant relationship with his son, however, may be coloring his self-deprecating view. He may, given his early upbringing, be someone who is self-protective and does not easily interact with people.

I called him a year later, however, and found him in a more upbeat mood. "The chief complaint with the elderly is that life can be lonely. But, if you make up your mind, you don't have to be. I made a decision to not sit at home but to get out after waiting the proper mourning period after my wife died. A year later, I met Edith," he told me. Tom said he met men in his community and that he would ask them to join him for dinner occasionally on the nights he was on his own. He does not do sports, but he will also sit and talk with men and women. "Talking is a wonderful means of exercise both verbally and physically," he told me. He also helps out in the community by driving the police car on the community watch once a week.

What Has He Learned from His Father?

Even though his father died when he was five, I asked Tom if he learned about friendships from his father. I wanted to know if his mother ever talked about his father, and if his father's surviving friends were involved with raising him.

In his answer, I got a renewed sense of the extent to which he was left on his own during his early years. "My father died of lung cancer. I never got any indication from my mother about his friends. My older brothers had lots of friends, but they never connected to me. I was pretty immature for a good part of my early life and looked like I was 14 when I went into the service."

He felt uncomfortable around people, and his immaturity may have added to his reliance on his wife for friends and also, as he later admits, may have hampered his relationship with her. It also may have affected his relationship with his son. He mentioned his rocky relationship with his son when we first met and again when I interviewed him on the phone. Tom accepted responsibility for his behavior. "My son has his own friends. He and his wife have their own circle. As a salesman, he is great with people and his children—he has an eight-year-old and a six-year-old. My son loves me, but he does not particularly like me—I find it difficult to talk with him. It is not a relationship where you can sit back and talk. Maybe it is my fault—maybe that is the way it is—I don't know. I don't hear from my grandchildren, but maybe they have busy lives."

I tried to get him to tell me more about his relationship with his son, wondering if building closeness between father and son would help his loneliness. His response tells me it is not going to happen. "I take him for what he is and that is all there is to it. He is angry about my not being a good father or good husband—I probably was not. As I get older, I get wiser. I would do it differently if I had to do it again. My attitude toward his mother affects his relationship with my girlfriend. I was not a very attentive husband; I was too selfish, never unfaithful. But he is angry at that and tolerates me."

What Has He Learned from Women?

The interview ended with comments about women's friendships. "I get along pretty well with women. I go to a singles program in a church, and I am one of a few men. I associate with these people, and they treat me with respect and civility, which I like. Being masculine does not stop me having friendships with women. They don't look at me about having an angle. Everyone is nice until proven otherwise. You only learn once about a person's character. Women are better than men at making friendship— I have seen Edith talk up people while we are waiting for a table. She can talk to anyone and inside of 15 minutes they have exchanged names, where they live, etcetera. It works for me because who she meets, I meet, too."

Tom believes that women are different from men in terms of making friends. He grew up in an era when roles were more clearly defined. As a product of that era, his reliance on a woman to do the emotional work for the couple (taking care of the arrangements and handling discussions having to do with feelings) is obvious.

Tom's life is greatly enhanced, as this last comment shows, by his relationship with Edith. She is his *must* and, to a large extent, his only friend aside from the *just* friends he sees. This is typical of men who live into their 80s, given how few men live this long. But, at the end of our initial talk, and even after talking about Edith, he says, "Living alone can be a pretty lonely life."

After our second talk a year later, he is more upbeat. I tell him this. He doesn't remember much about our previous talk but does feel that life is good for him now.

Conclusion

People in old age are often left with few options for *must* friends. Tom initially imparted a sense of loss and loneliness, but looked at life with a rosier perspective the next time we talked. (This emotional shift is the nature of such interviews—people's lives can markedly change from one time to the next.) He has had few meaningful relationships in his life and has fewer now. He has never made friends easily and, because of this, does not seem particularly open to making new *must* friends at this stage in his life, perhaps because he believes he can't. From his reflections on his early life, it is clear that such attempts at new friendships would be a significant stretch for someone who never felt he was good with people and was a loner growing up. At the end of the day, he is down to one person— Edith—although he does have others in his life on a more superficial basis. For men in their 80s, activities like Tom's—assisting in the community, exercising, interacting with others, and going out to dinner—are key to both maintaining health and building better relationships. Making the conscious decision to go out after his wife died was, without a doubt, the best way for Tom to combat loneliness and approach friendships. Other men could follow his lead in making friends. As physical as well as mental capacities diminish, a positive spirit, even when friendships are difficult to form, may be the most important friend-making attribute.

14

Fred in His 90s: Thinking Maybe It's in the Genes

My circle of companionship has shrunk as I get older.

By the time a man reaches his 90s, he is a rarity. Less than 1% of American men reach that age, and women in their 90s outnumber them by more than two to one.[8] Out of a group of 100 men who were friends and classmates at high school graduation, only one or two might show up for the 75th reunion!

Where does a guy this age go for friends? The final stage of life leaves him searching—he must let go of those who have died and reach out to those who remain. It can be difficult for a generation of men shaped by wars, the Depression, and huge technological gains that both facilitate communication and intimidate those who are not able to get up to speed. These are men who were often raised to be independent, stoic, and to bear their discomfort in silence. Now, when they need others, finding peers and reaching out to them is difficult. At the same time, research on aging does show that traditional sex roles learned in young adulthood begin to change in later life. According to social worker Froma Walsh, men become more flexible and display increasing levels of passivity and greater needs for nurturance and affiliation in old age.[9] Some things do change that make it easier to reach out to others. While subsequent generations of men are having different experiences growing up and growing old, much is still to be learned from how these guys handle aging and their male friendships.

Fred, age 94 and white, is married to his first wife of 33 years, having remained a bachelor until age 61. He was a businessman most of his life.

Fred is remarkable in that he has been highly active all his life and played tennis until he turned 92. He still plays golf occasionally. His perspective on friendships is reflective of his age—friendships have a pace to them, he believes, and they start to slow down and are harder to form the older one becomes.

I interviewed Fred in his Washington, D.C., apartment where he and his wife have recently moved while they are building a new house. He doesn't really want a new house, he said, but his wife, who is in her late 70s, does. He shrugs his shoulders and smiles as if he has no choice. That is the kind of person he is—philosophical and easygoing.

Fred had very few friends until he went into the service in World War II. Unlike Tom (in Chapter 13), he does not blame himself for his lack of friends when younger. It was just the circumstances in which he found himself at the time. As such, he has always believed he was capable of making friends. He also has a younger wife, and they are still active as a couple. In his depiction of his life, he makes a clear distinction between the *must* and the *just* friends.

How Does He Define *Friendship* and *Friend*?

"I have had a rather unusual life when it comes to friends. My first friend was in elementary school—we had moved from New York to Philadelphia. He was really the only good friend I had until I went to high school. My classmates were black, Jewish, Italian, and Irish. They absolutely disregarded me, so for four years I had no friends. I then went to college because my neighbor, who was a coach, said I should go to Villanova, which is a Catholic college. I am Jewish, and there was only one other Jew at Villanova, and I commuted from over two hours to go to school there. So, it was hard to make connections. I had friends, but I guess I should call them acquaintances (*just* friends). I couldn't get to their parties, and I wasn't invited anyway. I went through four years of that. I had no chance, aside from in the neighborhood, to make good friends. I then commuted to graduate school at Penn—I had no male friends because I was in a school of education, which was largely female."

With his formal education over, Fred began working. But his difficulty forming close friendships continued. Fred referred to the status differential between him and his co-workers. "I took a job in South Philadelphia, and I couldn't be friends with people at work because I was the boss at 28.

That froze every type of friendship." Why did that freeze it? I asked. "I was head of the Company and making a lot of money and the people either admired me, resented me, or kowtowed to me, so I couldn't make friends. I then had a chance to go to Cincinnati, and that was interesting because I made one very good friend there. He was my only true friend since the friend I made in grade school."

Fred defines his friendships in terms similar to those expressed by the other men interviewed in this section: friends anticipate your needs without you asking them for anything specifically. A *must* friend knows you well enough that he anticipates your needs. "I met other men, but I would only call them acquaintances—to me there's a big difference. A (*must*) friend goes out of his way without you asking him to do anything for you. Other people will do things for you, but you have to ask them to and the same way they ask you to do things for them. But it is that spontaneous giving that makes it a friend."

Fred enlisted during World War II and served in military intelligence. He was surprised to be in intelligence near Germany, because Jews were not assigned there. "I found out I was the only Jew. I didn't look Jewish, and I had gone to a Catholic college. I didn't resent that, but because I was Jewish, I didn't have any friends. On Sunday, they would all go to church, and I was the only one left alone. And they would date Catholic or Christian girls, but I didn't go with them or get invited to the parties." His age was also a barrier to friendships, as he was in his early 30s and most of the men were younger. He did make friends, Fred said, with four other men in military intelligence with whom he worked closely.

How did he know they were his friends? His answer mirrors his earlier statement: that friends do things for each other. "We were very close. We had to take care of each other. We discussed personal matters, and we would lend each other whatever money was needed. We did all those little things that friends do—can I have the car tonight? Sure, but have it back by 12. Do you have any extra cigarettes? We were very close in that respect. I enjoyed World War II, because I contributed and I made friends. I know that sounds funny—to enjoy a war—but it is true."

Despite the terrible hardships of war, that experience was the first time that Fred felt he had friends. He felt connected to other people in a common cause. Males get this same feeling of connection through sports also, whether they are playing together on a team or rooting for the local franchise.

How Does He Maintain Friends?

I wondered to what extent he had stayed close with friends from his service years. "Paul got married after the war, and we stayed in contact and then it just died off. I don't know what happened. Another guy in Harrisburg got a job and had five children, and that took care of his time. (Fred was single at this time, which would have put further distance between him and this friend.) Jesse, another guy from the war, was very religious, and we hung out together and then that ended. But I am still in contact with Blaine. I can't call him a real (*must*) friend, but we were very close." He is no longer as close to Blaine as he was because, "I am not able to do anything for Blaine, and he cannot do anything for me. It is hard to be close when we are 1,500 miles apart."

To the question about whether he had ever lost a friend after a falling out, Fred said that whatever disagreements occurred were quickly forgotten, "I have lost an occasional friend—Mark and I had a falling out because he did not get a special assignment in World War II—I got it, and he got upset, but we dropped it in a minute and went on from there." This is consistent with Fred's self-contained nature—friends are important but he has learned to get by without them for significant periods of his life. Thus, he does not become overly concerned when friendships hit a bump in the road. Because of this approach, potential problems with friends don't escalate, and things work themselves out more quickly. Given his age, it is remarkable how few disputes Fred recounts, but it is consistent with the way many men approach their relationships. They try to keep them low-maintenance, make them work when they can, and let them go when they cannot make them work.

What Does He Do with Friends?

The notion that friends "do things for each other" is common among men, especially men at Fred's stage of life. It harkens back to the shoulder-to-shoulder notion of friendships, but also to an older notion that friendships meant physically helping each other out. It has been only recently that friendships have been pursued for the emotional value they provide, not just the physical assistance with moving, lending money, and doing home repairs.

From talking to Fred for more than an hour, I began to wonder if I had misread him—I thought he did not have friends because he did not fit in socially, but now I wonder if it is because he had not sought out friendships. I asked about his need for others as friends. "I am self-contained. I was in high school for four years and never had friends. In college, no friends to speak of—I was friendly, but no close friends. I didn't say, 'Hey are you going to this party and do you want to come?' When I became head of the company, there was that resentment I described before. So I did stick within myself a great deal."

Does He Have Enough Friends?

Fred believes he has enough friends. "I have Curt and Ted. Now Ted has aged (he is in his mid 80s), but I see Curt, and we play golf together. I see him once a week maybe, and we talk on the phone a little but if something is important we will get together to talk about it. We go to symphony, theater, and dinner together with our wives. I can't golf right now because I am weak with pneumonia. I will play golf with him in Florida and will drive across to the East Coast where he lives, and we will play there. But what else can you do at our age with your friends? We will talk on the phone about what happened to so and so. We don't call each other to chat; it is more to make plans to meet face-to-face. I am not much of a telephone person, so we go over to each other's places to chat."

Fred very poignantly sums up his answer to the question about having enough friends: "I do have enough friends, but remember—I am 94 years old. It is a little bit different if you are your age (pointing to me in my 50s). When I was younger, there were so many things I liked to do. I used to love to travel. I don't have that energy now. I used to go play golf or tennis a few times a week; I would go play football or baseball with my friends. I gave up tennis last year. I would play with people I knew, I wouldn't call them friends but they were golf or tennis partners (these are *just* friends). I would go out, and I don't do that any more. This change doesn't happen over night—it is an evolution or devolution, I don't know what you'd call it. My circle of companionship has shrunk as I get older. I talk with friends, and I think it has happened for them, too. Your business contacts stop, and your friends are gone. Attrition takes place, either naturally or through death, and you don't mind it because you yourself feel less able to do things. Maybe that is why you need fewer 'friends,' but you still need a *friend* (Fred's emphasis). Believe me, you do."

What Has He Learned from His Father?

Fred's level of self-containment is more easily understood when he explains his father's influence on his friendships. "I did not learn anything about friendships from him—he was a Prussian in every sense of the word. He was very well educated. He was arrogant, and I don't think people loved him at all. He had well-placed relatives, but they were not friends. My mother had a few friends, though no male friends. My father had very few friends. His brothers were very successful, but they were not close at all with each other. I, in turn, am not close to any relatives."

I wondered to what extent his father influenced him in making friends, and asked if he grew up telling himself he wanted to have friends because his father did not have friends. "No, not at all. I just saw how it was. I think I learned to be on my own because my father was arrogant and very alone and did not become proud of me until I became head of the company. When they told me I could take over the company and oust people, I didn't have the heart for it, so I left that company—where I was doing well—and went to Cincinnati. My father thought I was crazy. My brothers did not have many friends, very few. Maybe it is in the genes, I don't know. I never thought of it that way."

Fred learned, as a result of his father's behavior and the limited opportunities for friendships available to him, to be self-contained as a survival technique. His father rarely expressed pride in Fred. And when Fred first experienced his father's pride, even after having served in a war, he lost it by not appearing tough enough to fire people. The sense from Fred is that he was not "man enough" for his tough Prussian father.

What Has He Learned from Women?

When it comes to women's friendships, Fred is most amazed at their level of intimacy. He admires their ability for closeness, but does not feel it would work for him. "I think women do friendships very well. I think they discuss their personal lives socially and politically much more than men do.

My wife goes out and plays tennis and golf and must know 100 women, and she can tell me about what each of these women did. Some of the things she said were so personal, I would never discuss them with anyone."

Conclusion

As we concluded the interview, I asked Fred for any final thoughts, and he again returned to the theme of doing things for others as the measure of a true friendship, "Most of the people I have ever known did not know the meaning of friends. Most of them are not (*must*) friends—they will not do something for someone without being asked. Maybe women will do it—most men won't. Now, many, many men, if you ask them to do something for you will do it, but you have to *ask* them to do it. Men would not say 'I will do something for you' without being asked. There is one heck of a difference between the two. No one has ever done it for me—I don't resent it either. Maybe I didn't need it. That's part of ego, I guess. I really don't think men know the real meaning of friends!"

I believe that these older generations were raised at a time when asking was too threatening, a situation that is different from the one that exists now for younger men. Today, younger men have more role models to show them how to make their needs known and this, to me, bodes well for the future.

Regardless of how long we live, we need to work on building relationships with men and women that will sustain and nurture us. Fred has found great happiness in his marriage, and he continues to maintain one or two close male friendships. He remains, as many of us do, a product of his upbringing and perhaps, as he suggested, of his genes. He feels he does not need many people in his life and believes that is due to both the way he was raised in his family but also to his genetic makeup.

I asked Fred what advice he would give to other men in their 90s on how to make friends. His answer reflected what other men have said—that friendships take many years to build. And at his age, he also is not sure he wants to invest the effort in it, "It takes too long, years to do it. You can't do it. All my friends were made many years ago. You have to go way back with people. It will be easy to make new acquaintances (*just* friends) but not (*must*) friends. And I think, 'Do I want to make the effort to make new friends?' I would not avoid it, but I wouldn't seek it."

IV

MAKING AND MAINTAINING FRIENDSHIPS

15

Men's Fellowship at a Saturday Morning Church Group

A few years ago, I was a member of a panel at a professional conference on male depression and suicide. With me was a pastor who had heard me talk about men's friendships, and he asked me to give the same presentation to his church's men's fellowship group. Their reactions to the study and their own discussion of the topic provide insights into how men's friendships can be discussed in a group setting.

About 20 men met every Saturday morning in a suburb 30 miles outside of Baltimore for prayer, a breakfast meeting, and discussion. The men ranged in age from their mid-30s to early 80s, with most older than 55. They are a white, Protestant group composed mostly of plumbers, electricians, firefighters, and businessmen, World War II and Vietnam veterans. Friendly and welcoming to me, a lot of good-natured kidding goes on between them. But they are also a supportive group, as befits their pastor's demeanor and their own nature. Two of the members are brothers.

After a meal of eggs and bacon cooked by the men, I began my talk with references to Aristotle's writings on friendships.[1] I then talked about the social sciences research on why men have difficulty forming friendships.[2] I followed this with quotes from other men in my study, about how friendships were defined.

An hour's discussion later, I had learned a great deal more about friendships and how they operate, both in groups like this and for the individuals in the room, almost all of whom contributed to the discussion with questions and comments.

What follows are some of the significant remarks these men made as they reflected—in no particular order—on their friendships, past and present.

As with other men in the previous chapters, I have changed the names of the participants.

After I talked about Aristotle's belief that you can be friends only with a peer, Steve said, "I consider the Pastor a friend, but I don't consider him a peer—I hold him in reverence because he is closer to God as a minister. I have him up on a pedestal."

Hank asked, "With Aristotle, are we talking about his society or this one? Was peers defined by him back then?"

Jerry answers, "Yes, but they are less defined today (pause)—now you can even be friends with a plumber (laughter)."

I then raised Aristotle's point that you should not have too many friends, that friendship is such a pure state, it can only be achieved with a few people. The pastor chimed in, "Some poet once said that if you can count the number of friends on one hand, you have wealth beyond all measure." Frank added, "I try to tell my children that same thing when they tell me about friends they have made I say, 'Wait a minute! You have only known these guys for three weeks—they aren't your friends.' I have worked with a bunch of guys, but I only consider one or two true friends."

"Aren't there levels of friends?" Bill wondered. "To me, in a time of need, I can count on that person, that (*must*) friend—no questions asked—he will come and help me. Once in Virginia, on the Fourth of July, my RV cable to my car breaks down. I call my friend, who leaves his family on the Fourth of July, and drives all the way down and picks me up. That's a friend."

"How many people do you have like that?" I ask.

Bill holds up his hand. "One."

Hank spoke again, "There are different levels of friends. There's the top level, the closest (*must*) friends—that's my perception—all these gentlemen here are my friends. I have functions at my house, and a lot of them come over, and that's friends. We all have that. When you first meet a person, you might stand away from them, but as you get closer, you stand closer to them (*trust* friend). And if they become really close (*must*) friends, you might be able to stand toe-to-toe with them and not back off. As you become more comfortable, and the friendship grows, the sphere becomes more open."

Murray jumped in, "I see it like a sphere, too—you are in the center and your friends are next closest to you and then the outer loops may be people who help you through random acts of kindness. I may do something for Steve, but it might happen because it is just out of the blue and I may feel good about it that day. But he couldn't count on me the same way that I would go down to Virginia on the Fourth." This, to me, is one of the classic ways to differentiate *must* friends from others. You can call the *must* friend on the Fourth of July and ask for help.

I described the friendship categories of the Buddy System. Steve responded, "That doesn't diminish the levels of friendships—you do different things with different people. That is just how it is. I have my football friends and my church friends. Many of you don't like football, but you are still my friends for other things."

The pastor moved the discussion on, "To put the five *(must)* friends that you can count on your hand into a relationship, you have to go to the Bible, where it asks, 'What greater love does one person have for another but that he would give up his life for another?' If you are talking about those people as your friends, would you give up your life for them?"

Steve responds, "Probably not. For my wife and kids, yes, but for a plumber? (pause again) No." (Laughter all around.)

Danny spoke up for the first time: "I would say, yes [I would give my life for a friend], if you are in the military."

"That is one of Aristotle's points," I stated. "To be friends, you have to share salt with another."

"Salt is also life," the pastor comments. "If you have really shared life in its most intense moments, like war, then you have shared salt with them."

Murray responded to the notion of the number of friends, "As you were saying, you could only have five friends, I disagree. I have more than five friends who would do anything for me. But how do you define friends?" he asked the group.

"One of my points," I responded, "is that it varies greatly from one person to the next."

Hank answered, "I like the friends in slots idea—that you have certain friends for certain things you do." At this point, as a number of conversations are carried on simultaneously, the men generally agree that different definitions of friendships exist. I then gave the social science definition about why men have trouble making friends—the lack of role models, fear of being vulnerable, fear of competition, and fear of appearing gay. There was general laughter at the reference to the fear of appearing gay, followed by a few jokes and some good natured hugging between men.

Hank asked, "Isn't the gay thing exclusive to this society? Didn't ancient societies, including the Greeks, have this as being okay?"

I confirmed that touching between men seems to be a much greater threat to men here than in many European or African countries.

Steve opened up further at this point, "I have seen great change here from when I first went into the military and today's society. But I also can tell you that my daughter's gay, and I went to a birthday party with her and I met eight women there, all of whom were gay, and I was extremely impressed with the people I met there from all walks of life. I took them all out and treated them to dinner, and it was amazing and not once was there an outward sign of affection, no hand holding or hugging. If you saw these women, and some of them were some dynamite lookers, you wouldn't know they were gay—but it is not something our society accepts."

Hank responded "Now, I think it is more acceptable for females to be gay than for men to be gay in our society. Why is that?"

Murray answered, "Maybe it is that men are envisioned as weak if they go to a situation and cry. I was in the military in the special forces, and you had to be tough—if you broke a leg, you smiled and kept on running."

The pastor then stated, "I think the fear is that, today, if you are a man and you come in contact with a woman who is a lesbian, it cannot possibly rub off and make you a lesbian, but if you meet a man who is gay, you are afraid you will somehow 'catch it' or someone is going to think you are gay."

I read some quotes from the men who were interviewed for the book. I had purposefully selected a few that made reference to spirituality and God, and I read one man's statement that he didn't need friends as he had God. The pastor picked up on that and said, "That doesn't hold up theologically. But I was thinking last night about today's talk. . . . why did Jesus pick 12 men of varying abilities to be his friends and begin this new religion? There was a three-year bond of friendship with the disciples, and all but one went to their death with their beliefs, so it was kind of like the original men's group. It was the forerunner of what we have here today."

Steve returned to an earlier theme by asking, "How many people actually want to live out in the woods in Northern Canada without friends? I don't think most individuals do. Is it one-thousandth of 1%? As a whole, people need that interaction with other people. A few centuries ago, everyone was pretty self-sufficient—you had to go out and hunt for food, but we don't do that anymore. I go to the store when I want to eat. That's why solitary confinement is the worst punishment. I believe that no interaction with anyone else, and I've talked to a lot of P.O.W.s from Vietnam, and that was the worst punishment—solitary confinement. You can go nuts and lose it."

The discussion moved on when Hank asked a question that reflects his personal situation, one that resounded with other men. The question centered on divorce and the sense of loss of friends that comes with divorce. "How come you move to a neighborhood for 20 years, and you have very good friends, and you get divorced, and you lose all that. It is all flushed down the toilet, all gone? Did you really have them as friends to begin with?"

Benjamin, who had not spoken yet, agreed and adds that children play a role in friendship building. "I had a similar experience to that. When you first move into a development, you are sharing experiences with all those people around you, raising children, a lot in common with those people. And then you move to another development, and you have not shared those experiences. Friendship is sharing experiences with others, and when you move into the new area you really don't have this common experience."

Steve chimed in: "So, what you are saying is that your commonality changes. I moved from Rosedale 10 years ago, where I raised my kids, to near here. And my kids are all grown now. I have only kept in touch with one person from the old neighborhood!"

Murray added, "Children can open the doors to those friendships, and when the children get older, it doesn't happen as much." Stanley, also new to the discussion, added two disconnected thoughts, one in relation to the impermanence of friendships and the other a small piece of advice. "Those friendships may not hold. When I was married 23 years and we split, the friends went with her and the kids. I didn't have any friends. I get married again, and all of a sudden, I have new friends. But the second group didn't know what went on with the first marriage, and I thought it was none of their business in the first place. But you have to make friends for yourself."

These four men are describing the shifting alliances that are formed and end with marriage or with children leaving the nest (or with a change of job or new neighborhood). As Robert Putnam suggests, this can contribute to a breakdown in community connectiveness. As friendships are dropped with changing circumstances, people are less apt to know and assist each other.

The pastor returned to the connection made through the military, "Steve and I share the Vietnam war experience together and, with any other vet you meet, there is an immediate camaraderie. It is a form of friendship and—I hate to say it—but the whole Band of Brothers thing pulls you together. There is a lot to that."

Hank rejoined the conversation, "I was in a situation with other trades-men, and we would go out together after work, go to one another's home for cookout, go to dances. I got promoted and that ended."

Steve, supporting Hank, said, "There is a clear distinction between the worker bees and management. In the military, they teach you that you cannot lead and guide the troops unless you had their respect and you separate yourself from the normal partnering. There was a bit of separation between you and the other guys."

Hank asked, "Isn't that what Aristotle was saying about peers?"

Steve responded, "Yes. When you move up, you may have wanted to continue the friendship, but they have a tendency to feel that they don't want to watch what they say. If you are management now, it may get back and hurt them in some way."

Reinforcing this theme, Murray stated, "In the military, the higher you go, the fewer friends you have—they even say, that you should not make friends."

Benjamin moved the conversation back to his situation and the difficulty he had maintaining friends in a new environment, "Before my brother moved down here, we weren't close (his brother is sitting next to him and nods). Now we are close and, being my brother, he is my friend also. But I feel uncomfortable. If two women want to go out and eat together, no one thinks anything of it. But take two guys, and people will think we're gay and that isn't right. And some times it really bothers me—I want to turn around and say, 'What are you looking at?'"

The topic changed back to the boss–peer discussion raised by Hank and Steve. Bob was a fire chief and said he was invited to parties with the other firefighters and had to stop going, "I felt like I couldn't get too chummy with people outside of the firehouse because they wouldn't listen to any-thing I would tell them to do at work. It eroded my authority."

The talk meandered for a while as people got more coffee. Murray returned to the topic when he said he puts God, family, and friends in the middle of his sphere, not himself. He believed that circumstances change those circles and who is close to you.

Steve reinforced that idea, "Yes. Everything will change as you see different dynamics—your close friend is brought together by camaraderie." He then moved the discussion on to siblings: "Look, I may be a different animal than most of you guys here because I am an only child. It is only me—so I have a couple of close friends, people I can talk to [who are not siblings]. A true friend won't say to you 'You're full of crap.'"

I was about to ask him if he ever wanted a friend who *would* tell him when he is full of crap, when a new man entered the discussion for the first time, Fred. "Well, I have two brothers who I talk to a lot—that's something you miss as an only child."

Steve responded, "Yeah—who can I turn to? You don't talk to your parents when you're a teen, and I can't talk to them now."

Fred answered: "Shared history with your brothers—as you grow up you have the commonality, and you can talk to each other. My siblings and I live apart, but we know we can count on each other."

Another new man entered the discussion, Fritz, who immigrated to the United States from Switzerland three years ago. He told about his travels and what constitutes a friend for him. "When I left for the States, I left all my friends behind—I only have maybe one friend. So, I think the question that separates friends from less close friends is: Who is the one you call first if you have something very important happen to you? That clearly says who your friend is. And if you go back to your old town, as I did, and you only have three days, who do you see? It can be with them like you were never separated."

I wanted to follow this thread, too, about prioritizing friends, when the pastor stepped in with some humor. "Nowadays, it is who you have plugged in on your cell phone that constitutes a friend."

Steve turned to Fritz, patted him on the back, and supported his journey by saying, "You made a decision to come to the States and to give up everything, and I think that takes a heck of a lot of courage. You are taking that step forward, and it is like falling off a cliff. And we are glad to have you." This encouraged Fritz, who replied, "We talk about friendships as only being in times of war, but it can also be other times. One of my friends was there for me at a difficult time when I was writing my master's thesis and something happened. So, friendships can be built at other times of crisis. I was completely blocked in my writing and this guy jumped in and helped me write. And that is a friendship. And we all have different situations in our lives where we have such friends."

The pastor answered with, "Actually I would hope that we could have brotherhood without war."

Benjamin returned to an earlier theme about sharing commonalities and how the sense of community is disintegrating. "The Masons, the Knights of Columbus, the Elks, were such places, but over the last 50 years these organizations have mostly died."[3]

I spoke up when people began wondering why those organizations died and offered the opinion that the family has morphed considerably over past half-century, with changing roles for women and men within the family. Men do not go off to men's clubs and leave women with children the way they did in the past.

Murray took the discussion in a new and important direction when he said, "A friendship is not something that, once you obtain it, you have it. It's not a goal; it is a journey, and you have to cultivate it or lose it. But, as I am talking, I am wondering if you really lose it if, 10 years later, a person is still your friend?"

As the meeting ended, the men continued to talk about friendships.

What can we conclude about male friendships from this day in the life of a church-based men's group? The men talked about the common bonds that can be built in the military or at a time of crisis. They talked about the difficulties of being friends when someone is not a peer, and they spoke about feeling uncomfortable when spending time with each other for fear of appearing gay. Another clear message, however, was the hurt that some felt when their life circumstances changed and they lost friends. Men who divorced or moved found themselves bereft of friendships and wondered if these friendships were ephemeral after all. It may have confirmed for some their deepest fears: that male friends were not there for them and that they were not liked for who they were—only for the circumstance they found themselves in by dint of marriage, children, or residential proximity.

These men, who have voluntarily joined the group, and perhaps many others, may do better when friendships are structured, so that less doubt exists about one's own likability. In the fellowship group, in the military, in the sports arena, men come together and enjoy each other's company within a structure that makes it safe to interact without the fear of rejection, which may occur "outside" the group, when the ground rules change. For all of us, the ultimate challenge in life remains: How close do I get to people, and how much of myself do I share while coping with the fear of rejection? These men are willing to charge ahead and try to connect with other men. They probably do it most comfortably in the context of a church group or a structured setting, where a leader or a defined purpose is present. At the same time, some of the men have definite close ties with men outside the group, men on whom they can rely—the story of the Fourth of July trip to Virginia comes to mind.

In these ways, these men represent a cross-section of men in the book. Some are a little wounded by past rejections, shy of new friendships, and approaching them with their shields up. Other men are held slightly at bay but remain an important part of their lives, as is evidenced by the group's comments. Others seek out and maintain important and deep bonds (*must* friendships) that were forged by common experience. Many of these men may have been buffeted by negative experiences, but they are able to shake them off and look ahead. To all men present, friendships are important—how they think about and act on them, however, varies.

16

Stepping Up to the Plate With Your Friendships

By this point, I hope that you have gained some helpful insights into men's friendships. In this final chapter, I offer observations about friendships and suggestions for how to make and maintain friendships with other men. Some of these suggestions are supported by the more than 500 men and women interviewed for the book, and some are my own ideas derived from my observations and interviews.

Observations About Men's Friendships

- Men want friends. Most guys will make attempts, sometimes clumsily, to make friends because they wish they had more of them. Their attempts are clumsy because they fear being rejected when they reach out to potential male friends. If men are competitive with each other, it is difficult to reach out to another man and ask him to join you for a ball game or lunch. Reaching out makes a man vulnerable, and some men are uncomfortable being vulnerable with another man.

- Many men have significant friendships—they just don't express them in the same way women do. Contrary to the opening quotes from men and women who thought this would be a short book, men have a great deal to say about friendships. These men's friendships are not defective or unfulfilling because men are less expressive than women—their friendships are just different from and of lower maintenance than women's.

- At the same time, some men definitely feel lonely and unable to communicate their feelings to other men (and sometimes even to their wife or significant other). These men's feelings are not easily revealed during interviews, and men may need more of a relationship before they can share. When I meet men and talk to them about the book, many men say they are interested in the topic and want to learn more about their own friendships. The topic strikes a chord. Unless these men learn to connect more with other men (and women), they may continue a more isolated and potentially less healthy existence.

- Men's friendships come and go in importance throughout a lifetime. When men are young (teens and early twenties), friendships are very important. As we age and become involved with a wife (or significant other), children, career, and home care, we have less time for friends. When we get older and the marriage or relationship solidifies, the children need less attention, and our career is more settled, increased time is available for friends. In later life, and with retirement, there is a greater need for friends to provide companionship. Recent research cites the impact that caring and companionship can have on living a longer, healthier life. Connecting with people throughout life may be lifesaving, particularly in times of personal and community crisis. Note the many stories of survival from people who helped each other during Hurricane Katrina as one example. Associating with others is in; isolation is out!

- Older men are more apt to describe situations in which they helped others rather than being helped themselves; they describe friends as being people who understand them and offer them help without their asking for it. Younger men may be better at asking for help and admitting vulnerabilities. This may bode well for future generations of men.

- Some men have their wives as their best friends. I am happy for them. I don't believe there is a primordial, cave man need for men to commune with men throughout life. Although I would like to believe that people need to commune with somebody, from the interviews, I know at least a few men say they are content with not having close friends. We must be careful about any kind of one-size-fits-all mentality when we speak of the need for friends or the importance of men having other men as their best friends.

- Some men envy women for the intimate friendships that women have with each other, but a lot of men don't want that level of closeness or sharing. These men think women's friendships are too emotional, too intense, and too mercurial.
- Homophobia and the fear of appearing gay remain significant impediments to having close and intimate relationships for some men.
- Some men remain stuck in an adolescent phase of friendship, one in which they never get beyond the interactions and activities they pursued with friends when they were younger. Although maintaining an adolescent level of interaction often keeps a guy feeling young, brings back youthful memories, and is fun, it should be coupled with the ability to act age-appropriately in the right context with that friend. I believe it is not beneficial to be stuck in an adolescent phase all the time—men should continually evolve levels of communication with those they love and with their male friends. But, too often for some men, an emotional regression occurs when they get together, which may be a defense against exploring other ways of relating on a deeper level.
- Men have the capacity to form significant relationships late in life, but they usually choose not to. Trust is very important to men, and it is difficult to establish trust with new friends late in life when those men have other or competing friendships that go back many years. Men instinctively compare the new friendships with the old. New friendships lack the many fond memories related to youth that older friendships bring back. Although sticking with the familiar and comfortable is an understandable tendency, it closes men off to forming new friendships that may nourish and sustain them in the future.
- Spirituality plays an important part in many men's lives and, in some cases, replaces the need for friends. A few men specifically indicated they do not need friends because they have a relationship with God. The religious venue, as in the example of the church fellowship group in the previous chapter, provides opportunities for men to make friends within a spiritual community. For people looking for greater meaning in their lives in these uncertain times, the link between spirituality and friendships is clear—both can help provide meaning.
- Race-based differences between men's friendships can be discerned in some cases. It is human nature that members of a minority group are more apt to rely on each other than are members of groups in

the majority. African Americans historically have relied more on community connections for their sustenance and survival than have whites. Here, the African-American men appear to form bonds more quickly with each other than do the white men with each other. Cross-racial friendships are more difficult to characterize, but appear generally to be on the rise in the United States. At the same time, although race can help determine the nature of friendships, a man's upbringing, role models, and disposition are also predictors of the type of friendships that he will have. Ultimately, it may be that what men look for in other people is trustworthiness, dependability, and loyalty. These characteristics may come to trump differences based on race (as well as differences based on religion, class, or sexual orientation).

- Women are puzzled by men's friendships. They want to understand them to a greater extent than men are interested in understanding women's friendships. Over the past five years, since I began writing this book, many women have said to me that they don't understand their husband's or their friends' friendships. Women want to understand the men they care about as well as their friendships, which sometimes interfere with the relationships the women have with the men.

- Reading about how other men make friends and what their friendships are like can help any man make friends. If you have read what other men have said and have not reflected at all on your own male relationships, go back to the beginning and start again.

The Buddy System: *Just, Rust, Trust,* and *Must* Friends

Every new encounter begins at the level of acquaintanceship or *just* friendship and holds the potential for growing into a more intimate relationship (*trust* or *must*). For those men open to new friendships, this could be the goal of every encounter.

Just Friends

Some men, depending on the context, have no intention of growing their relationships. For example, many men at work wish to keep people at the level of a *just* friendship. Their co-workers are enjoyable to be around and are necessary to interact with for the functioning of the workplace. But there is little desire to interact with them outside of work or to trust them in the workplace. The more competitive the workplace, the less the trust, and the less likely a closer friendship will be formed. Why trust a colleague with the news that you are looking around for another job if that news could get back to the boss and result in her giving a plum assignment to someone else? In addition, and thinking back to Aristotle's discussion that a man can only be friends with a peer, the boss–employee relationship is also unlikely to become one characterized by a *trust* or *must* friendship. By definition, these relationships must be kept at a distance.

Other men have no desire to change their *just* friends into closer friendships because they are content with that level of friendship with those particular people or they have other, close friendships. Clearly, many men only have so much time and emotional resources for very close friends. Having friendships at a casual level is all they are interested in. Some of the guys with whom I play golf are an example—nice guys, fun on the golf course, but I do not want a greater level of intimacy with them. We don't share the same interests (outside of golf) and the same values. If they wanted to go away for a golf weekend, I would probably skip it as I wouldn't want to spend that much time with them. There's nothing wrong with this—it is just the level of friendship I wish to pursue with them. These *just* friends are seasonal friends—I see them a great deal during golf season and then go for six months with no contact. Men with second homes have seasonal friends also—they see them during the winter when, for example, they go south, and then they don't see them again until the next year.

For men who want to change their *just* friendships to closer ones, specific suggestions are included in the next section. These tips will teach guys how to build friendships and how to maintain and deepen them.

Rust Friends

Rust friends are the old-timers. When men are with *rust* friends, they revert to the age they were when these bonds were the strongest—unless the *rust* friend has developed into a *trust* or *must* friend. As I write about in my poker game, some of my *rust* friends have gone on to become my closest friends. This is one natural evolution of old friends with whom someone has stayed close. Many friendships, though, don't grow past the level of high school, college, or fraternity acquaintance as adulthood approaches. Yet, these people continue to be part of our lives, as we see them in the neighborhood or at reunions. They remember us when we were at our most imbecilic, sophomoric, or heroic, as the case may be. We are strongly imprinted in each other's psyches.

Men have ideas about how they should act that are often formed and crystallized in childhood. When with their *rust* friends, some men revert back to those types of actions rather than acting as they usually do, as more mature adults. Some guys find it difficult to be their more adult selves if they are being treated as if they are still in their adolescence. I see a guy around town from time to time who knew me as a kid and thought I was a complete jerk. Every time I see him, I still think he sees me as a jerk. (Let's assume for the sake of discussion, please, I am not a jerk any more.) I feel uncomfortable, and maybe I begin acting like a jerk when I am around him or maybe I revert back to feeling some of the same insecurities I felt as a teen. I could argue that he is more of a *rust* enemy than friend, but this same process works with friends, too.

This behavioral imprinting can often be reprogrammed with *rust* friends. Think about the high school nerd who returns to his 20th reunion as the president of his company or inventor of the latest lifesaving device. Think about the high school quarterback who returns 40 pounds over-weight. Talk with them, always being open to the possibility that they have changed; this open communication can reduce the knee-jerk reaction of treating them like the nerd or the 17- year-old quarterback they once were. Conversations and openness work both ways. As we learn about how others have changed, they learn how we have changed.

Trust Friends

Trust friends are, for some men, quite enjoyable because they are fun to be around, they are trustworthy, and energy permeates the relationship. Mick talks about it in Chapter 10, when he describes the sheer delight of friendship with both his *must* and *trust* friends. *Trust* friends don't demand as much as *must* friends, and the expectations are not as high on a *trust* friendship. These friendships are a little safer for men, as they are often slightly less intimate and revealing. It is kind of like dating someone and enjoying the contact but keeping love out of the equation. Most tales in this book about men getting hurt in friendships with men involve *must* friendships, in which someone let someone else down.

Recently, I interviewed one of my own *trust* friends, who heard about the book and wanted to be interviewed. He is a 60-year-old family sociologist living and teaching in another state. I'll call him Louis. Louis' wife became very ill last year with a heart problem. He called his only *must* friend to tell him about her illness. This friendship is quite close—they kayak, have dinner alone once a week, and work on campus together. Louis has no children, and his friend is single and 20 years his junior. They are both of Italian descent and are quite comfortable giving each other a hug. The problem arose when Louis' friend did not call Louis back within a few days of the operation to see how his wife was doing. Louis was hurt and called the friend on it. "What's going on, guy? I tell you about my wife and you don't call? I thought we were friends." A *must* friendship leaves a man open to this sort of possible hurt. Louis' expectations would not have been as high if it had been a *trust* friendship. They worked it out, but it set the friendship back a few notches for a while. If they had not worked it out, it might have convinced Louis to not get that close again with a guy.

Trust friends can also be "friends-in-training" to move up to being *must* friends. People should have a large cadre of such friends, because they can be cultivated when the time comes for a man to expand his circle of closest friends. Particularly as we age and as opportunities open up for more friendships, *trust* friends are those who can be called upon and either maintained at that level or pursued for a higher level of intimacy.

Must Friends

Men define themselves by the people who occupy their highest level of friendship, the *must* friends. Who we are as men is reflected in who our friends are. If we return to Aristotle one final time, we see that, for him, friendships are a high calling and something that only people of character can have. If our closest friends are people of character, we are apt to be people of character. Making and nurturing friends who are good people is very important to building a better community. It is something we all must strive for, both in our own lives and in the lives of those to whom we are closest.

Observations on Friendships with Family

A number of men (and women) said their families (brothers, cousins, sisters, wives) were their best friends. Family members fall into a different category of friend. They can not be considered in the same light because these relationships are so much more complicated. Most friends you can drop if something goes haywire. With family members, it is a bit more difficult.

Strong and nurturing family relationships definitely reduce the need for friends, as we heard throughout the study. Dysfunctional or nonexistent relationships within the family often increase the need for friends. There are various views on why friendships may or may not develop between family members.

Psychiatrist Murray Bowen[4] describes how family interactional patterns are handed down from one generation to the next. By drawing a family tree, one can look at how people in previous generations related to each other. Let's use a Make Believe Guy (MBG) to illustrate how this works. MBG's father was never very close with his own siblings and taught John that his aunt and uncle should not be trusted. Maybe some money problem or nasty competition engendered by MBG's grandparents scared MBG's father away from being close to his brother and sister. It will be difficult for MBG to trust his own siblings, given what he learned from their father, so he seeks friends outside of his family.

In contrast, I received a different message from my father—although he had few close male friends, he was very close with his younger brother. I, in turn, am close with my brother, while also maintaining some *must* friends. I believe this is not happenstance: my brother and I are close because we learned from our father and uncle that brothers stick together.

Bowen teaches us that families can, with insight and understanding of familial patterns, pull together for mutual benefit. If you are stuck with a family pattern that you do not like, and you are not close with your siblings, Bowen would encourage you to try and understand your family patterns and take steps to change them by talking with family members and learning new ways to interact. Another psychiatrist, Ivan Boszormenyi-Nagy,[5] thinks of family history as a ledger—if you did not get enough love or affection from your parents when you were young, and you think your siblings got too much, you will carry that feeling of negligence into adulthood. It will be hard for you, as an adult, to be friends with your siblings because you will continue to focus on what they got that you did not get—love. Insight into what, in the past, upset you about a sibling can help you in working it through in the present. An awareness of the family's culture can also be helpful, as some cultures historically value closeness and community, whereas others value separation and autonomy. When people from different cultures marry, multiple, conflicting messages may be passed down. If you have a mixed-culture family, it may be especially difficult to figure out why closeness is valued by some part of the family, while distance and self-reliance are valued by another part.

Virginia Satir,[6] a social work and family therapist, zeroed in on the importance of clear communication between people as the basis for building healthy relationships. In her model, people with good self-esteem communicate well with others and can have adult conversations with them. If communication within your family is not as good as it could be, she has a series of exercises for understanding poor communication patterns and working to improve them. For example, having trouble communicating with your sibling? Try sitting back to back in chairs and talking without being able to see each other. You will no longer be able to rely on the old cues like height or facial expression that have been such an integral part of your communication over the years. This will force you to more clearly say what you are feeling and not present a mixed message.

Sometimes friend relationships are easier to change than family relationships—less history is present and less is at stake. But, by working on family issues, a guy can get a better grasp of his relationships with and need for friends.

Suggestions for Making and Maintaining Friendships

I have broken these suggestions down into three broad categories for easier understanding. To make friends, you have to first understand what is going on in your own life. The first set of suggestions centers on steps to take before starting the friendship-building process. The next set has to do with how to make friends, and the third with how to maintain the friends that you have made.

Understanding Yourself

- What type of relationships do you want to have with your friends in terms of the level of feedback you give and receive? Will it be the "all accepting" or the "tell it like it is" friendship? It is possible to combine both, being quite honest while also being accepting, but that requires a high level of trust and connection between two people. Remember—as the poet Emerson noted, the best way to have a friend is to be one.[7]

- Think about how you define friendship and if you are applying that definition to your friends. Can you be yourself with your friends, do you have mutual sharing with them?

- Consider whether you are too tied to high school friends to the exclusion of more recent ones. If so, you may be shutting off many opportunities for new connections. On the other hand, if you want nothing to do with your high school friends, this is a clear sign of unhappiness with them or yourself at that stage of your life. You should be aware that such a cut-off from your past, although it may be justified, may have an impact on your tolerance for making friends in the present. You may be overprotective of yourself in your current friendships.

- Understand your own family's history of friendships and see if that history applies to your current patterns of friendships. Did your father (or mother) have a lot of friends? Were friends valued in your home when you were growing up? Did you make friends easily when you were growing up? Your history can affect the ease with which you move in and out of friendships with others.

- Does reading about other men's views of their fathers cause you to reflect on your own father? If your father is still alive, ask him about his friendships, and use what you learn to reflect on your own friendships. If he has died, ask relatives or other men who knew him whether he had friends and how he treated them. Recognize that his influence may still have a powerful effect on decisions you make about how you value friendships.

- Think about the role that women play in the friendships you have made in the past. Have your observations of them resulted in your improving your own friendships? Are you emulating their friendships, or trying to avoid like the plague having friendships like theirs? Ideally, you fall somewhere in the middle and are taking from your knowledge of women's friendships ideas that apply to your situation and your personality.

- As women enter the workforce in increasing numbers, more opportunities are available to interact with them in a shoulder-to-shoulder context. By understanding how women's and men's friendships are similar and different, better communication can occur in the work environment. For example, you may observe a female colleague over lunch listening and giving support for a friendship-related problem, when you would be apt to give concrete suggestions. This is a natural difference. In turn, a woman colleague may not understand why you are not keeping in more frequent contact with a friend. These are the differences in how some men and women carry out their friendships, and you can learn from them.

- If you are a father, use what you have learned about friendship to more consciously influence your children in how you would like them to value friendships. Although this chapter has focused on men's relationships with their own fathers, it has significant application to what happens to the next generation of men (and women). Consider what you would want your legacy to be to your children or those cousins, students, or younger men with whom you are in contact. What would you want them to say that they learned from you about friendships?

- Figure out if you are more comfortable relating to one person or relating to men in a group. Understand that this is part of your nature, and do not try to force yourself into making friends in a way that you do not feel suits your personality.

- As far as masculinity is concerned, define it for yourself and make connections with people who feel comfortable to you. Notions about masculinity can change with age and with the friends who someone makes. If you believe your beliefs about masculinity are preventing you from feeling comfortable making friends, you should consider changing those beliefs.

- Realize that some men you want to become friends with may have family and career responsibilities and demands that may interfere with their availability to you.

- Consider whether fears about appearing gay are holding you back from friendships. If they are, *slowly* and *incrementally* try reaching out to other men to make friends with them and then see if those fears are realistic. In addition, you may try getting together with men in small groups rather than one-on-one if that feels too intense. Also, think about where those messages came from in your own life and decide if you still wish to have those messages prevent you from making more friends.

- Dismiss the idea that men do not have friends—the previous chapters prove they do.

Making Friends

- If you want to make more friends, review what other men in this book had to say about how to make and maintain friendships. Find a level of closeness with men that feels comfortable to you—will you call or email each other every day, every week, or every month? How much will you share about your personal life? How much physicality is comfortable? Look for commonalities as well as an appreciation of differences. It is sometimes great fun to have a friend who is quite different from you, if you can both revel in that difference.

- If you want to make new friends, the solutions are straightforward, although not always easy to obtain. Using what you've learned from the men in the study, you should: find commonalities, get involved in activities (knowing about sports is a plus), be open to new experiences, be open to meeting people both at work and through friends and other community contacts, be true to yourself, be upbeat, and communicate with people.

- Think in small increments of change. Do not try and remake your life or your friendships in big leaps; instead, take small steps that will bring you closer to people you care about. Radical and too rapid change will scare away some of your friends. Call a friend right now to chat or make plans to see him. Consider sharing something more personal with him than you have shared in the past (without shocking him by sharing something too personal or out of character with what you have shared with him in the past).

- Do you have enough (*must* and *trust*) friends, and do you have a good balance between the time you are putting into work, family, and friendships? Ideally, you will have all three of these facets of your life in balance. If you do not, making friends will be more difficult, as you will tend to shortchange something in your life and all parts of your life will suffer.

- If you do not see your father as a role model for making friends, find other adult mentors or peers whom you can emulate. Many examples of good friendship-building skills exist. Find a style that matches your approach.

- Consider making friends with people who are older and younger than you. The age difference can be enriching.

- If you do not have platonic friendships with women, start searching for them if your life's situation will allow it. People who are in committed relationships with women may have a harder time with this if it causes jealousy, but my concern is that you not cut yourself off from more friendships—just keep the boundaries clear. Look for common and safe activities in which to build friendships—work committees, church-related activities, or hobbies like bridge are good places to begin.

- Be prepared to give something of yourself to build a friendship.
- Remember that trust is one of the basic requirements for making friends. Once it is broken, it is hard to repair.
- Do not pursue friendships with people who do not make you feel good about yourself.
- Be a good listener and be supportive. Throughout the book, communication between people was seen as a key component of initiating and maintaining friendships. It will be difficult to make friends if the guys you meet do not believe you are hearing what they are saying. Being open and agreeable to others were, according to one study,[8] key components of building friendships. Simple steps like these are effective in the workplace, too. Dale Carnegie's classic 1936 book on human relations at work, *How to Win Friends and Influence People*, offers straightforward suggestions for getting along with people and getting them to like you. Two of them are smile and become interested in other people.
- People generally like to be around people who like themselves and are upbeat. If you tend to complain or look at the darker side of things, consider whether this is impeding your relationships and take steps to change (perhaps by considering therapy)[9].
- Be comfortable with the fact that some men are accustomed to silence. Do not assume that silence means disinterest.[10]

Maintaining Friendships

- You cannot let your friendships wither. Many men recount that they can pick up a friendship from 10 years earlier as if they had not lost a moment. But why wait that long if the potential for meaningful connection exists? Friendships get stronger, I believe, when you stay in touch through phone calls, e-mails, and getting together.

Communication is how we let people know we are thinking about them and care about them.

- If you are losing friends, figure out where you set the bar in a relationship. Do you hold people to a standard that is too high or too low? What would cause you to give up on a friend? Thinking this through may help you appreciate the friends you have.
- Appreciate the duality of "being there" and "helping out" a friend. These are both nurturing as well as traditional masculine behaviors. If you appreciate the extent to which you can be nurturing, you will open yourself up to nurturing your friends in other ways that will enhance your friendships.
- If you are married or in a significant relationship, discuss with your partner the role that friends can play in your life, so that a good balance exists among your multiple relationships.
- Remember a friend's birthday or anniversary by sending him an e-mail or giving him a card—this is how friendships are maintained.
- Hug a friend if a meaningful event has occurred—a death, birth, anniversary, birthday.
- Do not focus *only* on turning new acquaintances into *must* friends— work on strengthening the friendships you have.
- Generate activities and reach out to your friends with concrete suggestions for things to do. Be the person who organizes get-togethers. Passivity is not likely to result in people wanting to do things with you or be your friend.
- Look at women's friendships and borrow from them what is comfortable for you to try in terms of interactions with your own friends.
- If your wife or girlfriend is interfering with your male friendships, evaluate why this is happening. Is she raising reasonable impediments to your friendships, or is she inappropriately blocking you from having such friendships?
- Finally, consider the Buddy System of *must, trust, rust,* and, *just* as ways of understanding the patterns of friendships and why you feel differently about some friends than you do about others. Only through such an understanding will you be able to appreciate who your friends are and work on improving the friendships that you have or want to build.

Changing Friendships

How can we change how men perceive making, relating to, and keeping friends? We need to start at a young age, with the next generation of men. We cannot continue to make the same mistakes, through the messages that boys receive now, about what it means to be a man and to be masculine. We need to help boys learn to relate to others, so that they can reach out and both offer and receive help when needed, which, according to psychologist William Pollack, is the foundation of a healthy person.[11] Boys need to learn to be vulnerable and nurturing, key cornerstones of any close relationship. Telling them to be tough and strong, to suck it up, and to not cry will only constrain them in the future.

Youth in our communities cannot be marginalized, isolated, and alienated. They need to learn to communicate in ways that will connect them to others, not distance them. This requires a high level of commitment from men and women who will mentor others and speak out against unhealthy child-rearing practices (not just for boys) in all communities. Adults in the community must become the role models for how friendships can work effectively between men and between men and women. With better friendships, we can break down walls that contribute to misunderstanding and loneliness.

Robert Putnam suggests that, to build better communities, we need greater civic engagement and social connectedness. How to do this? His recommendations include making the workplace friendlier to families and communities, designing communities that reduce commuting time to work, building tolerance between different groups, moving away from passive and isolating television watching, and engaging in more community activities that include art, politics, and volunteering.[12] These suggestions underpin the purposes of this book—to build better friendships to sustain people throughout life and improve our health and happiness.

Ultimately, this book is about connection and the need for men of all ages to build better friendships with others. Given the uncertainty of the times, it is the ability to relate to others in a supportive way, to be there for them, to be trustworthy and dependable that will shape the course of a man's life and improve the quality of the communities in which we all live.

And, when thinking about your own future as a friend, consider Rick's optimistic statement to the police chief, Captain Louis Renault, in the 1942 movie *Casablanca* as they stroll off into the fog having just thwarted the Nazis—and after each has just seen the other as an adversary—"Louis, I think this is the beginning of a beautiful friendship."

V
APPENDICES

Appendix A
About the Study

Study Methodology

Twelve open-ended questions were used to gain an understanding of adult male friendships. Student researchers in a graduate social work course taught from 2002 to 2004 were each asked to interview 10 men aged 21 and over, previously known or unknown to them, for the purpose of gaining a perspective on male friendships from a nonclinical sample.[1] Asking open-ended questions in a qualitative interview format is a form of naturalistic inquiry that is similar in many ways to the therapeutic interview.[2] It can yield useful information when not much is known about the topic. The open-ended questions form anchors that allow the interviewees to respond to broad topic areas.

Thirty-nine students completed interviews with men (an additional question was added to the interview in a later semester, so that not all the subjects were asked the same questions). Prior to conducting the interviews, students practiced interviewing each other to ensure that they fully understood the nature of this type of interview and the importance of not trying to influence the responses. Students then went out and interviewed one person and returned to the class to discuss that process before conducting more interviews. This approach resulted in 386 useable interviews. Four interviews were excluded because they were either incomplete or, in one case, the interviewee was only 19 years old, when the cut-off age was set at 21. Each student typed up the interview and shared it with other students during the class meetings, which helped to build an understanding of the questions and the possible ways of interpreting the questions to the interviewees. This iterative process builds on the interviewers' understanding of the topic. Students discussed their findings and impressions each week. In class, students began a content analysis of the key themes raised during the interviews and then grouped the responses into broader categories.[3] Each student made a class presentation at the end of the semester and wrote a 15–20 page paper focused on their findings and their interpretations of the findings. During the past few years, I have reviewed these papers to ensure that I continue to capture the interviewers' thoughts about the findings and that major themes are captured. Students from subsequent semesters have read earlier semesters' papers also and have built their own impressions of the data from these papers as well as their own analysis of the data that they collected. With the information entered into a database, means and comparisons between groups were derived. Other students in 2004 and 2005, doing independent research projects without the benefit of the group process, reviewed the coding to ensure that it was valid. This verification process and triangulation are common in this type of research.

For the eight men who were interviewed in the second section of the book, and for the church group, the broad format of the questions was followed to initiate discussion. But a constant comparative approach was also used, in which I began to try out hypotheses on the interview subjects.[4] The men were not interviewed in order from youngest to oldest or oldest to youngest, so the questions and discussions vary from one interview to the next based on impressions I gained and the ideas and hypotheses I was working with at the time. For example, I began to realize midway through this set of interviews that older men (60s to 90s) seemed to have a harder time specifically asking friends for help than the younger men (20s to 50s). I could pursue this with some of the men being interviewed but for others, I had to use a post-hoc analysis so common to this type of research.

Coding the open-ended responses of 386 men can be difficult. Some men gave one-word answers that were not further probed by the student interviewers, whereas other men were highly descriptive in their open-ended responses. For example, for the question, "Have you learned anything about friendships from observing female friendships?" answers were coded four ways. The first category was for responses that were affirmative of the value of observing female friendships. To be included in this category, the sense had to be that something positive was learned from observing women's relationships. The second category was for respondents who said that nothing had been learned and gave no further response. The third category was used for men who clearly indicated that they had a negative impression of women's friendships. The fourth category was used for an "other" category, for those who said friendships were the same for men and women or that men and women each had strengths and weaknesses when it came to friendships.

This last category, which could overlap with the second one, indicated that the respondent was not placing a positive or negative value on any differences that might exist between men and women's friendships.

For another question, concerning whether men made close friends through their significant women partners (those who were single were excluded from this particular analysis), responses were coded dichotomously, with respondents either agreeing or disagreeing that they have made close friends. This question turned out to be one of the weakest in the study, as it was difficult to know if the women were attempting to help the men make friends without alerting them to this fact.

For the women's study, 12 students interviewed between 10 and 11 women and asked similarly worded questions as the men's. The analysis involved students reviewing the literature, sharing interviews, discussing themes, presenting their findings to the class, and completing a 15-20 page paper in which they interpreted their results.

The women presented similar challenges in coding their responses but not to the same extremes. Women tended to give longer responses, which allowed the coders more opportunity to more clearly interpret those responses.

Grouping respondent's demographic information can also be difficult. For example, the men were asked where they grew up. Although more than half said they grew up outside of Maryland, how would someone classify himself if he moved to Maryland at 12 versus 21? Four percent were born outside of the United States. Some of the countries of origin include Canada, Sierra Leone, Israel, El Salvador, Qatar, Holland, Indonesia, and Iran. But at what age and under what conditions did they come to the United States, and how does that immigration affect their friendships? Slightly over half said they were raised in an urban area, with the rest indicating they were raised in a suburban environment (38%) or a rural one (10%). What if they moved from a rural to a suburban area at the age of 12? How would they answer the question? Most were currently living in the Maryland and Washington, D.C. area, but a number were interviewed by students when the students returned home and interviewed people there (particularly New York, New Jersey, and Pennsylvania). Living arrangements are often dynamic, so someone may be in a new state for only a few weeks or months when they were interviewed (we did not ask how long they had lived at their address). Although this makes them a resident of that most recent state, how do we interpret their geographic location?

Sexual orientation is also difficult to classify, as some people who were interviewed might not wish to reveal such information. Ten of the male respondents disclosed they were gay, over 2.5% of the sample. It is impossible to know if others in the sample are also gay. Two-thirds indicated they were married or living with someone, and a handful of those not married were divorced.

Sample Description

Men. The majority of the 386 subjects (85%) were known to their interviewer. Sixty-five percent of the subjects were white, 29% were African-American, and the rest were Latino (2%), Asian (2%), or Arab (2%). The subjects' average age was 38, and ages ranged from 21 to 85. Four percent of the sample is either 21 or 22 years old and 4% is 71 and over. Regarding education, 15% of the sample had between a 6th grade and a high school education, 17% had attended some college, 34% had graduated college, and another 34% had some education beyond college, with 3% of the total sample having a doctoral degree. A range of job categories were represented, with 21% being professionals; 44% working in sales, business, or other nonprofessional white-collar professions; 22% occupying blue-collar positions; and the rest being classified as students, unemployed, or retired. The majority (82%) identified as Christian/Protestant; 12% were Jewish, 2% were Muslim, and the rest were atheist/agnostic.

Women. The women subjects also had an average age of 38, with half being 31 and younger and 16% being 55 and older. Seventy-two percent were known to their interviewer. The oldest was 83. Seventy-two percent are white, 18% are African-American, and the remaining are either Latina, Asian, or self-identified as mixed-race. Ten percent have a high school diploma only, twenty percent had some college education, thirty percent graduated from college, and forty percent had some education beyond college. Most held professional jobs (39%), were in sales (18%), secretarial work (22%), or were students (14%). Few described themselves as unemployed, retired, or housewife. Most (76%) are Christian/Protestant, 16% are Jewish, and the other 8% are Hindu, Buddhist, or atheist/agnostic. Slightly over half (52%) are married (or living with someone), and most of the unmarried women (80%) have never been married. The remainder are widowed or divorced.

Student Interviewers. The student interviewers were a highly diverse group—slightly more than half are white, over one-third are African-America, and the remainder are Latina. Five out of six interviewers of the men are female, and they ranged in age from their 20s to their 50s. The women's sample was interviewed by 11 women and one man.

Limitations

Limitations of these data gathering approaches may affect the findings and their interpretation. For example, subjects might want to give socially desirable responses (as cited, 85% of the men and 72% of the women were known to their interviewer). Another limitation could be related to the gender of the interviewer. Female interviewers might draw different responses from subjects than male interviewers, as it has been noted that males often feel more comfortable talking to females. During the in-class discussions of the interviews, this was explored; no significant differences were noted at the time between what the male students and female students were hearing from the subjects, although more subtle differences could exist. This was not seen as a problem for those interviewing the female sample. Some men were reluctant to be interviewed. Butera[5] encountered a great deal of difficulty getting men to agree to be interviewed and hypothesized it was because she was female, that men don't like to talk about feelings, don't have many friends, and are pressed for time. The student interviewers did not seem to encounter this level of reluctance, perhaps because they were not requiring as much time for the interview process as Butera was. Although not explored specifically, it is my impression that women were more interested in being interviewed than were men, as Butera had also found. Another limitation could be some variation in questioning and recording from one interviewer to the next, as so many interviewers were involved. Variations could also exist from one group of students to the next. As there was a great deal of information sharing, and as each subsequent class read the interviews completed by the previous class, this type of interviewer variability was most likely kept to a minimum. At the same time, such variability, where it exists, could be seen as a strength of this research, because the purpose was to gain a broad understanding of friendships from a diverse group of men.

This is largely a white and African-American sample. By 2008, there are more Latinos in the United States than African-Americans. I have tried to include subjects who are Latino, Asian, and Arab in the accounts, but these groups are under-represented overall in the study. The voices of an important and growing population of men, particularly Latinos who come from historically *macho* communities, are not heard. The book would have been better with their inclusion. For those wishing more information about these populations, I suggest reading Gerami[6] for Muslim masculinities, Gutmann and Vigoya[7] and Coltrane[8] for Latino masculinities, and Taga[9] for East-Asian masculinities.

An additional limitation may be that the definitions of friendships are not consensually validated and vary by region of the country and culture.[10] Butera[11] notes in her article on the difficulties of interviewing Australian men about their friendships that the use of the term "mate" was preferred to the term "friend" and that, when referring to a relationship, men often were referring to a romantic partner, not a friend/mate. Everyone has some concept of what a friendship is, but they may not agree on its meaning. Thus, even asking someone to comment about friendship can bring up widely differing perceptions from those who consider teammates or work colleagues as friends to those who consider only childhood friends as meeting the definition of "friend." Terms used to describe friendship, like trustworthiness, could also have cultural and even community-based differences in their meaning. Regional differences may also exist.[12] Most of the interviews took place in the metropolitan Maryland area. This is an area known for not being highly transitory. It may mean that residents have lived in the region longer than those who might be interviewed in California, for example, where mobility is greater. Thus, it may be easier to sustain friendships in the Baltimore area if people are less apt to move, or it may be easier to hold to a standard that a friendship must be of a certain duration(e.g., since childhood) for it to be considered a friendship.

Cross-sectional surveys only capture a person's thoughts at one point in time. As in the case of Tom, the man in his 80s who is featured in Chapter 13, answers changed between the first and second interviews, which were conducted a year apart. One protection against this is the use of a large sample. So, although my impressions of an individual man and his impressions of his friendships may vary over time, enough men are captured at one time to permit a fairly good impression of men's answers in general.

When I cite percentages of men and women who responded to questions, I did not run χ^2 statistics for fear that this would give the impression of attempting to validate a method that is more interpretive than objective. I also have smoothed out the actual language used, removing repeated words and phrases used while the speaker was thinking ("ums" and "ahs"), to make the text easier reading. I urge the reader thus to consider the presentation of these data as merely suggestive of how men and women might respond to these questions.

Finally, I have had to examine my own process in interpreting the data. Such interpretations are never 100% objective and, with a topic of this nature, can be highly influenced by feelings, selective readings of the literature, and unintended biases. As a result, I urge the reader to consider his (or her) own reaction to the men's (and women's) words and to draw conclusions that will help him (or her) become better friends to others.

Appendix B

Questions for Men's Groups and Classroom Discussion

Questions to Use for Discussion Groups for Men, Women, and Youth

These questions are discussed in the book.

1. What is a friendship—what does a friend mean to you?
2. Are friendships important to you?
3. Do you believe you have enough male friends?
4. How have friends helped you (are they a source of social support)? How have you helped friends?
5. What are examples of what you do with your male friends?
6. How do you establish friendships with men, and how do you maintain them?
7. Do you ever lose male friends and, if so, how do you get them back (if you do)?
8. Did (does) your father (or other significant adult male) have many friends and, if so, what messages did (do) you receive about friendships from him? What about your mother and her friendships?
9. Do you have friendships with women that are nonsexual in nature?
10. Do you learn about friendships from observing female friendships?
11. If you are married or have a significant other, have you made friends through that person?
12. Is there a link between masculinity and male friendships?
13. To what extent does a fear of appearing homosexual affect your friendships?
14. To what extent do you agree with Aristotle on the following:
    a. Friendship is the highest order of relationship.

   b. You can only be friends with a peer.

   c. You have to have known someone for a long time before they are a true friend.

   d. You have to "share salt" with someone before you can become close friends.

   e. You can only have a few close friends, as true friendships require a lot from you.

15. Do you have enough time for your friends?

Other Questions

These are not discussed in the book.

16. Would you give your kidney to your best friend?
17. Is there anything you don't tell your close friend about yourself that would make you seem weak or vulnerable?
18. To what extent do you compete with your close friends?
19. Do you have to be careful about who you introduce some of your close friends to?
20. Do some people in your life wonder why you consider certain people as friends?
21. Are you proud to describe your friends as your friends?
22. Many men only get together with men in group situations. Can you be friends with someone with whom you have never been alone?

Questions for Classroom Discussions

It is recommended that the literature be reviewed before considering these questions:

1. Hegemonic masculinity, according to Connell (2005a), affects how men interact with each other. Connell defines hegemony as the dynamic by which one group in essence controls other groups. In relation to masculinity, Connell continues, "Hegemonic masculinity can be defined as the configuration of gender practice which embodies the currently accepted answer to the problem of the

legitimacy of patriarchy which guarantees … the domination of men and the subordination of women" (p. 77). While not always the case, Connell notes, the top levels of power in military, business, and politics usually exemplify masculinity (p. 77). Within this understanding, some men will have power over others in terms of socially acceptable behavior and may exclude men from groups based on their behavior (p. 78).

To what extent do you think hegemonic masculinity assists or impedes men's ability to form friendships?

2. Peterson's (2007) Philadelphia-based men's group has been meeting for more than 20 years. It is comprised of white and African-American men who live in urban and suburban areas. They operate under four informal expectations: "no telling of jokes that demean another person or group, no discussion of professional sports, no self-aggrandizement through 'hero' stories, and no networking for personal gain" (p. 74). These expectations are put in place to compel men to forge new ways of relating to each other.

What do you think about these ways of relating?

3. A number of authors (e.g., Kaplan, 2007) have noted the common assumption that men do not have intimate relationships with other men because men do not engage in verbal self-disclosure. Self-disclosure is seen as a prerequisite to intimacy.

Can men have intimacy with other men without verbal self-disclosure?

4. Some experts believe that by studying differences between men based on race, class, sexual orientation, religion, culture, and age, we will learn a good deal more about men and their friendships. Others believe (e.g., Mike Donaldson, personal communication) that such explorations will end up parsing people too finely into small groups that have little meaning. Rather, commonalities based on how people consider friendships (some place great importance on trust, for example) should be the basis for comparisons.

Which direction is best for future research on men's friendships?

5. E. Anthony Rotundo's book, *American Manhood: Transformations in Masculinity from the Revolution to the Modern Era* (1993), provides an excellent history and a way of understanding how white Northern men's behaviors toward each other have changed. For example, by the middle of the 19th century, young men who had very close relationships with each other understood that they would lose these relationships with marriage and career. Rotundo

writes, "There were several reasons why close friends assumed that their ties would be broken by manhood, and all of them were related to the task of taking on a man's duties" (p. 88). These included marriage and career. Once these commitments were made, childhood was left behind (p. 90).

To what extent is it still true that men give up their childhood friendships with marriage (or commitment) and career?

6. Recent studies have described women as talking more than men, being more emotionally expressive, and more interested in relationships.

   To what extent should the way that women construct their friendships be used as a basis for comparison with how men construct theirs?

7. Robert Putnam's book, *Bowling Alone*, describes how Americans have become less connected to each other over the last generation. He calls for new public and private structures and policies to get people more engaged and more connected as individuals (2000, p. 403). I argue that building better friendships is one way to achieve greater connection between people.

   To what extent can the problems related to social disengagement be addressed through public and private institutions?

8. One notion with this book is that reading about other men's experiences and gaining insight into friendships can change the way one interacts with friends.

   To what extent do you think learning about the Buddy System or another way of interacting can result in a man changing the way he interacts with his friends?

Notes

INTRODUCTION

1. Psychoanalyst and author Judith Viorst, in her book, *Necessary Losses*, describes the nature of female friendships and provides possible insight into men's friendship categories as well. She describes six types of friendships: 1. convenience friends—those at work or next door who help out in a pinch but are not intimate; 2. special-interest friends—people we get together with for various activities (sports, book clubs, etc.); 3. historical friends—people we have known for years, whom we may not see that often but whom we don't want to lose touch with; 4. crossroads friends—those we meet at critical junctures in our lives; 5. cross-generational friends—older and younger friends who serve as surrogate parents or children; and 6. close friends—people who are emotionally and geographically near us and with whom we sustain ongoing contact and great levels of intimacy.

Psychologist Jan Yager, in *Friendships: The Power of Friendships and How It Shapes Our Lives*, has three classifications—best, close, and casual. To Yager, as the number of people in one category grows, the value of friendship decreases. One can also have more than one best friend, as there can be best friends from various periods in one's life.

2. Approval for the research was gained from the University of Maryland Institutional Review Board, and all study participants were given a consent form.

3. In 2005, the U.S. population was 67% white, 14.4% Latino, and 13.5% African American (U.S.Census Bureau, 2006a).

4. The sample was more highly educated than the U.S. population, wherein 32% have no education past high school and an additional 15% have not completed high school (U.S. Census Bureau, 2007).

PART I

1. For various studies and commentaries showing these connections, see e.g., Berkman & Syme (1979), Carstensen (1991), and Winefeld et al. (1992), Betcher & Pollack (1993). Christiakis and Fowler (2007), in a well-reported article in *The New England Journal of Medicine*, found the reverse also true—that people with obese friends were more apt to become obese themselves than people without obese friends.

2. Florian et al (1995) found people with effective social support systems had greater emotional security when compared with those who were more isolated. Social support and social network research can be connected to the study of friendship (Farrell, 1985).

3. See Addis & Mahalik (2003), Harrison (1978), and Williams (2003) who all, in various ways, connect men's socialization and difficulty with vulnerability to help seeking.

4. In one survey of 162 undergraduates, men and their male friends were found to be more competitive than women and their female friends or people in cross-sex friendships. Singleton & Vacca (2007) believe this to be consistent with gender role expectations, in which masculinity is more competitive than femininity.

5. Burleson (2003), p. 5.

6. Putnam (2000). In *Bowling Alone*, Putnam documents the decline of connections between people but also challenges Americans to reverse them.

7. McPherson, Smith-Lovin, & Brashears (2006). Boarse et al. (2006) put the median number of core ties at 15 and the number of significant ties (these are less important contacts than core ties) at 16.

8. Pahl & Pevalin (2005).

9. Tiger (1999) writes that the hunter-gatherers "courted and chose other men as working and fighting partners, and as recreational companions, and how one feature of male bonding was the exclusion of females" (p. 244). This changed with the development of stable communities.

10. Plato (1992), p. 9.

11. Aristotle (1998), p. 138.

12. At times, and across history, people in need have referred to each other as friends when they really were not. Consider the phrase, "The enemy of my enemy is my friend." Then consider, for example, what happens in Homer's *Odyssey*. Eurymachus, a suitor of Odysseus's wife Penelope, upon realizing that Odysseus has unexpectedly returned home from the Trojan Wars and is going to kill him and all the other suitors for attempting to marry Penelope and plunder his home, calls upon his "friendship" with men who have been his competition for Penelope until that point. In his call for assistance, he shouts, "My friends, there's no quarter coming from those ruthless hands (referring to Odysseus). He has got the strong bow and the quiver and will shoot from the threshold floor till he has killed us all." Eurymachus calls them friends, but they were not friends before. Only in this context and when imminent death looms does the idea of "friendship" arise. Needless to say, Eurymachus doesn't make it into the next chapter.

13. Nardi (1992), p. 2.

14. Hansen (1992), p. 42. Letters written in the early 18th Century between Alexander Pope and William Wycherly and Jonathan Swift have also been

analyzed and are further examples of love being frequently expressed between heterosexual men (Stephanson, 1997).

15. Shenk (2005).

16. Hansen (1992), p. 54.

17. See, e.g., Hansen (1992); Kimmel (1996); Nardi (1992); Plummer (1999);Rotundo (1993); Stearns (1990).

18. Rotundo (1993).

19. Kimmel (1996), p. 122.

20. Kimmel (1996), p. 121.

21. Rotundo (1993).

22. Masculinity is also defined differently by people who were raised in other countries and moved to the United States. For example, one Iranian-born 57-year-old who now works in the United States as a bartender told us when asked about masculinity and friendship, "In my culture, there were not a lot of supported relationships between sexes and so you only did hang out with, in my case, the guys. We, I believe, are a much more expressive people and touch more between men without there being any sort of strange connotation then maybe exists in America." Butera (2006a) argues that masculinity is changing in Australia, too. Calling someone a mate is being replaced by calling someone a friend – she believes the latter is a more feminized version of the once masculine feeling "mate" which was never used to refer to women. Friend is more androgynous.

23. Knoester, Haynie, & Stephens (2006), pp. 1248–1249. In their literature review, Knoester et al. point out that if children and parents do not have a good relationship with each other, the parents' influence on friendships will be greatly reduced.

24. E.g. Myers (2005); Weiten (2007).

25. One Mexican study of 8,068 heterosexually active males between the ages of 15 and 24 found that over half identified none or one confidants when asked to describe someone who they could talk to or seek advice from about an important personal problem (Marston, Juarez, & Izazola, 2004, p. 414). Clearly many male youth, in at least some parts of world, are not deeply embedded in trusting relationships with others.

26. McPherson, Smith-Lovin, & Cook (2001) use the term *homophily* to describe associations based on similarities. In an increasingly diverse world however, differences can also sometimes attract. I met a medical doctor, Raju, from India on an airplane; he talked about his preference for people different from himself. Most of his friends here are U.S. citizens. To him, the heterogeneity of backgrounds is what makes friends so useful. Raju, an immigrant to the United States, wants diversity. "When I help my American friends, I do not do it from an Indian perspective. I try and offer them an American view. In addition, if I have a complicated situation, I am not helped

from any single perspective by their comments. All of my American friends have traveled extensively outside of the U.S. So they do have that in common, but it is more a world view that they offer and that I offer, and not one specifically bound by culture."

27. Rushton & Bons (2005) studied monozygotic and dizygotic twins' preferences for friends and spouses. In response to a series of questions, monozygotic twins chose people as friends and spouses who more closely resembled each other than did dizygotic twins, leading them to conclude that people are genetically inclined toward people who are genetically similar to them.

28. Verbrugge (1977) refers to a proximity principle that states that people who are *similar* are more apt to become friends. She found, through a 1970s study of a U.S. and German city, that people of similar status are apt to be friends, a point made by Aristotle about peer friendships. In the text, I am using *proximity* to mean geographic proximity.

29. Finchum (2005). In her study of mobile women over 45, e-mail was a major method of keeping the friendship alive; The Pew Internet & American Life Project (see Boarse et al., 2006) concludes that e-mail enables friendships to be maintained as people can communicate quickly and at their leisure. They claim social networks have been maintained by e-mail.

30. Cheng, Chan, & Tong (2005) studied online friendships in Hong Kong.

31. Goleman (2006).

32. Levi, La Vechhia, & Saraceno (2003).

33. Moeller-Leimkuehler (2003). .

34. Rubin (1983) points out that cultures in which men are physically close are often those in which women's roles are fairly rigidly determined. She also points out that physical closeness may not mean emotional closeness.

35. Rybak & McAndrew (2006).

36. Burleson (2003).

37. Hollinger (2006).

38. Franklin (1992); Duneier's (1992) study of African-American men who hang out together in a Chicago diner also speaks to this point.

39. Burleson (2003).

40. Roberts (1994). Mattis, Murray, Hatcher et al (2001) found in their study of 171 African American men and their friendships that those who shared more with male friends felt more support from friends than those who were less sharing.

41. Gutmann & Vigoya (2005).

42. Coltrane (2001).

43. Morgan (2005) refers to class as the "unequal distribution of life chances" (p. 167).

44. Stearns (1990), p. 115.

45. Cohen (1992), p. 128.

46. Nardi (2007).

47. Wright & Cho (1992).

48. Nardi (2000), p. 357.

49. Wright & Cho (1992), p. 88.

50. Myers (1996).

51. Myers (1996).

52. Biesanz, West, & Millevoi (2007).

53. Kimmel (1996), p. 173.

54. Davis (1985).

55. Muraco (2006), p. 1313; She looks at friendships across sexual orientation also and supports my belief that people who do not feel supported by their family will look to build friendship networks to compensate.

56. Salmon's (2003) study indicates that birth order may be linked with friendship interests. In a study of 245 college students, middle-born children felt less positively toward family and more positively toward friends than did their older or younger siblings. It was hypothesized that parents raised them differently, putting greater emphasis on first- and last-born, which is why they were more externally focused.

57. Sherman, Lansford, & Volling (2006).

58. Mendes De Leon (2006).

59. Lewis (1978); Morin &Garfinkel (1978); Pease (2000); Tognoli (1980).

60. Sherman et al. (2000); Meth (1990). I met Richard about the time his book came out, and he helped me validate some of my thoughts about therapeutic work with men.

61. Roy et al. (2000).

62. Wright (1982), p. 8, provides the first reference I could find to the notion of men's side-by-side or shoulder-to-shoulder friendships as compared with women's face-to-face friendships. See pp. 16–17 for his suggestion that both qualities are present in longstanding relationships.

63. Messner (2001), p. 94.

64. Pollack (2006).

65. Connell (2005), p. xix. Time I spent at the University of Sydney in 2007 has influenced my thinking about masculinities.

66. Sheets & Lugar (2005).

67. Wall et al (1984).

68. Ward et al (2003).

69. Rubin (1986), p. 166.

70. Rubin (1985).

71. Dindia & Allen (1992).

72. Carstensen (1991).

73. Baumeister & Sommmer (1997).

74. Seibert et al (1999).

75. Vaughan & Nowicki (1999). One very broad definition of friendship for both men and women, "those individuals who you feel close to, who you interact with frequently, those who you would seek out for some type of social activity" (p. 363) was used in a study by Brewer & Webster (1999) to explore how common it is to forget friends living in a college dormitory when asked to recall them. Such definitions are common in research and often do not capture more meaningful connections that people build with friends.

76. Tognoli (1980).

77. Roy et al. (2000).

78. Agrawal et al. (2002).

79. Cahill (2005).

80. Bazelon (2008) cautions that this study has never been replicated.

81. Schmitt, Realo, Voracek, & Allik (2008) found in their research that 55 nations with higher levels of human development were those where women and men had greater personality differentials. This counterintuitive finding was found in other studies also. In essence, when more freedom exists, more divergence between men and women may emerge. It is, however, not purely genetic. The authors suggest that a gene–environment interaction exists that must be weighed in understanding the emergence of differences between men and women on certain personality characteristics.

82. Baumeister (2007) said in a speech, and I agree, " it's best to avoid value judgments . . . they have made discussion of gender politics very difficult and sensitive, thereby warping the play of ideas."

83. Morris (1978), p. 23.

84. Richard Lingeman (2007) dedicates an entire book to friendships among American writers.

85. Michaelis (1983), p. 270.

86. Albom (1997), pp. 175–176.

87. Albom (1997), pp. 183–184.

88. Taken from the *Reader's Digest Treasury of Modern Quotations* (1975), p. 660.

89. Farthing's (2005) description of costly signaling theory is one way to consider risk taking. He writes that men take foolish risks as a way of signaling to women (and other men) their health and vigor. If someone can succeed at a foolish risk, they will also succeed at more practical ones that might result in protecting women and children. A good risk taker would also prove to be a good friend to another man in time of crisis. Butch and Sundance continually signal to each other the pros and cons of risk taking, making fun of each other along the way.

90. Matthews (1986) describes the lack of consensus about how to define a friend as one of the gaps in the literature.

91. Putnam (2000).

92. Stroud (2006), p. 503. She goes on to write that the ethics of the friendship mean that you *owe* it to the friend to publicly defend him.

93. The American Medical Association Web site does not list surgery as one of the top seven specialties for women, and there are 10 women in internal medicine and seven in pediatrics for every one in surgery. According to the Census Bureau (2006b), there are 143,000 fathers taking care of children at home, as compared with 5.6 million mothers in that role—a ratio of one stay-at-home dad for every 39 stay-at-home moms.

94. Norah Vincent, a reporter, went "underground" as a male for 18 months. In her book, *Self-made Man*, she describes her experiences with joining an all-male bowling league. Despite her bowling incompetence, she felt totally accepted by the men and could take a humorous look at herself, too, as Isuko does. "They made me look ridiculous to myself, and they made me laugh about it. And for that I will always be grateful to them, because anybody who does that for you is a true and great friend" (2006, p. 61).

95. Gladwell (2002), p. 177.

96. Coleman, Ganong, & Rothrauff (2006).

97. Some of these quotes appear in my 2006 article in the journal *Family Therapy*.

98. Raewyn Connell (2005a, b, c; and Connell and Wood, 2005), for example, has written a great deal on the topic from a global perspective.

99. Putnam (2000).

100. Versions of some of the quotes here also appear in Greif (2006).

101. The "roast" is another way that men (and women) who are friends publicly get together and tease each other through insults. As Oppenhemier (2007) writes, to really roast someone you have to know your friends' vulnerabilities and his most notable mistakes.

102. Bearman & Parigi (2004), p. 538.

103. Bearman & Parigi (2004).

104. In Chapter 5, we show that about one-third of those who are married make friends through their wife. Note that all the men in the survey were not married.

105. Boarse et al (2006)

106. See Putnam (2001).

107. Matthews (1986), p. 79.

108. Gay (1989), p. 55.

109. *Bartlett's Familiar Quotations* (1992), p. 450.

110. Totten (2003).

111. Collins, Noble, Poynting, & Tabar (2000), in describing Arab youth gangs in Sydney, believe that an intersection of masculinity, ethnicity, and class exists in many gangs, in which the purpose is to provide protection for each other. The marginalization of a racially specific nonmajority group, in this case Lebanese,

pulls the members together. They protect each other with the threat of violence against others who interfere with their lives. Criminal activity to gain material things in this community means being tough, being adult, and being masculine, according to the authors. Respect from others is an important component of manhood (masculinity), and respect is also gained from being tough. U.S. gangs are usually race- and class-specific also and serve as a source of protection from others.

112. Kindlon & Thompson (1999). p. 113.

113. Pollack (1998).

114. E.g. Dubowitz, Lane, Greif, Jensen, & Lamb (2006).

115. This point, that these are estimates, needs to be emphasized and is discussed in greater depth in the Methodology section of the Appendix. It is hard to draw definitive conclusions from interview material, and so findings should be seen as suggestive for trends.

116. Putnam (2000), pp. 81–84.

PART II

1. Brizendine (2006), p. 5.

2. Derks, Dolan, Hudziak, et al. (2007).

3. Cahill (2005).

4. Even in Canli, Desmond, Zhao, & Gabrieli's (2002) study of 12 men and 12 women whose MRIs showed sex-related differences in retaining memories of emotionally laden pictures they were shown, environmental factors, like cognitive training, were cited as one possible way to affect the outcome.

5. Petersen (2003).

6. One study in the 1980s of friendships of men and women in the U.S., Great Britain, Germany, Italy, and Hungary found almost no gender specific differences – "At the same time, remarkabale variations in the features of friendship networks were found across nations" (Bruckner & Knaup, 1993, p. 263). This is another example of the impact of the social context on friendships.

7. Menaker (1986), p. 615.

8. Kupers (1992), pp. 132–133.

9. Seidler (1992), p. 30.

10. Carstensen (1991).

11. Dindia & Allen (1992).

12. Baumeister & Sommer (1997).

13. Lewis (1978); Rubin (1986).

14. Lewis (1978).

15. Kimmel (1996); Barton (2000).

16. Pentz (2000).

17. Vaughn & Nowicki (1999).

18. Swain (1992).

19. Carey (2007), p. 8.

20. McGoldrick (1989), p. 32. Jordan et al (1991), support this when they write, "(T)heories of 'human development' which espoused increasing capacity for separation, autonomy, mastery, independence, and self-sufficiency as indications of health and maturity consistently portrayed women as too emotional, too dependent (and), lacking in clear boundaries." p. v.

21. Taylor, Klein, Lewis et al (2000), in a review of existing research, believe that women, when under stress, "tend and befriend." Women are more likely to affiliate with each other than men under these conditions and this may be due to a biological predisposition. This is an example of how biology arguably shapes the social context. Clearly both contexts matter, though it is unclear and to what extent they affect each other.

22. Viorst (1998). Viorst also cites six types of friendship, which are endnoted in Part I, endnote 1.

23. Rubin (1985), p. 163.

24. *Ibid*, pp. 62–63. Rubin's research was completed in the 1980s, so these findings may be different now.

25. Putnam (2000), p. 200. Full-time work, however, will reduce the amount of time women can spend in such community associations.

26. Liang et al (2002).

27. Knickmeyer et al. (2003).

28. Berzoff (1989).

29. Wright (1982), p. 19.

30. With the women, this question was asked earlier in the interviews.

31. The appendix explains the limitations in depth. The method used for the women's research was the same as used for the men's.

32. See, e.g. Tannen (2006).

33. This point, that these are estimates, must be emphasized and is discussed in greater depth in the Methodology section of the Appendix. It is hard to draw definitive conclusions from interview material, so findings should be seen as suggestive for trends. In relation to this particular question, mothers may have had many friends at one point in the respondent's life and not at another, thus making it difficult to draw definitive conclusions about respondents' answers. At the same time, we were asking for impressions, which are what we received from the respondents.

PART III

1. Curtis (2006) writes that more than one in five men in Great Britain in their late 20s live with parents.

2. Pease (2002), p.136. Adams (1994), in reviewing the literature on men's friendship patterns, found that people who work have more social support than retirees.

3. Sheehy (1998), p. 20.

4. Hoare (2002), pp. 192–193.

5. In addition to citations provided earlier in this book, Adams (1994), in her literature review on older men's friendships, learned that men with friends adapted better when placed in a residential setting than did those without friends.

6. Matthews (1986), p. 117.

7. Matthews (1986), p. 14.

8. U.S. Census Bureau (2006c), Table S0101.

9. Walsh (1989), p. 326.

PART IV

1. I drew heavily on *Nichomachean Ethics* for the discussion.

2. See, e.g. Lewis (1978) and Messner (2001), whose thoughts appear in Chapter 1.

3. Kimmel (1996) also makes this point, as noted in Chapter 1.

4. Nichols & Schwartz (2007).

5. *Ibid.*

6. *Ibid.*

7. Enright & Rawlinson (1991), p. 342.

8. Hevl (2004), in a study of 737 middle-aged and older participants in Heidelberg, found that openness in middle age and agreeableness in older age contribute to friendship involvement.

9. Gordon and Pasick (1990) write about what the process of therapy can be like for men seeking to enhance their friendships. They also write about men's groups as being therapeutically helpful. One piece of their advice is to not denigrate traditional ways that men make friends—through work and sports—and to use those venues to strengthen friendships.

10. Taylor (2006).

11. Pollack (2006).

12. Putnam (2000), pp. 402–416.

PART V

1. Institutional Review Board approval was received from the University of Maryland and students were aware the research was for a book.

2. Padgett (1998).

3. Strauss & Corbin (1990).

4. Strauss & Corbin (1990).
5. Butera (2006b).
6. Gerami (2005).
7. Guttman & Vigoya (2005).
8. Coltrane (2001).
9. Taga (2005).
10. Adams, Blieszner, & DeVries (2000).
11. Butera (2006b).
12. Adams et al (2000).

References

Adams, R. G. (1994). Older men's friendship patterns. In E. H. Thompson (Ed.)., *Older men's lives* (pp. 159–177). Thousand Oaks, CA: Sage.

Adams, R. G., Blieszner, R., & De Vries, B. (2000). Definitions of friendship in the third age: Age, gender and study location effects. *Journal of Aging Studies, 14,* 117–133.

Addis, M. E. & Mahalik, J. R. (2003). Men, masculinity, and the contexts of help seeking. *American Psychologist, 58,* 5–14.

Adler, B. (2007). *Boys and their toys: Understanding men by understanding their relationships with gadgets.* New York: American Management Association.

Agrawal, A., Jacobson, K. C., Prescott, C. A., & Kendler, K. S. (2002). A twin study of sex differences in social support. *Psychological Medicine, 32,* 1155–1164.

Albom, M. (1997). *Tuesdays with Morrie.* New York: Doubleday.

Aristotle. (1998). *Nichomachean ethics.* Ontario: Dover.

Bartlett's Familiar Quotations. (1989). New York: Little, Brown and Co.

Barton, E. R. (2000). Parallels between mythopoetic men's work/men's peer mutual support groups and selected Feminist theories. In E. R. Barton (Ed.)., *Mythopoetic perspectives of men's healing work* (pp. 3–20). Westport, CT.: Bergin & Garvey.

Baumeister, R. F. (2007). Is there anything good about men? Invited address at the American Psychological Association, August 24, San Francisco.

Baumeister, R. F. & Sommer, K. L. (1997). What do men want? Gender difference and two spheres of belongingness: Comment on Cross and Madson (1997). *Psychological Bulletin, 122,* 38–44.

Bazelon, E. (2008). Hormones, genes, and the corner office. *New York Times Book Review,* March 9, p. 11.

Bearman, P. & Parigi, P. (2004). Cloning headless frogs and other important matters: Conversation topics and network structure. *Social Forces, 83,* 535–557.

Berkman, L. F. & Syme, S. L. (1979). Social networks, host resistance, and mortality: A nine year follow-up study of Alameda County residents. *American Journal of Epidemiology, 109*, 186–204.

Berzoff, J. (1989). The therapeutic value of women's adult friendships. *Smith College Studies in Social Work, 59*, 267–279.

Betcher, W. & Pollack, W. (1993). *In a time of fallen heroes*. New York: Atheneum.

Biesanz, J. C., West, S. G., & Millevoi, A. (2007). What do you learn about someone over time? The relationship between length of acquaintance and consensus and self-other agreement in judgments of personality. *Journal of Personality and Social Psychology, 92*, 119–135.

Blinn, William. (1972). *Brian's song*. New York: Bantam.

Bly, R. (1992). *Iron John: A book about men*. New York: Vintage.

Boarse, J., Horrigan, J. B., Wellman, B., & Rainie, L. (2006). *The strength of internet ties*. Washington, DC: Pew Internet & American Life Project.

Bowen, M. (1976). Theory in the practice of psychotherapy. In P. J. Guerin (Ed.), *Family therapy: Theory and Practice* (pp. 42–90). New York: Gardner Press.

Brewer, D. D. & Webster, C. M. (1999). Forgetting of friends and its effects on measuring friendship networks. *Social Networks, 21*, 361–373.

Brizendine, L. (2006). *The female brain*. New York: Morgan Road Books.

Bruckner, E. & Knaup, K. (1993). Women and men's friendships in comparative perspective. *European Sociological Review, 9*, 249-266.

Burleson, B. R. (2003). The experiences and effects of emotional support: What the study of cultural and gender differences can tell us about the close relationships, emotion, and interpersonal communication. *Personal Relationships, 10*, 1–23.

Butera, K. (2006a). The disappearance of 'mateship' in the 21st century. Paper presented at the Mateship: Trust and exclusion in Australian History Conference, Monash University, Melbourne, February 16.

Butera, K. (2006b). Manhunt: The challenge of enticing men to participate in a study on friendship. *Qualitative Inquiry, 12*, 1262–1282.

Cahill, L. (2005). His brain, her brain. *Scientific American, 292*(5), 40–48.

Canli, T., Desmond, J. E., Zhao, Z., & Gabrieli, J. D. E. (2002). Sex differences in the neural basis of emotional memories. *Proceedings of the National Academy of Sciences of the United States of America, 99*, 10789–10794.

Carey, B. (2007, October 2). Friends with benefits, and stress too. *The New York Times*, pp. D5 and D8.

Carnegie, D. (1981). *How to win friends and influence people*. New York: Simon & Shuster Inc.

Carstensen, L. L. (1991). Selectivity theory: Social activity in life-span context. *Annual Review of Gerontology and Geriatrics, 11*, 195–217.

Cheng, G. H. L., Chan, D. K. S., & Tong, P. Y. (2005). Qualities of online friendships with different gender compositions and durations. *Cyber Psychology & Behavior, 9*, 14–21.

Christakis, N. A. & Fowler, J. H. (2007). The spread of obesity in a large social network over 32 years. *The New England Journal of Medicine, 357*, 370–379.

Cohen, T. (1992). Men's families, men's friends: A structural analysis of constraints on men's social ties. In P. M. Nardi (Ed.), *Men's friendships* (pp. 115–131). Newbury Park, CA: Sage.

Coleman, M., Ganong, L. H., & Rothrauff, T. C. (2006). Racial and ethnic similarities and differences in beliefs about intergenerational assistance to older adults after divorce and remarriage. *Family Relations, 55*, 576–587.

Collins, J., Noble, G., Poynting, S. & Tabar, P. (2000). *Kebabs, kids, cops & crime*. Annandale, Australia: Pluto Press.

Coltrane, S. (2001). Stability and change in Chicano men's family lives. In M.S. Kimmel & M. A. Messner (Eds.), *Men's lives* (pp. 451–466). Boston: Allyn & Bacon.

Connell, R. (2005a). *Masculinities*, second edition. Berkeley: University of California Press.

Connell, R. (2005b). Growing up masculine: Rethinking the significance of adolescence in the making of masculinities. *Irish Journal of Sociology, 14*, 11–28.

Connell, R. (2005c). Change among the gatekeepers: Men, masculinities and gender equality in the global arena. *Signs: Journal of Women in Culture and Society, 30*, 1801–1825.

Connell, R. W. & Wood, J. (2005). Globalization and business masculinities. *Men and Masculinities, 7*, 347–364.

Curtis, P. (2006, February 21). More men in 20s living at home. *The Guardian*, p. 1.

Davis, K. E. (1985). Near and dear: Friendship and love compared. *Psychology Today*, February, 22–30.

Derks, E. S., Dolan. C. V., Hudziak, J. J., Neale, M. C., & Boomsma, D. I. (2007). Assessment and etiology of attention deficit disorder and oppositional defiant disorder in boys and girls. *Behavior Genetics, 37*, 559–566.

Dindia, K. & Allen, M. (1992). Sex difference in self–disclosure: A meta-analysis. *Psychological Bulletin, 112*, 106–112.

Dubowitz, H., Lane, W., Greif, G. L., Jensen, T. K. & Lamb, M. E. (2006). Low-income African American fathers' involvement in children's lives: Implications for practitioners. *Journal of Family Social Work, 10*, 25–41.

Duneier, M. (1992). *Slim's table: Race, respectability, and masculinity*. Chicago: The University of Chicago Press.

Enright, D. J. & Rawlinson, D. (Eds.). (1991). *The Oxford book of friendship*. New York: Oxford University Press.

Epstein, J. (2006). *Friendship: An exposé*. New York: Houghton Mifflin Company.

Farrell, M. P. (1985). Friendship between men. *Marriage and Family Review, 9(3/4)*, 163-197.

Farthing, M. (2005). Attitudes toward heroic and nonheroic physical risk takers as mates and as friends. *Evolution and Human Behavior, 26*, 171–185.

Finchum, T. D. (2005). Keeping the ball in the air: Contact in long-distance friendships. *Journal of Women and Aging, 17*, 91–106.

Florian, V., Mikuloncer, M. & Bucholtz, I. (1995). Effects of adult attachment style on the perception and search for social support. *The Journal of Psychology, 129*, 665–676.

Franklin, C W. (1992). Hey, home—Yo, bro: Friendship among black men. In P. M. Nardi (Ed.), *Men's friendships* (pp. 201–214). Newbury Park, CA: Sage.

Gay, P. (1989). *Freud: A life in our time*. NY: Doubleday.

Gerami, S. (2005). Islamist masculinity and Muslim masculinities. In M.S. Kimmel, J. Hearn, & R.W. Connell (Eds.), *Handbook of studies on men and masculinities* (pp. 448–457). Thousand Oaks, CA: Sage.

Gladwell, M. (2002). *The tipping point: How little things can make a big difference*. New York: Back Bay Books.

Goleman, D. (2006, October 10). Friends for life: An emerging biology of healing. *The New York Times*, p. D5.

Gordon, B. & Pasick, R. S. (1990). Changing the nature of friendships between men. In R. L. Meth & R. S. Pasick (Eds.), *Men in therapy: The challenge of change* (pp. 261–278). New York: Guilford.

Greif, G. L. (2006). Male friendships: Implications from research for family therapy. *Family Therapy, 33*, 1–15.

Gutmann, M. C. & Vigoya, M. V. (2005). Masculinities in Latin America. In M.S. Kimmel, J. Hearn, & R.W. Connell (Eds.), *Handbook of studies on men and masculinities* (pp. 114–128). Thousand Oaks, CA: Sage.

Halberstam, D. (2003). *The teammates: A portrait of a friendship*. New York: Hyperion.

Hansen, K. V. (1992). "Our eyes behold each other": Masculinity and intimate friendships in Antebellum New England. In P. M. Nardi (Ed.), *Men's friendships* (pp. 35–58). Newbury Park, CA: Sage.

Harrison, J. (1978). Warning: The male sex role may be dangerous to your health. *Journal of Social Issues, 34*, 65–80.

Heyl, V. (2006). Friendships in middle and older adulthood: The long arm of early childhood experiences. *Zeitschrift fur Gernotologie und Geraitrie, 37*, 357–359 (taken from translated abstract).

Hoare, C. H. (2002). *Erikson on development in adulthood*. New York: Oxford University Press.

Hollinger, D. A. (2006). From identity to solidarity. *Daedalus, 135*(4), 23–31.

Iggulden, N. & Iggulden, C. (2007). *The dangerous book for boys.* New York: Harper Collins.

Isaacs, F. (1999). *Toxic friends-true friends: How your friends can make or break your health, happiness, family, and career.* New York: William Morrow and Company.

Jordan, J. V., Kaplan, A. G., Miller, J. B., Stiver, I. P., & Surrey, J. L. (1991). *Women's growth in connection: Writings from the Stone Center.* New York: Guilford.

Kaplan, D. (2007). Folk models of dyadic male bonds in Israeli culture. *The Sociological Quarterly, 48,* 47–72.

Kimmel, M. (1996). *Manhood in America: A cultural history.* New York: The Free Press.

Kindlon, D. & Thompson, M. (1999). *Raising Cain: Protecting the emotional life of boys.* New York: Ballantine Books.

Knickmeyer, N., Sexton, K., & Nishimura, N. (2002). The impact of same-sex friendships on the well-being of women: A review of the literature. *Women & Therapy, 25,* 37–59.

Knoester, C., Haynie, D. L., & Stephens, C. M. (2006). Parenting practices and adolescents' friendship networks. *Journal of Marriage and Family, 68,* 1247–1260.

Kupers, T. A. (1992). *Revisioning Men's Lives: Gender, intimacy, and power.* New York: Guilford.

Levi, F., La Vecchia, C., & Saraceno, B. (2003). Global suicide rates. *European Journal of Public Health, 13,* 97–98.

Lewis, R. A. (1978). Emotional intimacy among men. *Journal of Social Issues, 34,* 108–121.

Liang, B., Tracy, A., Taylor, C. A., Williams, L. M., Jordan, J. V., & Miller, J. B. (2002).The relational health indices: A study of women's relationships. *Psychology of Women Quarterly, 26,* 25.

Lingeman, R. (2007). *Double lives: American writers' friendships.* New York: Random House.

Marston, C., Juarez, F., & Izazola, J. A. (2004). Young, unmarried men and sex: Do friends and partners shape risk behaviour? *Culture, Health & Sexuality, 6,* 411–424.

Matthews, S. H. (1986). *Friendships through the life course: Oral biographies in old age.* Beverly Hills, CA: Sage.

Mattis, J. S., Murray, Y. F., Hatcher, C. A., Hearn, K. D., Lawhon, G. D., Murphy, E. J., & Washington, T. A. (2001). Religiosity, spirituality, and the subjective quality of African American men's friendships: An exploratory study. *Journal of Adult Development, 8,* 221–230.

McGoldrick, M. (1989). Women and the family life cycle. In B. Carter and M. McGoldrick (Eds.), *The changing family life cycle: A framework for family therapy*, 2nd edition (pp. 29–68). Boston: Allyn and Bacon.

McPherson, M., Smith-Lovin, L., & Brashears, M. E. (2006). Social isolation in America: Changes in core discussion networks over two decades. *American Sociological Review, 71*, 353–375.

McPherson, M., Smith-Lovin, L., & Cook, J. M. (2001). Birds of a feather: Homophily in social networks. *Annual Review of Sociology, 27*, 415–444.

Menaker, E. (1986). Some observations regarding men's contemporary views on women. *The Psychoanalytic Review, 73*, 614–617.

Mendes de Leon, C. F. (2005). Why do friendships matter for survival? *Journal of Epidemiology and Community Health, 59*, 538–539.

Messner, M. A. (2001). Boyhood, organized sports, and the construction of masculinities. In M. S. Kimmel & M. A. Messner (Eds.), *Men's lives*, 5th edition (pp. 88–99). Boston: Allyn and Bacon.

Meth, R. L. (1990). The road to masculinity. In R. L. Meth & R.S. Pasick (Eds.), *Men in therapy: The challenge of change* (pp. 3–34). New York: Guilford.

Michaelis, D. (1983). *The best of friends*. New York: William Morrow.

Moeller-Leimkuehler, A. (2003). The gender gap in suicide and premature death or: Why are men so vulnerable? *European Archives of Psychiatry & Clinical Neuroscience, 253*, 1–8.

Morgan, D. (2005). Class and masculinity. In M.S. Kimmel, J. Hearn, & R.W. Connell (Eds.), *Handbook of studies on men and masculinities* (pp. 165–177). Thousand Oaks, CA: Sage.

Morin, S. F. & Grafinkel, E. M. (1978). Male homophobia. *Journal of Social Issues, 34*, 29-47.

Morris, W. (1978). *James Jones: A friendship*. New York: Doubleday.

Muraco, A. (2006). Intentional families: Fictive kin ties between cross-gender, different sexual orientation friends. *Journal of Marriage and Family, 68*, 1313–1325.

Myers, D. G. (2005). *Social psychology*, 8th edition. New York: McGraw-Hill.

Nardi, P. M. (1992). Seamless souls: An introduction to men's friendships. In P. M. Nardi (Ed.), *Men's friendships* (pp. 1–14). Newbury Park, CA: Sage.

Nardi, P. M. (2000). Friendship. In G. E. Haggerty (Ed.), *Gay histories and cultures: An encyclopedia* (pp. 357–358). New York: Garland Publishing, Inc.

Nardi, P. M. (2007). Friendship, sex, and masculinity. In M. Kimmel (Ed.), *The sexual self: The construction of sexual scripts* (pp. 49-57). Nashville: Vanderbilt University Press.

Nichols, M. P. & Schwartz, R. C. (2007). *Family therapy: Concepts and Methods*, 8th Edition. Boston: Allyn and Bacon.

Oppenheim, N. (2007). Rules of the roast. *Men's Health, 22(2)*, 101, 105, 107.

Padgett, D. K. (1998). *Qualitative methods in social work research: Challenges and rewards.* Thousand Oaks, CA: Sage.

Pahl, R. & Pevalin, D. J. (2005). Between family and friends: A longitudinal study of friendship choice. *British Journal of Sociology, 56,* 433–450.

Pease, B. (2002). *Men and gender relations.* Victoria, Australia: Tertiary Press.

Pentz, M. (2000). Heuristic and ethnographic study of the ManKind Project: Initiating men into a 'new masculinity' or a repackaging of dominant controlling patriarchy. In E. R. Barton (Ed.), *Mythopoetic perspectives of men's healing work* (pp. 204–225). Westport, CT.: Bergin & Garvey.

Petersen, A. (2003). Research on men and masculinities: Some implications of recent theory for future work. *Men and Masculinities, 6,* 54–69.

Peterson, T. J. (2007). Another level: Friendships transcending geography and race. *The Journal of Men's Studies, 15,* 71–82.

Plato. (1992). *Republic.* Translated by G. M. A. Grube. Indianapolis: Hackett Publishing Co.

Plummer, D. (1999). *One of the boys: Masculinity, homophobia, and modern manhood.* New York: Harrington Park Press.

Pollack, W. S. (1998). *Real boys: Rescuing our sons from the myths of boyhood.* New York: Random House.

Pollack, W. S. (2006). The "war" for boys: Hearing "real boys'" voices, healing their pain. *Professional Psychology: Research and Practice, 37,* 190–195.

Price, J. (1999). *Navigating differences: Friendships between gay and straight men.* New York: Harrington Park Press.

Putnam, R. D. (2000). *Bowling alone: The collapse and revival of American community.* New York: Simon and Schuster.

The Reader's Digest Treasury of Modern Quotations. (1975). New York: Reader's Digest Press.

Roberts, G. W. (1994). Brother to brother: African American modes of relating among Men. *Journal of Black Studies, 24,* 379-390.

Rotundo, E. A. (1993). *American manhood: Transformations in masculinity from the revolution to the modern era.* New York: Basic Books.

Roy, R., Benenson, J. F., & Lilly, F. (2000). Beyond intimacy: Differences in same-sex friendships. *The Journal of Psychology, 134,* 93–101.

Rubin, L. (1983). *Intimate strangers: Men and women together.* New York: Harper Perennial.

Rubin, L. (1985). *Just friends: The role of friendship in our lives.* New York: Harper & Row Publishers.

Rubin, L. (1986). On men and friendship. *Psychoanalytic Review, 73,* 165–181.

Rushton, J. P. & Bons, T. A. (2005). Mate choice and friendship in twins: Evidence for genetic similarity. *Psychological Science, 16,* 555–559.

Rybak, A. & McAndrew, F. T. (2006). How do we decide whom our friends are? Defining levels of friendship in Poland and the United States. *Journal of Social Psychology, 146,* 147–163.

Salmon, C. (2003). Birth order and relationships: Family, friends, and sexual partners. *Human Nature, 14,* 73–88.

Satir, V. (1983). *Conjoint family therapy.* Palo Alto: Science and Behavior Books.

Schmitt, D. P., Realo, A., Voracek, M., & Allik, J. (2008). Why can't a man be more like a woman? Sex differences in Big Five Personality Traits across 55 cultures. *Journal of Personality and Social Psychology, 94,* 168–182.

Seidler, V. J. (1992). Rejection, vulnerability, and friendship. In P. M. Nardi (Ed.), *Men's friendships* (pp. 15–34). Newbury Park, CA: Sage.

Sheehy, G. (1998). *Understanding men's passages: Discovering the new map of men's lives.* New York: Random House.

Sheets, V. L. & Lugar, R. (2005). Sources of conflict between friends in Russia and the United States. *Cross-cultural Research, 39,* 380–398.

Shenk, J. W. (2005). *Lincoln's melancholy: How depression challenged a president and failed his generation.* Boston: Mariner Books.

Sherman, A. M., deVries, B., & Lansford, J. E. (2000). Friendship in childhood and adulthood: Lessons across the life span. *Journal of Aging and Human Development, 51,* 31–51.

Sherman, A. M., Lansford, J. E., & Volling, B. L. (2006). Sibling relationships and best friendship in young adulthood: Warmth, conflict, and well-being. *Personal Relationships, 13,* 151–165.

Siebert, D. C., Mutran, E. J., & Reitzes, D. C. (1999). Friendship and social support: The importance of role identity to aging adults. *Social Work, 44,* 522–533.

Singleton, R. A. & Vacca, J. (2007). Interpersonal competition in friendships. *Sex Roles, 57,* 617–627.

Steinbeck, J. (1937). *Of mice and men.* New York: Spangler.

Stephanson, R. (1997). Epicoene friendship: Understanding male friendship in the early Eighteenth century, with some speculations about Pope. *Eighteenth Century: Theory and Interpretation, 38,* 151-170.

Strauss, A. & Corbin, J. (1990). *Basics of qualitative research: Grounded theory, procedures and techniques.* Newbury Park, CA: Sage.

Stearns, P. N. (1990). *Be a man! Males in modern society,* 2nd edition. New York: Holmes & Meier.

Stroud, S. (2006). Episystemic partiality in friendship. *Ethics: An International Journal Of Social, political, and Legal Philosophy, 116,* 498–524.

Swain, S. O. (1992). Men's friendships with women: Intimacy, sexual boundaries, and the informant role. In P. M. Nardi (Ed.), *Men's friendships* (pp. 153–172). Newbury Park, CA: Sage.

Taga, F. (2005). East Asian masculinities. In M.S. Kimmel, J. Hearn, & R.W. Connell (Eds.), *Handbook of studies on men and masculinities* (pp. 129–140). Thousand Oaks, CA: Sage.

Tannen, D. (2006). *"You're wearing that?: Understanding mothers and daughters in conversation.* New York: Random House.

Taylor, B. A. (2006). Gendered training: Men and men's issues in marriage and family therapy programs. *American Journal of Family Therapy, 34,* 263–277.

Taylor, S. E., Klein, L. C., Lewis, B. P., Gruenewald, T. L., Gurung, R. A. R., & Updegraff, J. A. (2000). Biobehavioral responses to stress in females: Tend-and Befriend, not fight-or-flight. *Psychological Review, 107,* 411-429.

Tiger, L. (1969). *Men in groups.* New York: Vintage Books.

Tiger, L. (1999). *The decline of males.* New York: Golden Books.

Tognoli, J. (1980). Male friendship and intimacy across the life span. *Family Relations, 29,* 273–279.

Totten, M. (2003). Girlfriend abuse as a form of masculinity construction among violent, marginal male youth. *Men & Masculinities, 6,* 70–92.

U.S. Bureau of Labor Statistics. (2006). Household Data Annual Averages: 3. Employment Status of the civilian non-institutional population by age, sex, and race. Washington, DC: Government Printing Office.

U.S. Census Bureau. (2006a). USA Statistics in Brief–Race and Hispanic Origin (last revised 12/10/2006). Washington, DC: Government Printing Office.

U.S. Census Bureau. (2006b). Table SHP-1: Parents and Children in Stay-at-Home Parenting Groups: 1994 to Present, May. Washington, DC: Government Printing Office.

U.S. Census Bureau. (2006c). United States: S0101. Age and Sex—2006 American Community Survey. Washington, DC: Government Printing Office.

U.S. Census Bureau. (2007). *Statistical Abstract of the United States: 2007.* Washington, DC: Government Printing Office.

Vaughn, E. & Nowicki, S. (1999). Close relationships and complementary interpersonal styles among men and women. *The Journal of Social Psychology, 139,* 473–478.

Verbrugge, L. M. (1977). The structure of adult friendship choices. *Social Forces, 56,* 576–597.

Vincent, N. (2006). *Self-made man: One woman's year disguised as a man.* New York: Penguin Books.

Viorst, J. (1998). *Necessary losses: The loves, illusions, dependencies, and impossible expectations that all of us have to give up in order to grow up.* New York: Alfred Knopf.

Wall, S. M., Pickert, S. M., & Paradise, L. V. (1984). American men's friendships: Self-reports on meaning and changes. *The Journal of Psychology, 116,* 179–186.

Walsh, F. (1989). The family in later life. In B. Carter and M. McGoldrick (Eds.), *The changing family life cycle: A framework for family therapy*, 2nd edition (pp. 311–332). Boston: Allyn and Bacon.

Ward, C. A., Bergner, M., & Kahn, J. H. (2003). Why do men distance? Factors predictive of male avoidance of intimate conflict. *Family Therapy, 30*, 1–11.

Weiten, W. (2007). *Psychology: Themes and Variations*, 7th edition. Belmont, CA: Wadsworth.

Williams, D. R. (2003). The health of men: Structured inequalities and opportunities. *American Journal of Public Health, 93*, 724–731.

Winefeld, H. R., Winefeld, A. H. & Tigggerman, M. (1992). Social support and psychological well-being in young adults: The multi-dimensional support scale. *Journal of Personality Assessment, 58*, 198–210.

Wright, P. H. (1982). Men's friendships, women's friendships and the alleged inferiority of the latter. *Sex Roles, 8*, 1–20.

Wright, E. O. & Cho, D. (1992). The relative permeability of class boundaries to cross-class friendships: A comparative study of the United States, Canada, Sweden, and Norway. *American Sociological Review, 57*, 85–102.

Yager, J. (1997). *Friendshifts: The power of friendship and how it shapes our lives*. Stamford CT: Hannacroix Creek.

Index

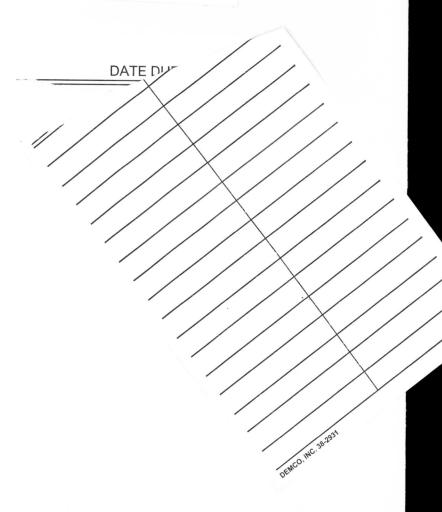

DATE DUE

DEMCO, INC. 38-2931